Study Guide for the French and German Tests

▶ ▶ ▶ ▶ ▶ ▶ ▶ ▶ ▶ ▶ ▶ ▶

A PUBLICATION OF ETS

Table of Contents
Study Guide for the French and German Tests

▶   ▶   ▶   ▶   ▶   ▶   ▶   ▶   ▶   ▶   ▶   ▶

TABLE OF CONTENTS

German: Content Knowledge Test
Chapter 11

Chapter 12

Chapter 13

Chapter 14

German: Productive Language Skills Test
Chapter 15

Chapter 16

Chapter 17

Chapter 18

Chapter 19

Appendix A

Appendix B

Chapter 1
Introduction to the French and German Tests and Suggestions for Using This Study Guide

▶   ▶   ▶   ▶   ▶   ▶   ▶   ▶   ▶   ▶   ▶   ▶

Introduction to the French and German Tests

The Praxis French and German tests assess beginning teachers' understanding of these languages and the cultures of the countries and regions where the languages are spoken.

The *French: Content Knowledge* test (0173) consists of 120 multiple-choice questions based on audio recordings and printed materials in French. Some questions (on language analysis) are in English. The test covers four major areas, in the following proportions:

Content Category	Approximate Number of Questions	Approximate Percentage of Examination
■ Interpretive Listening (in French)	32	27%
■ Structure of the Language (Grammatical Accuracy, in French and English)	34	28%
■ Interpretive Reading (in French)	31	26%
■ Cultural Perspectives (in French)	23	19%

You have two hours to complete the test.

The test is not intended to assess teaching skills but rather your competence in various language skills and your knowledge of the cultures of France and French-speaking countries and regions.

The *French: Productive Language Skills* test (0171) consists of nine questions: six questions that you must answer in spoken French—the Presentational Speaking section of the test—and three questions that you must answer in written French—the Presentational Writing section. The test covers these two sections in the following proportions:

Content Category	Number of Questions	Percentage of Total Test Score	Minutes
■ Presentational Speaking	6	60%	25 (approximate)
■ Presentational Writing	3	40%	35

You have one hour to complete the test.

The test is not intended to assess teaching skills but rather your ability to speak and write French.

The *German: Content Knowledge* test (0181) consists of 120 multiple-choice questions based on audio recordings and printed materials in German. It covers four major areas, in the following proportions:

Content Category	Approximate Number of Questions	Approximate Percentage of Examination
■ Interpretive Listening (in German)	32	27%
■ Structure of the Language (Grammatical Accuracy, in German and English)	34	28%
■ Interpretive Reading (in German)	31	26%
■ Cultural Perspectives (in German)	23	19%

You have two hours to complete the test.

The test is not intended to assess teaching skills but rather your competence in various language skills and your knowledge of the cultures of Germany and German-speaking countries.

The *German: Productive Language Skills* test (0182) consists of nine questions: six questions that you must answer in spoken German—the Presentational Speaking section of the test—and three questions that you must answer in written German—the Presentational Writing section. The test covers these two sections in the following proportions:

Content Category	Number of Questions	Percentage of Total Test Score	Minutes
■ Presentational Speaking	6	60%	25 (approximate)
■ Presentational Writing	3	40%	35

You have one hour to complete the test.

The test is not intended to assess teaching skills but rather your ability to speak and write German.

Suggestions for Using This Study Guide

These language tests are different from final exams or other tests you may have taken for other courses because they are comprehensive—that is, they cover material you may have learned in courses during your entire undergraduate program. They require you to synthesize information you have learned from many sources and to understand the subject as a whole.

Therefore, you should review and prepare for the test you plan to take, rather than merely becoming familiar with the question formats. A thorough review of the material covered on the test will significantly increase your likelihood of success. Moreover, studying for your licensing exam is a great opportunity to reflect on and develop a deeper understanding of your field before you begin to teach. As you prepare to take the test, it may be particularly helpful for you to think about how you would apply the study topics and sample exercises to the teaching experiences you obtained during your teacher preparation program. Your student teaching experience will be especially relevant to your thinking about the materials in the study guide.

We recommend the following approach for using this study guide to prepare for the tests.

- **Become familiar with the test content.** Learn what will be assessed in the test you plan to take, covered in chapter 3 (for the *French: Content Knowledge* test), 7 (for the *French: Productive Language Skills* test), 11 (for the *German: Content Knowledge* test), or 15 (for the *German: Productive Language Skills* test).

- **Assess how well you know the content in each area.** After you learn what topics the test contains, you should assess your knowledge in each area. How well do you know the material? In which areas do you need to learn more before you take the test? It is quite likely that you will need to brush up on most or all of the areas.

- **Develop a study plan.** Assess what you need to study and create a realistic plan for studying. You can develop your study plan in any way that works best for you. A "Study Plan" form is included in appendix A at the end of the book as a possible way to structure your planning. Remember that these are licensure tests that cover a great deal of material. Plan to review carefully. You will need to allow time to find books and other materials, time to read the materials and take notes, and time to go over your notes.

- **Identify study materials.** Most of the materials covered by these tests are contained in standard introductory textbooks. If you do not own introductory texts that cover all the relevant areas, you may want to borrow some from friends or from a library. You may also want to obtain a copy of your state's standards for French or German. (One way to find these standards quickly is to go to the Web site for your state's Department of Education.) The textbooks used in secondary classrooms may also prove useful to you, since they often present the material you need to know. Use standard school and college introductory textbooks and other reliable, professionally prepared materials. Don't rely heavily on information provided by friends or from searching the World Wide Web. Neither of these sources is as uniformly reliable as textbooks.

- **Work through your study plan.** You may want to work alone, or you may find it more helpful to work with a group or with a mentor. Work through the topics and descriptions of question types outlined in chapters 3, 7, 11, and 15. Rather than memorizing definitions from books, be able to define and discuss the topics and question types in your own words and understand the relationships among diverse topics and concepts. If you are working with a group or mentor, you can also try informal quizzes and questioning techniques.

- **Learn about the test format in chapters 4, 8, 12, or 16.** For each of the four tests, this guide also includes a chapter about the test's format—multiple choice for the *French: Content Knowledge* and *German: Content Knowledge* tests, and constructed response for the *French: Productive Language Skills* and *German: Productive Language Skills* tests. For you to succeed on multiple-choice questions, you must focus carefully on the question, avoid reading things into the question, pay attention to details, and sift patiently through the answer choices. For you to succeed on constructed-response questions, you will want to learn how constructed-response tests are scored, and you will also want to read valuable tips on taking a test in this format.

- **Proceed to the practice questions.** Once you have completed your review and familiarized yourself with the format for your test, you are ready to benefit from the "Practice Questions" portions of this guide, chapters 5, 9, 13, and 17.

Suggestions for Using the "Practice Questions," "Right Answers," and "Sample Responses" Chapters

- **Answer the practice questions in chapters 5, 9, 13, or 17.** Work on the practice questions in a quiet place without distractions. Remember that the practice questions are only examples of the way the topics are covered in the test. The actual test will have different questions.

- **Score the practice questions.** If you have answered the practice questions for the *French: Content Knowledge* or *German: Content Knowledge* test, go through the detailed answers in chapters 6 or 14, and mark the questions you answered correctly and the ones you missed. Look over the explanations for the correct answers to the questions you missed and see if you understand them. If you have answered the practice questions for the *French: Productive Language Skills* or *German: Productive Language Skills* test, look in chapters 10 or 18 to see sample responses that scored well, scored poorly, or scored in-between. By examining these sample responses, you can focus on the aspects of your own practice response that were successful and unsuccessful. This knowledge will help you plan any additional studying you might need.

- **Decide whether you need more review.** After you have looked at your results, decide whether there are areas that you need to brush up on before you take the actual test. Go back to your textbooks and reference materials to see if the topics and skills are covered there. You might also want to go over your questions with a friend or teacher who is familiar with the subjects.

- **Assess your readiness.** Do you feel confident about your level of understanding in each of the areas? If not, where do you need more work? If you feel ready, complete the checklist in chapter 19 ("Are You Ready?—Last Minute Tips") to double-check that you've thought through the details. If you need more information about registration or the testing situation itself, use the resources in appendix B: "For More Information."

Note: Every effort is made to provide the most recent information in this study guide. However, The Praxis Series tests are continually evaluated and updated. You will always find the most recent information about these tests, including the topics and skills covered, number of questions, time allotted, and scoring criteria, in the *Test at a Glance* materials available online at http://www.ets.org/praxis/prxtest.html.

Chapter 2

Background Information on The Praxis Series™ Subject Assessments

► ► ► ► ► ► ► ► ► ► ► ►

What Are The Praxis Series Subject Assessments?

The Praxis Series Subject Assessments are designed by ETS to assess your knowledge of specific subject areas. They are a part of the licensing procedure in many states. This study guide covers assessments that test your knowledge of the actual content you will be expected to teach once you are licensed. Your state has adopted The Praxis Series tests because it wants to confirm that you have achieved a specified level of mastery in your subject area before it grants you a license to teach in a classroom.

The Praxis Series tests are part of a national testing program, meaning that the tests covered in this study guide are required in more than one state for licensure. The advantage of a national program is that if you want to move to another state, you can transfer your scores from one state to another. However, each state has specific test requirements and passing scores. If you are applying for a license in another state, you will want to verify the appropriate test and passing score requirements. This information is available online at www.ets.org/praxis/prxstate.html or by calling ETS at 800-772-9476 or 609-771-7395.

What Is Licensure?

Licensure in any area—medicine, law, architecture, accounting, cosmetology—is an assurance to the public that the person holding the license possesses sufficient knowledge and skills to perform important occupational activities safely and effectively. In the case of teacher licensing, a license tells the public that the individual has met predefined competency standards for beginning teaching practice.

Because a license makes such a serious claim about its holder, licensure tests are usually quite demanding. In some fields, licensure tests have more than one part and last for more than one day. Candidates for licensure in all fields plan intensive study as part of their professional preparation: some join study groups, others study alone. But preparing to take a licensure test is, in all cases, a professional activity. Because a licensure exam assesses the entire body of knowledge for the field you are entering, preparing for the test takes planning, discipline, and sustained effort.

Why Does My State Require The Praxis Series Assessments?

Your state chose The Praxis Series assessments because the tests assess the breadth and depth of content— called the "domain"—that your state wants its teachers to possess before they begin to teach. The level of content knowledge, reflected in the passing score, is based on recommendations of panels of teachers and teacher educators in each subject area. The state licensing agency and, in some states, the state legislature ratify the passing scores that have been recommended by panels of teachers.

What Do the Tests Measure?

The Praxis Series Subject Assessments are tests of content knowledge. They measure your understanding and skills in a particular subject area. Multiple-choice tests measure a broad range of knowledge across your content area. Constructed-response tests measure your ability to provide in-depth explanations of a few essential topics in a given subject area. Content-specific pedagogy tests, most of which are constructed-response, measure your understanding of how to teach certain fundamental concepts in a subject area. The tests do not measure your actual teaching ability, however. They measure your knowledge of a subject and of how to teach it. The teachers in your field who help us design and write these tests, and the states that require them, do so in the belief that knowledge of your subject area is the first requirement for licensing. Teaching combines many complex skills, only some of which can be measured by a single test. While the tests covered in this study guide measure knowledge of your subject area, your teaching ability is a skill that is typically measured in other ways—for example, through observation, videotaped practice, or portfolios.

How Were These Tests Developed?

ETS began the development of The Praxis Series Subject Assessments with a survey. For each subject, teachers around the country in various teaching situations were asked to judge which knowledge and skills a beginning teacher in that subject needs to possess. Professors in schools of education who prepare teachers were asked the same questions. The responses were ranked in order of importance and sent out to hundreds of teachers for review. All of the responses to these surveys (called "job analysis surveys") were analyzed to summarize the judgments of these professionals. From their consensus, we developed guidelines, or specifications, for the multiple-choice and constructed-response tests. Each subject area had a committee of practicing teachers and teacher educators who wrote the specifications, which were reviewed and eventually approved by teachers. From the test specifications, groups of teachers and professional test developers created test questions that met content requirements and satisfied the *ETS Standards for Quality and Fairness.**

When your state adopted The Praxis Series Subject Assessments, local panels of practicing teachers and teacher educators in each subject area met to examine the tests and to evaluate each question for its relevance to beginning teachers in your state. This is called a "validity study" because local practicing teachers validate that the test content is relevant to the job. During the validity study, the panel also provides a passing-score recommendation. This process includes a rigorous review to determine how many of the test questions a beginning teacher in that state would be able to answer correctly. Your state's licensing agency then reviewed the panel's recommendations and made a final determination of the passing-score requirement.

Throughout the development process, practitioners in the teaching field—teachers and teacher educators—participated in defining what The Praxis Series Subject Assessments would cover, which test would be used for licensure in your subject area, and what score would be needed to achieve licensure. This practice is consistent with how professional licensure works in most fields: those who are already licensed oversee the licensing of new practitioners. When you pass The Praxis Series Subject Assessments, you and the practitioners in your state will have evidence that you have the knowledge and skills required for beginning teaching practice.

* *ETS Standards for Quality and Fairness* (2003, Princeton, NJ) are consistent with the "Standards for Educational and Psychological Testing," industry standards issued jointly by the American Educational Research Association, the American Psychological Association, and the National Council on Measurement in Education (1999, Washington, DC).

Chapter 3
Study Topics—*French: Content Knowledge*

► ► ► ► ► ► ► ► ► ► ► ►

Introduction to the Test

The Praxis *French: Content Knowledge* test is designed to assess the knowledge and competencies necessary for beginning or entry-year teachers of French. You will be required to answer questions based on recorded conversations and narrations. You will also be required to read, interpret, and correct written French and to identify errors and error patterns in grammar, structure, mechanics, word choice, and register. You will be asked questions about the geography, history, and culture of France and French-speaking countries and regions.

The purpose of this chapter is to provide guidance on how to prepare for the test. A broad overview of the areas covered in the Praxis *French: Content Knowledge* test is followed by detailed lists of the specific topics that are covered under each broad area.

You are not expected to be an expert on all aspects of the topics that follow. However, you should understand the major characteristics or aspects of each topic and be able to recognize them in various kinds of examples or selections.

Here is an overview of the areas covered on the test, along with their subareas:

Interpretive Listening
27% of the questions

> Short Conversations
> Short Narrations
> Long Conversations and Long Narrations

Structure of the Language
28% of the questions

> Speech Analysis
> Writing Analysis
> Language Analysis
> Grammar Analysis

Interpretive Reading
26% of the questions

> Content and Organization
> Implied Content
> Use of Language

Cultural Perspectives
19% of the questions

> Geography
> Lifestyles and Societies
> Sociolinguistic Elements of French
> History
> Literature and the Arts

Interpretive Listening

The Interpretive Listening section of the test is divided into three different parts: short conversations, short narrations, and long conversations and long narrations. Selections will be read by native speakers of French, followed by questions read orally. Answer choices will appear only in your test book.

Short Conversations

For these questions, you will be asked to listen to a recorded dialogue between two native speakers of French speaking at a normal rate of speech. To complete this task successfully, you must be able to interpret stress and intonation; understand the meanings of key words; understand high-frequency vocabulary, idiomatic expressions, and figures of speech; recognize questions and instructions; understand verb tenses; identify main ideas; and understand conversations on a number of topics.

- Recognize the meaning carried by stress and intonation
  - Rising intonation is used to ask a question, whereas unchanging intonation is used to make a statement. For example, consider the expression *Ça va?* or *Ça va,* which varies in meaning according to the intonation of the voice.
  - Intonation can indicate a particular emotion, including surprise or discontent.
- Understand the meaning of an utterance based on key words
  - What key indicators dictate formal vs. informal speech?
    - Use of *tu* versus *vous*
  - What verb conjugations indicate different time sequences?
    - Use of imperfect to indicate ongoing or habitual action in the past
      - *Quand j'étais jeune, j'aimais aller au cinéma. ("When I was young, I liked to go to the movies.")*

- Use of the *passé composé* to indicate a completed, finite occurrence in the past
  - *Je suis allé cinq fois au cinéma au mois de juillet.*
- What key words allow you to determine where a particular situation may be taking place or what information is being requested? For example, if you hear key words such as *nos billets d'avion, cherchons nos valises,* and finally, *allons au contrôle des passeports,* you will know from the conversation that the speakers are at an airport.
- What are common patterns for cognates in English/French?
  - "-ly" endings in English ("exactly") usually are conveyed by a *-ment* ending in French *(exactement).*

- Understand high-frequency vocabulary, idiomatic expressions, and figures of speech
  - Understand vocabulary used in common, everyday situations, such as at school or at home
  - Interpret idiomatic expressions that cannot be translated literally from English to French, such as
    - *Ça va,* which can be interpreted as "I'm fine."
    - *Je me suis lavé les cheveux.* ("I washed my hair.")
    - *Cette robe me plaît.* ("I like this dress.")
    - *Il fait beau.* ("The weather is nice.")
    - *Il tombe des cordes.* ("It's raining cats and dogs.")

- Recognize verb tenses and what they indicate
  - What key words distinguish the past from the present or future?
    - Use of the periphrastic future (*aller* + infinitive, as in *Je vais partir mardi prochain.*)

◆ Use of certain phrases with past tenses, such as

— *tous les jours* + imperfect

— *hier* + preterite

■ Identify the main idea of an informal conversation

▶ Can you determine the main idea through repeated or related words and phrases?

▶ Can you identify a problem, understand a situation, and recognize the resolution of a problem or situation?

▶ Can you make inferences based on key information, such as the place where the conversation occurs or the given time frame?

■ Understand conversations on a variety of everyday topics, such as

▶ Ordering food in a restaurant

▶ Asking for advice

▶ Making a phone call

▶ Talking about entertainment and leisure activities

▶ Discussing health

Short Narrations

For these questions, you will be asked to listen to one native speaker of French speaking at a normal rate of speech. This person may be telling a brief story, speaking about an event, making an announcement, or providing the type of information you would hear on a radio or television broadcast. To answer these questions successfully, you will use many of the same skills involved in answering questions following short conversations.

Long Conversations and Long Narrations

For the questions referring to long conversations, you will be asked to listen to two native speakers of French conducting an extended conversation. For the questions referring to long narrations, you will hear a native speaker of French speaking at a normal rate of speech for an extended period of time. To answer these questions successfully, you will use many of the same skills involved in answering questions that follow short conversations or narrations.

Structure of the Language (Grammatical Accuracy)

This section of the test is divided into four different parts: Speech Analysis, Writing Analysis, Language Analysis, and Grammar Analysis.

Speech Analysis

For these questions, you will be asked to analyze errors in material recorded by nonnative speakers of French. To complete this task successfully, you must be able to detect, describe, and correct errors in grammar, word choice, and pronunciation. You will need to

■ Demonstrate the ability to detect, describe, and correct grammatical errors in spoken French. This may include errors involving

▶ Use of gender or number

◆ Definite and indefinite articles

◆ Possessive and demonstrative adjectives

▶ Use of the contracted forms of articles

◆ *de* and *le* combine to become *du*

◆ *à* and *le* combine to become *au*

▶ Placement of adjectives or adverbs in a sentence

◆ Adjectives expressing beauty, age, goodness, and size precede the word they describe.

◆ Certain adjectives change in meaning depending on where they are placed in a sentence.

— *un homme pauvre* ("a man who is poor") does not express the same idea as *un pauvre homme* ("a pitiful, miserable man")

- ◆ Adverbs may directly follow the verb of a sentence or be placed at the beginning or end of the sentence, depending on the expression.
    - — *Nous jouons <u>souvent</u> au tennis.*
    - — *Nous jouons au tennis <u>de temps en temps</u>.*
- ► Use of adjectives, including
    - ◆ Irregular forms of adjectives
        - — *beau* becomes *bel* in front of a vowel or a mute *h: un bel hôtel*
        - — *international* becomes *internationaux* in the plural: *des hôtels internationaux*
    - ◆ Comparative or superlative forms of adjectives
        - — *bon(ne)(s)* becomes *meilleur(e)(s)*
- ► Use of the partitive
    - ◆ *du, de la, de l', des: Donne-moi <u>du</u> pain.* ("Give me some bread."); *Je vais mettre <u>de l'</u> eau sur la table.* ("I'll put water on the table.")
    - ◆ Expressions of quantity usually followed by *de* instead of *des*
        - — *Beaucoup de gens aiment ce film.*
    - ◆ Negative expressions in which the partitive generally changes to *de*
        - — *J'ai fait <u>du</u> ski* but *Je n'ai pas fait <u>de</u> ski.*
        - — *Je vais acheter <u>des</u> tomates* but *Je ne vais pas acheter <u>de</u> tomates.*
- ► Use of different negations
    - ◆ Negations that can be substituted for *ne...pas* but not combined with it
        - — *Je n'ai vu <u>personne</u>.*
        - — *<u>Personne</u> n'aime ce film.*
    - ◆ Correct word order for negative expressions
        - — *Je n'ai rien vu* but *Je n'ai vu personne.*
- ► Use of prepositions
    - ◆ After certain verbs that require *à* or *de* or change in meaning according to the preposition used
        - — *Il <u>essaie de</u> trouver un emploi.*
        - — *Est-ce que tu penses à tes études?* ("Are you thinking about your studies?"); *Qu'est-ce que tu penses de tes études?* ("What do you think of your studies?")
    - ◆ With dates, seasons, and time
        - — *lundi,* for example, indicates a specific date, as opposed to *le lundi,* which signifies repetition: *Je viendrai te voir lundi.* ("I'll visit you on Monday."); *Je joue au tennis le lundi.* ("I play tennis every Monday.")
    - ◆ With names of cities and countries
        - — *à* is used with most cities: *Elle habite à Paris.*
        - — *en, au,* and *aux* are the prepositions used with most countries, according to the gender of the country: *Nous irons en Suède ou au Danemark cet été.*
- ► Use of pronouns
    - ◆ Distinction between direct and indirect object pronouns in simple sentences
        - — *Je vais <u>lui</u> téléphoner.*
        - — *Il <u>la</u> regarde.*
    - ◆ Correct placement or word order of object pronouns in a sentence
        - — Direct or indirect object pronoun: *Il <u>me</u> téléphone souvent.*
        - — Double object pronoun: *Je veux mon stylo. Tu peux <u>me le</u> donner?*
    - ◆ Correct use of disjunctive or stress pronouns
        - — *Nous allons au théâtre avec <u>eux</u>.*
        - — *<u>Moi</u>, je préfère le chocolat.*
    - ◆ Correct use of reflexive pronouns according to the subject of the sentence
        - — *Nous <u>nous</u> amusons.*

♦ Correct use and placement of pronouns with the imperative

— *Donne-lui le livre; Montre-moi tes photos.*

— In the negative: *Ne lui donne pas le livre; ne me montre pas tes photos.*

♦ Correct use of the pronouns *y* and *en*

— *y* and *en* used for places: *Je viens du Canada; J'en viens / Je vais à Québec; J'y vais.*

— *y* used to replace an indirect object following a verb: *Tu penses à faire tes bagages? Oui, j'y pense.*

— *en* replacing the partitive: *J'ai trouvé des stylos. J'en ai acheté quelques-uns.*

♦ Interrogative pronouns

— *Laquelle de ces voitures est en panne?*

▶ Use of verb forms

♦ Correct use of auxiliaries with compound past tenses

— *Il a quitté son appartement à 8h* is correct since *quitter* uses *avoir* as an auxiliary.

— *Il est sorti à 8h* is correct because the verb *sortir*, when intransitive, is conjugated with the auxiliary verb *être* in compound past tenses.

— *Il a sorti ses valises* is correct since *sortir* is a transitive verb in this sentence.

♦ Correct use of past participles

— Verbs such as *prendre, mettre, voir, ouvrir* are only a few of the many verbs in French that have irregular past participles.

♦ Correct conjugation of irregular verbs in the present and future tenses

— Some common examples include *aller, venir, faire, avoir, être, voir.*

♦ Correct usage of tenses in *quand* or *si* clauses

— *Quand,* used with the future tense in one clause, requires the second clause of the sentence to also be in the future tense: *Quand j'irai en France, je visiterai Paris.*

— The present tense is required in the *si* clause when a future action is expressed in the main clause: *Si je vais en France, je visiterai Paris.*

♦ Correct distinction between the *passé composé,* which expresses a single, completed action in the past, and the imperfect tense, which expresses repeated or habitual actions in the past or the circumstances of an event

— *J'allais à Paris chaque été.* ("I used to go to Paris every summer.")

— *Je suis allé à Paris l'été dernier.* ("I went to Paris last summer.")

■ Demonstrate the ability to detect, describe, and correct errors in word choice. This may include errors involving

▶ False cognates

♦ Certain English and French words look alike but have different meanings.

— *Une location* means a rental and not a location.

— *Une place* means a seat or a (town) square.

— *Attendre* means to wait, while to attend is translated in French by *assister à.*

▶ The use of colloquial language in formal situations

♦ Certain informal expressions in French are not acceptable in formal situations, and if used, are considered impolite.

— For example, in a store, you would not say to a sales person, *Je voudrais voir vos fringues.* Rather, *vêtements* would be the appropriate word to use.

— Similarly, *une bagnole* is a common expression for a car in informal, colloquial situations, but *une voiture* is the phrase to use when talking with a car dealer.

▶ The use of unacceptable anglicisms

♦ Certain French grammar constructs are very different from English.

— *Je m'intéresse à la musique.* ("I am interested in music.")

— *Je me suis cassé le bras.* ("I broke my arm.")

■ Demonstrate the ability to detect, describe, and correct faulty pronunciation in spoken French

▶ Common errors may include the pronunciation of certain letters that should not be pronounced in French, or the lack of pronunciation of certain letters that should be pronounced.

♦ Most consonants at the end of a word are not pronounced: *gran(d)*, *peti(t)*, *de(s) chapeau(x)*.

♦ The mute *e* at the end of a word is silent, but the consonant that precedes it is pronounced: *grande, petite, une robe*.

♦ The endings in the present tense of *-er* verbs—first, second, and third person singular and third person plural—are pronounced the same

— *Je regard(e). Tu regard(es). Elle regard(e). Ils regard(ent).*

♦ Some "liaisons" are compulsory, while others are forbidden:

— *les enfants; ils arrivent* (compulsory liaison)

— *Les élèves ont bien travaillé; un livre et un cahier* (no liaison)

— The letter *h* is never pronounced in French. Most of the time, it is muted and there must be a liaison with the preceding word.

▾ *un hôtel / l'hôtel, un homme / l'homme* (liaison and elision)

— In some cases, the *h* is aspirated (*aspiré*), and, though not pronounced, behaves like a consonant (no elision, no liaison):

▾ *le héros; le haricot* (no liaison, no elision)

♦ The nasal sounds [ã], [õ], [ĩ] are pronounced without actualization of the *n* sound.

— *américain; un enfant; le ballon*

♦ The *n* is pronounced without nasalization of the preceding vowel when followed by another *n*, a mute *e*, or another vowel.

— *Elle est américaine; une bonne banane; un animal*

Writing Analysis

For these questions, you will be asked to analyze errors in writing samples from nonnative writers of French. Answering these questions requires you to use the same skills you used in answering Speech Analysis questions. In this section you will have to

■ Demonstrate the ability to detect, describe, and correct basic grammatical errors in written French. This may include errors involving

▶ The agreement of adjectives

♦ Spelling of regular adjectives where *e* or *s* is added for feminine and plural items

— *Ce livre est intéressant; cette voiture est intéressante; ces livres sont intéressants; ces voitures sont intéressantes.*

♦ Spelling and application of adjectives with different ending changes

— *sportif* and *sportive*

— *sérieux* and *sérieuse*

— *mensuel* and *mensuelle*

♦ Spelling and application of irregular adjectives

— *un bel hôtel, de beaux hôtels*

▶ The correct spelling of demonstrative adjectives

- ♦ Appropriate forms
  - — *cet élève, ce petit élève*
- ♦ Correct spelling and distinction from words that sound similar
  - — *ces / c'est / ses*

▶ The appropriate spelling of plural nouns

- ♦ Regular nouns in which *s* is added to create the plural
  - — *une table, des tables*
- ♦ Regular nouns in which *x* is added to create the plural
  - — *un bureau, des bureaux*
- ♦ Nouns that change from the singular to the plural
  - — *un cheval, des chevaux*

▶ The correct spelling of adverbs

- ♦ Many adverbs are derived from the feminine form of adjectives.
  - — *sérieuse* becomes *sérieusement*
- ♦ Some adverbs do not use the feminine form of adjectives.
  - — *élégamment*
  - — *poliment*

▶ Appropriate usage and spelling of definite and indefinite articles

- ♦ Definite articles specify nouns or are used for general statements.
  - — *J'aime la musique.*
  - — *J'ai acheté le livre qui est sur la table.*
- ♦ Indefinite articles are used where an object is not specified.
  - — *J'ai acheté des livres.*
- ♦ Correct use and spelling of contractions

▶ The correct use of conjunctions and relative pronouns

- ♦ With the indicative to express certainty
  - — *Il est certain que Pierre va venir.*
  - — *Je crois que Pierre viendra.*

♦ With the subjunctive to express emotion, uncertainty, desire, necessity
  - — *Je souhaite que Pierre vienne.*
  - — *Je ne crois pas que Pierre vienne.*
♦ *J'espère* is usually followed by the future
  - — *J'espère que Pierre viendra.*
♦ *qui, que, dont, lequel*, etc.
  - — *J'ai des amis <u>qui</u> sont gentils.* ("who")
  - — *J'ai des amis <u>que</u> je connais depuis longtemps.* ("whom")
  - — *J'ai des amis <u>dont</u> j'ai visité la maison.* ("whose")
  - — *J'ai des amis <u>avec lesquels</u> j'aime aller au cinéma.* ("with whom")

▶ The correct spelling of words and expressions that sound similar in French

- ♦ *c'est / ces / ses ; est / et*
- ♦ Nasals *en, an, em, am – on, om – in, ain, aim* (*enfant, pain, lapin, faim, chambre, tomber*)
- ♦ *Passé composé* of *–er* verbs versus infinitive
  - — *Je suis <u>allé</u> au cinéma; je vais <u>aller</u> au cinéma.*

▶ Appropriate forms and spelling for all moods and tenses of regular and irregular verbs

- ♦ Compound past tense verbs using *avoir* as an auxiliary
- ♦ Verbs of motion using *être* as an auxiliary
- ♦ Reflexive verbs using *être* as an auxiliary
- ♦ Agreement of past participles
  - — *Ma copine est <u>allée</u> à la piscine.* The past participle here correctly agrees with the subject.
  - — *J'ai trouvé ces chaussures dans le placard. Qui les a <u>achetées</u>?* The past participle here correctly agrees with the direct object preceeding the verb.

- ◆ Nonagreement of past participles of reflexive verbs followed by a direct object
  - — *Martine s'est <u>lavée</u>,* compared to *Martine s'est <u>lavé</u> les mains.*
- ◆ Agreement or nonagreement of past participles of verbs that can be transitive or intransitive

- ■ Demonstrate the ability to detect, describe, and correct language that is inappropriate to the task and/or audience addressed
  - ▶ The use of *tu* versus *vous* in informal and formal situations
  - ▶ The use of appropriate vocabulary for a specific situation

Language Analysis

This section will require you to provide explanations for grammatical and word-use errors. Topics in this section may ask you to

- ■ Demonstrate knowledge of the structural components of the French language. This may include the identification of the correct use of structures, such as
  - ▶ Direct and indirect objects—their forms and correct placement
  - ▶ Placement of adjectives
  - ▶ Regular and irregular adjectives
  - ▶ The appropriate use of tenses
  - ▶ The use of *avoir* and *être* as auxiliaries in compound past tenses
  - ▶ Agreement of nouns and modifiers
  - ▶ Agreement of subject/verb
  - ▶ Idiomatic expressions
  - ▶ Cognates
  - ▶ Comparatives and superlatives

- ■ Demonstrate knowledge of the basic meaningful elements of words, such as
  - ▶ Verb usage
  - ▶ Verbs with spelling changes
  - ▶ Word roots
  - ▶ Prefixes and suffixes

- ■ Demonstrate knowledge of word order to form phrases, clauses, and sentences. This may include
  - ▶ Order of subject and verb in statements versus questions
    - ◆ Using inversion to create a question
      - — *Partez-vous bientôt?*
    - ◆ Using *est-ce que* to create a question
      - — *Est-ce que vous partez bientôt?*
  - ▶ Order of nouns and modifying adjectives
    - ◆ Adjectives that have different meanings when they precede or follow nouns

- ■ Demonstrate knowledge of the function of cognates and false cognates in the development of vocabulary

- ■ Demonstrate an understanding of the formation of contractions and compound words
  - ▶ *au/du*
  - ▶ *le portemanteau; l'abat-jour; le rouge-gorge*

Grammar Analysis

For these questions, you will read sentences or paragraphs from which words or phrases have been omitted. You will be asked to choose the answer that correctly completes the sentence. This part of the test requires knowledge of

- ■ The correct formation and use of regular and irregular verbs in all moods and tenses
  - ▶ Regular and irregular verbs in various tenses

- ▶ Differentiation between past tenses in the indicative (*passé composé* and imperfect)
- ▶ Use of the subjunctive, indicative, and imperative moods

■ The correct formation and use of nouns, adjectives, adverbs, and articles

- ▶ Noun and adjective agreement
- ▶ Derivation of adverbs
- ▶ Use of articles
- ▶ Use of indefinite and negative expressions

■ The correct formation and use of pronouns

- ▶ Use and placement of direct, indirect, and reflexive pronouns
- ▶ Use and placement of double object pronouns
- ▶ Use and placement of pronouns with imperatives

Interpretive Reading

This section is designed to measure how well you understand written French. Reading selections come from a number of sources, including academic texts; literary selections, ranging from classic to contemporary; prose; poetry; fiction and nonfiction; media sources such as magazines and newspapers or the Internet; and realia (posters, tickets, advertisements, etc.). The subject matter can be extensive, covering social sciences, cultural topics, humanities, science, education, history, or general interest. Depending on the type, density, and length of the reading selection, it may be followed by one to eight questions. You will be asked questions about content and organization, implied content, and use of language. The main topics to consider are presented below, followed by a sample reading selection.

You should be able to demonstrate the ability to

- ■ Determine the main idea or purpose of the selection

■ Identify other important ideas from the

- ▶ Content and key words
- ▶ Tone of the text
- ▶ Type of language used

■ Identify supporting details from the

- ▶ Content and key words

■ Identify paraphrases or summaries of ideas from the

- ▶ Content and key words
- ▶ Conclusion of the text

■ Identify relationships among ideas directly stated, such as

- ▶ Cause and effect
- ▶ Sequence of ideas
- ▶ Conclusion

■ Locate the place in a passage where specific information can be found from

- ▶ Key words
- ▶ The chronology of the text

■ Understand a variety of reading materials

You will need to bring the following skills to the reading selection:

- ■ The ability to distinguish what is implied from what is directly stated

- ■ The ability to make inferences from directly stated content

- ■ The ability to recognize the style or manner of expression
  - ▶ Literary
  - ▶ Narrative
  - ▶ Informational
  - ▶ Persuasive

- ■ The ability to distinguish fact from opinion

- The ability to recognize how the meaning of a word, sentence, or paragraph is affected by the context in which it appears

- The ability to determine the meaning of figurative language

- The ability to understand the function of key transition indicators, such as *cependant, mais, donc, par conséquent*

The following exercise and annotated sample are intended to give you practice in the kinds of interpretive thinking that are expected in this section of the test. Although the format of the annotation exercise is not like that of the multiple-choice questions on the test, the types and levels of understanding and evaluation needed to complete it are comparable. Read the passage and try to annotate key words, phrases, and sentences in the passage. Then, read the annotated version on the following page and compare it with your analysis.

This reading sample is from a work by Émile Zola.

Denise, depuis le matin, subissait la tentation. Ce magasin en face, si vaste pour elle, où elle voyait entrer en une heure plus de monde qu'il n'en venait à la boutique de sa famille en province en six mois, l'étourdissait et l'attirait ; et il y avait, dans son désir d'y pénétrer, une peur vague qui achevait de la séduire. En même temps, la boutique de son oncle où elle se trouvait à présent lui causait un sentiment de malaise. C'était un dédain irraisonné, une répugnance instinctive pour ce trou glacial de l'ancien commerce. Toutes ses sensations, son entrée inquiète, l'accueil aigri de ses parents, le déjeuner triste sous un jour de cachot, son attente au milieu de la solitude ensommeillée de cette vieille maison agonisante, se résumaient en une sourde protestation, en une passion de la vie et de la lumière. Et malgré son bon cœur, ses yeux retournaient toujours au Bonheur des Dames, le magasin en face, comme si la vendeuse en elle avait eu le besoin de se réchauffer au flamboiement de cette grande vente.

— *En voilà qui ont du monde, au moins, laissa-t-elle échapper.*

Mais elle regretta cette parole, en apercevant les Baudu près d'elle. Mme Baudu, qui avait achevé de déjeuner, était debout, toute blanche, ses yeux blancs fixés sur le monstre ; et, résignée, elle ne pouvait le voir, le rencontrer ainsi de l'autre côté de la rue, sans qu'un désespoir muet gonflât ses paupières.

Baudu, la bile au visage, se contenta de dire :

— *Tout ce qui reluit n'est pas d'or. Patience !*

Now, compare your annotations with the ones below.

The main idea of the passage comes across at the beginning with the words *magasin* and *tentation*, as well as with Denise's observation that the store attracts many customers.

This reading sample is from a work by Émile Zola.

Denise, depuis le matin, subissait la tentation. Ce magasin en face, si vaste pour elle, où elle voyait entrer en une heure plus de monde qu'il n'en venait à la boutique de sa famille en province en six mois, l'étourdissait et l'attirait ; et il y avait, dans son désir d'y pénétrer, une peur vague qui achevait de la séduire. En même temps, la boutique de son oncle où elle se trouvait à présent lui causait un sentiment de malaise. C'était un dédain irraisonné, une répugnance instinctive pour ce trou glacial de l'ancien commerce. Toutes ses sensations, son entrée inquiète, l'accueil aigri de ses parents, le déjeuner triste sous un jour de cachot, son attente au milieu de la solitude ensommeillée de cette vieille maison agonisante, se résumaient en une sourde protestation, en une passion de la vie et de la lumière. Et malgré son bon cœur, ses yeux retournaient toujours au Bonheur des Dames, le magasin en face, comme si la vendeuse en elle avait eu le besoin de se réchauffer au flamboiement de cette grande vente.

— *En voilà qui ont du monde, au moins, laissa-t-elle échapper.*

Mais elle regretta cette parole, en apercevant les Baudu près d'elle. Mme Baudu, qui avait achevé de déjeuner, était debout, toute blanche, ses yeux blancs fixés sur le monstre ; et, résignée, elle ne pouvait le voir, le rencontrer ainsi de l'autre côté de la rue, sans qu'un désespoir muet gonflât ses paupières.

Baudu, la bile au visage, se contenta de dire :

— *Tout ce qui reluit n'est pas d'or. Patience !*

She feels attracted by the store but scared at the same time.

To her, the store across the street represents passion, life, and light.

Denise cannot help observing aloud that the store across the street has many customers as opposed to her uncle's store.

Baudu is very angry, *la bile au visage*. He is hopeful that the glory and richness of the enemy store are only superficial and will not last.

Denise feels very uncomfortable about her uncle's store (*malaise, dédain, répugnance, trou glacial*).

We learn that Denise is a store clerk.

This makes the Baudu family very unhappy (adding insult to injury). Madame Baudu is especially upset by the simple vision of the "monster" store across the street.

Cultural Perspectives

Questions in the Cultural Perspectives section focus on the following areas: lifestyles and societies, sociolinguistic elements of French, literature and the arts, history, and geography. The following is a suggested list of possible topics that may appear in the Cultural Perspectives section. This list is in no way comprehensive, but it provides an idea of the type of topics related to the cultures of France and francophone countries that may appear in the test.

Lifestyles and Societies

For these questions, your knowledge of the way of life and customs in France and in other French-speaking countries and regions will be tested.

- Contemporary lifestyles
  - ▶ Food
    - ◆ Traditional dishes and specialties
    - ◆ Regional specialties
  - ▶ Meals
    - ◆ Eating habits: *l'entrée; le plat principal; la salade; le fromage; le dessert*
    - ◆ Times and names of the three main meals
  - ▶ Customs
    - ◆ Meeting people
    - ◆ Greeting people
    - ◆ Behavior in public places
  - ▶ Body Language
    - ◆ Common gestures and their meanings
  - ▶ Holidays
    - ◆ Religious holidays
      - — *Pâques*
      - — *Pentecôte*
      - — *l'Ascension*
      - — *la Toussaint*
      - — *Noël*
    - ◆ Public holidays
      - — *la Fête nationale (le 14 juillet)*
      - — *la Fête du Travail (le 1er mai)*

- ▶ Family relationships
  - ◆ Families and their homes
  - ◆ Relationships with people outside the family
  - ◆ Summer vacations
- ▶ Education
  - ◆ School systems
  - ◆ Higher education
- ▶ Regional variations

Sociolinguistic Elements of French

These questions test your knowledge and understanding of appropriate language and expressions. You may be given a specific social situation, formal or informal, or a task or audience. Questions address

- Customary usage of certain words or expressions in specific situations, such as the use of *vous* as opposed to *tu*

- Use of colloquial language

- Idiomatic expressions; common sayings; proverbs

Literature and the Arts

For these questions, your knowledge of major French authors and their works, as well as events related to the arts, will be tested.

- Major works and authors of the literature of France and other French-speaking countries, including
  - ▶ Medieval literature
    - ◆ *La chanson de Roland*
    - ◆ *Troubadours*
  - ▶ 16th–18th-century French literature
    - ◆ Rabelais
    - ◆ Corneille
    - ◆ Racine
    - ◆ Molière
    - ◆ Madame de Sévigné

- La Bruyère
- *L'Encyclopédie*
- Montesquieu
- Voltaire
- Rousseau
- Beaumarchais
- ▶ 19th–20th-century French and Francophone literature
  - Chateaubriand
  - Lamartine
  - Victor Hugo
  - Balzac
  - Baudelaire
  - Verlaine
  - Rimbaud
  - Mallarmé
  - Mauriac
  - Marcel Proust
  - Colette
  - Simone de Beauvoir
  - Léopold Senghor
  - Louis Aragon
  - Albert Camus
  - Jean-Paul Sartre
  - André Gide
  - Jean Cocteau
  - Ionesco
  - Saint-Exupéry

- ■ Significant figures, works, and events in the arts
  - ▶ Traditional theater
    - Molière
    - *La Comédie-Française*
  - ▶ Music
    - Popular: Georges Brassens, Jacques Brel
    - Classical: Lully, Berlioz, Debussy
  - ▶ Art and Architecture
    - Painting: Delacroix, Monet, Van Gogh, Matisse

- Sculpture: Rodin
- Architecture: Romanesque, Gothic, Contemporary
- ▶ Film
  - *La Nouvelle Vague:* Truffaut, Godard
- ▶ Popular Culture
  - Comics: *La Bande Dessinée*
- ▶ Dance
  - Regional traditions
  - *Ballet de l'Opéra*

History

For these questions, your knowledge of the historical facts and background of France and French-speaking countries and regions will be tested. This includes

- ■ The contributions of French culture to North America
  - ▶ Louisiana
  - ▶ Québec

- ■ Landmark contributions of French-speaking people to the history, economy, political life, and culture of the United States, including the role of France
  - ▶ During the colonial period
  - ▶ During the American Revolution
  - ▶ During the First and Second World Wars
  - ▶ In Vietnam

- ■ The most important events and principal historic figures of France and other French-speaking countries
  - ▶ Gaul and the Roman Empire
  - ▶ Charlemagne
  - ▶ Medieval France and the Crusades
  - ▶ Joan of Arc
  - ▶ Louis XIV
  - ▶ Louis XVI
  - ▶ French and Indian War
  - ▶ French Revolution
  - ▶ Napoléon

- ▶ French colonial period
  - ◆ Canada
  - ◆ Lousiana
  - ◆ Africa
  - ◆ Asia
- ▶ First World War
- ▶ Second World War
- ▶ Charles de Gaulle

■ Contemporary world politics and economics affecting France

- ▶ Role of major French political parties
  - ◆ Elections and voting
- ▶ Organization of the government in France
- ▶ *La francophonie*
- ▶ Relations with other EU countries
- ▶ Immigration issues in France
- ▶ French economy, business, and industry
  - ◆ Fashion
  - ◆ Perfumes
  - ◆ Food
  - ◆ Cosmetics
  - ◆ Tourism

Geography

In this section of the test, your knowledge of geographical facts will be tested. This involves

■ Locating France and other French-speaking regions and countries

- ▶ Continental France
- ▶ DOM-TOM
- ▶ Francophone Africa
- ▶ Francophone Asia

■ Identifying major geographical features of France and French-speaking regions and countries

- ▶ Rivers
- ▶ Mountains
- ▶ Regions
- ▶ Major cities

Once again, test takers are reminded that this is not an all-inclusive list and that these specific examples will not appear on every test. These are simply areas, topics, events, and figures that represent the major categories that are covered: lifestyles and societies, sociolinguistic elements of French, literature and the arts, history, and geography.

Chapter 4

Succeeding on Multiple-Choice Questions—
French: Content Knowledge

▶   ▶   ▶   ▶   ▶   ▶   ▶   ▶   ▶   ▶   ▶   ▶

Understanding Multiple-Choice Questions

When you read multiple-choice questions on the Praxis *French: Content Knowledge* test, you will probably notice that the syntax (word order) is different from the word order you are used to seeing in ordinary material that you read, such as newspapers or textbooks. One of the reasons for this difference is that many test questions contain the phrase "which of the following."

In order to answer a multiple-choice question successfully, you need to consider carefully the context set up by the question and limit your choice of answers to the list given. The purpose of the phrase "which of the following" is to remind you to do this. For example, look at this question.

Which of the following is a flavor made from beans?

(A) Strawberry
(B) Cherry
(C) Vanilla
(D) Mint

You may know that chocolate and coffee are also flavors made from beans, but they are not listed, and the question asks you to select from the list that follows ("which of the following"). So the answer has to be the only bean-derived flavor in the list: vanilla.

Notice that the answer can be substituted for the phrase "which of the following." In the question above, you could insert "vanilla" for "which of the following" and have the sentence "Vanilla is a flavor made from beans." Sometimes it helps to cross out "which of the following" and insert the various choices. You may want to give this technique a try as you answer various multiple-choice practice questions.

Looking carefully at the "which of the following" phrase helps you to focus on what the question is asking you to find and on the answer choices. In the simple example above, all of the answer choices are flavors. Your job is to decide which of the flavors is the one made from beans.

The vanilla bean question is pretty straightforward. However, the phrase "which of the following" can also be found in more challenging questions. Look at this question:

To modify the noun phrase *"un arbre,"* which of the following forms of the adjective is appropriate?

(A) *belle*
(B) *bel*
(C) *beau*
(D) *beaux*

The placement of "which of the following" tells you that the list of choices consists of several forms of an adjective. What are you supposed to find as an answer? You are supposed to find the choice that is appropriate to use to modify the noun phrase *"un arbre."*

ETS question writers and editors work very hard to word each question as clearly as possible. Sometimes, though, it helps to put the question in your own words. Here, you could paraphrase the question as "Which form of the adjective is the right one to attach to *'un arbre'?"* The correct answer is (B). (*"Arbre"* is masculine singular, but it begins with a vowel, so instead of the usual masculine singular *"beau"* you would use *"bel."*)

You may also find that it helps to circle or underline each of the critical details of the question in your test book so you do not miss any of them. It is only by looking at all parts of the question carefully that you will have all of the information you need to answer it. Circle or underline the critical parts of what is being asked in this question.

Which of the following adjectives always follows the noun it modifies?

(A) *rond*
(B) *grand*
(C) *bon*
(D) *vieux*

Here is one possible way you may have annotated the question:

Which of the following adjectives always follows the noun it modifies?

(A) *rond*
(B) *grand*
(C) *bon*
(D) *vieux*

After thinking about the question, you can probably see that you are being asked to look at four adjectives and to choose the one that always is written after the noun it modifies. The correct answer is (A). The important thing is understanding what the question is asking. With enough practice, you should be able to determine what any question is asking. Knowing the answer is, of course, a different matter, but you have to understand a question before you can answer it correctly.

Understanding Questions Containing "NOT," "LEAST," or "EXCEPT"

The words "NOT," "LEAST," and "EXCEPT" can make comprehension of test questions more difficult. They ask you to select the choice that *does not* fit. You must be very careful with this question type because it is easy to forget that you are selecting the negative. This question type is used in situations in which there are several good solutions or ways to approach something, but also a clearly wrong way. These words are always capitalized when they appear in The Praxis Series test questions, but they are easily (and frequently) overlooked.

For the following test question, determine what kind of answer you need and what the details of the question are.

Which of the following words does NOT have the same meaning as its English cognate?

(A) *attendre*
(B) *copier*
(C) *abandonner*
(D) *investir*

You're looking for a French word that does NOT mean the same as its English cognate—that is, the word in English that resembles it and that comes from the same root. (A) is the correct answer. *Attendre* means "to wait," not "to attend," whereas all of the other French words do mean the same as their cognates ("to copy," "to abandon," and "to invest").

> It's easy to get confused while you're processing the information to answer a question that contains a "NOT," "LEAST," or "EXCEPT." If you treat the word "NOT," "LEAST," or "EXCEPT" as one of the details you must satisfy, you have a better chance of understanding what the question is asking.

Be Familiar with Question Types Based on Recorded Excerpts

The first two sections of the *French: Content Knowledge* test will require you to listen to a recording of spoken French. The recording will be played **only once.** Although some of the recorded material will be printed in the test book, some will not, so it is important that you listen carefully to the spoken material. The questions based on the recorded material will be in several formats.

1. Interpretive Listening—Short Conversations

In this type of question, you listen to a recording of native French speakers conversing at a normal conversational rate of speed. You then are asked one or more questions based on what you have heard. Neither the dialogue nor the questions are printed in your test book. In the following example, first you hear the following dialogue:

(Man)   *Allô, Marie? C'est Robert. Tu sais, la météo prévoit une averse pour cet après-midi. Si nous faisions autre chose?*

(Woman)   *Je veux bien. D'ailleurs, j'ai pas mal à faire à la maison.*

(Narrator)   *De quoi s'agit-il?*

Then, in your test book you see the following choices:

     (A)   De la construction d'un bâtiment.
     (B)   D'une maladie subite.
     (C)   D'une sortie remise.
     (D)   D'une prédiction astrologique.

To answer, you must select the choice that best answers the narrator's question: what is it (the dialogue) about? The correct answer is (C), a postponed date or outing.

2. Interpretive Listening—Short Narrations

This question type is similar to the one discussed in the previous section, except that instead of a conversation you hear a short narration. The narration is not printed in your test book. After each narration, you will hear one or more questions, which are printed in your test book. You may find it useful to take notes in your test book as you listen to the narration.

Here is an example, which begins with the narrator speaking:

(Narrator) *Cette question se rapporte à l'information suivante.*

(Woman) *Après plusieurs semaines de préparatifs, trois alpinistes allemands se sont lancés à l'assaut de la face nord du Pic au Diable, un mur rocheux de plus de 800 mètres, barré d'énormes surplombs, dans les Alpes. L'ascension de cette paroi n'a jamais été réalisée en hiver.*

(Narrator) *De quoi s'agit-il?*

Then, in your test book you see the following choices:

(A)   D'une semaine de camping.
(B)   D'une aventure hasardeuse.
(C)   D'une partie de ski.
(D)   D'une avalanche dans les Alpes.

The correct answer is (B).

3. Interpretive Listening—Long Conversations and Narrations

These formats are the same as those discussed in the two previous sections, except that the narrative passages and conversations are longer. After each narration or conversation, you will hear several questions, which are printed in your test book.

4. Questions about Structure of the Language Based on Recorded Excerpts

Section II of the *French: Content Knowledge* test is called Structure of the Language (Grammatical Accuracy) and includes both listening and reading selections.

In the first part of section II, you hear recorded selections spoken by students who are learning French and who make errors in their speech. Their words are not printed in your test book. The following example begins with the voice of the narrator:

(Narrator)   Question 4 refers to the following selection about a student's school and vacation.

(Student)   *Je suis étudiant. J'étudie à l'université. J'aime la musique et les sciences. Dans été, je voyage avec mes parents.*

(Narrator)   Question Number 4: Correct the error in the following excerpt.

You hear again:

(Student)   *Dans été, je voyage avec mes parents.*

In your test book you read the following:

Question 4 refers to the following selection about a student's school and vacation.

4. Correct the error in the following excerpt.

(A)   Change *Dans* to *En.*
(B)   Change *je* to *nous.*
(C)   Change *voyage* to *voyagé.*
(D)   Change *mes* to *ma.*

The correct answer is (A). *Dans* is the wrong preposition for the phrase "in the summer"; the correct phrase is *"en été."*

Be Familiar with Question Types Based on Written Excerpts

1. Questions about Structure of the Language Based on Written Excerpts

In the second part of section II, you read paragraphs written by students who are learning French. The student writing contains errors, and your task is to identify, correct, or describe the type of error made in a particular sentence from the paragraph. Each sentence selected contains only *one* error. When you answer the question, it helps to consider the meaning of the sentence and the type of error in the context of the whole paragraph. You may find it useful to take notes in your test book.

Here is an example:

This question refers to the following selection about a birthday.

(1) Mon anniversaire est samedi prochain; c'est le premier de juin. (2) J'espère recevoir beaucoup   de cadeaux.

Correct the error in sentence 1.

(A)   Change *Mon* to *Ma.*
(B)   Change *prochain* to *prochaine.*
(C)   Change *le premier* to *la première.*
(D)   Change *de juin* to *juin.*

The correct answer is (D). The correct way to write "June first" is *"le premier juin"*; therefore *"de juin"* must be changed to *"juin."*

2. Fill-in-the-blank Questions

Some questions in section II feature French sentences or paragraphs in which words or phrases have been removed and replaced with a blank space. You are presented with four options for filling in the blank. Your task is to choose the option that results in the best sentence or paragraph in written French. Here is an example:

Je me souviens de cette histoire avec _____ précision que je pourrais vous la raconter en détail.

(A)   tant
(B)   tant de
(C)   tant que
(D)   autant que

The correct answer is (B). The phrase *"tant de,"* when it is followed by a noun and *"que,"* means "so much…that…."

3. Interpretive Reading Questions

In Section III of the *French: Content Knowledge* test, you read several selections in French. Each selection is followed by one or more questions. Your task is to answer each question based only on what is stated or implied in the selection. You may find it helpful to take notes in your test book.

Here is an example:

Cette question se rapporte à l'extrait suivant, écrit par un dramaturge en réponse à la critique d'une de ses pièces de théâtre.

Puis-je vous affirmer, Madame, qu'on ne gagne aucun argent au théâtre en attaquant la religion et que si le but de ma vie était de gagner de l'argent, je crois que j'aurais depuis longtemps changé de métier ? Vous faites erreur sur ma personne et sur mes intentions.

On peut déduire que la dame à qui ces remarques sont adressées

(A)   connaît bien le théâtre
(B)   est antireligieuse
(C)   a accusé le dramaturge de matérialisme
(D)   a compris les intentions du dramaturge

You are being asked to look at the dramatist's reply to his critic and deduce something about her. He has said that attacking religion in a play is not a way to earn money, and that if his purpose in life were to earn money, he would have changed his profession long ago. Therefore the correct answer is (C)—she has accused him of materialism.

Other Formats

New formats are developed from time to time to find new ways of assessing knowledge with multiple-choice questions. If you see a format you are not familiar with, read the directions carefully. Then read and approach the question the way you would any other question, asking yourself what you are supposed to be looking for and what details are given in the question that help you find the answer.

Other Useful Facts about the Test

1. You can answer the questions that do not require listening in any order. You can go through the questions with written prompts from beginning to end, as many test takers do, or you can create your own path. Perhaps you will want to answer questions in your strongest area of knowledge first and then move from your strengths to your weaker areas. There is no right or wrong way. Use the approach that works best for you.

You do not have this liberty with the questions that require you to listen to a recording. You must answer those questions in the order in which you hear them and in the time that the recording permits. You are not allowed to pause the recording for extra time.

2. There are no trick questions on the test. You don't have to find any hidden meanings or worry about trick wording. All of the questions on the test ask about subject matter knowledge in a straightforward manner.

3. Don't worry about answer patterns. There is one myth that says that answers on multiple-choice tests follow patterns. Another myth says that there will never be more than two questions with the same lettered answer following each other. There is no truth to either of these myths. Select the answer you think is correct based on your knowledge of the subject.

4. There is no penalty for guessing. Your test score for multiple-choice questions is based on the number of correct answers you have. When you don't know the answer to a question, try to eliminate any obviously wrong answers and then guess at the correct one.

5. It's OK to write in your test book. You can work out problems right on the pages of the book, make notes to yourself, mark questions you want to review later, or write anything at all. Your test book will be destroyed after you are finished with it, so use it in any way that is helpful to you. But make sure to mark your answers on the answer sheet.

Smart Tips for Taking the Test

1. Put your answers in the right "bubbles." It seems obvious, but be sure that you are filling in the answer bubble that corresponds to the question you are answering. A significant number of test takers fill in a bubble without checking to see that the number matches the question they are answering.

2. Skip the nonlistening questions you find extremely difficult. In the section of the test that does not require listening to a recording, there are sure to be some questions that you think are hard. Rather than trying to answer these on your first pass through this part of the test, leave them blank and mark them in your test book so you can come back to them later. Pay attention to the time as you answer the rest of the questions on the test, and try to finish with 10 or 15 minutes remaining so that you can go back over the questions you left blank. Even if you don't know the answer the second time you read the questions, see if you can narrow down the possible answers, and then guess.

3. Keep track of the time. In the part of the test that requires you to listen to a recording, you must answer within a specific period of time. For the rest of the test, however, you will need to budget your time for yourself. Take a watch to the test, just in case the clock in the test room is difficult for you to see. You will probably have plenty of time to answer all of the questions, but if you find yourself becoming bogged down in one section, you might decide to move on and come back to that section later.

4. Read all of the possible answers before selecting one—and then reread the question to be sure the answer you have selected really answers the question being asked. Remember that a question that contains a phrase such as "Which of the following does NOT..." is asking for the one answer that is NOT a correct statement or conclusion.

5. Check your answers. If you have extra time left over at the end of the test, look over each question and make sure that you have filled in the bubble on the answer sheet as you intended. Many test takers make careless mistakes that they could have corrected if they had checked their answers.

6. Don't worry about your score when you are taking the test. No one is expected to answer all of the questions correctly. Your score on this test is not analogous to your score on the SAT, the GRE, or other similar looking (but in fact very different) tests. It doesn't matter whether you score very high or barely pass this test. If you meet the minimum passing scores for your state and you meet the state's other requirements for obtaining a teaching license, you will receive a license. In other words, your actual score doesn't matter, as long as it is above the minimum required score. With your score report, you will receive a booklet entitled *Understanding Your Praxis Scores*, which lists the passing scores for your state.

Study Guide for the French and German Tests   35

Chapter 5
Practice Questions—*French: Content Knowledge*

► ► ► ► ► ► ► ► ► ► ► ►

Now that you have studied the content topics and have worked through strategies relating to multiple-choice questions, you should answer the following practice questions. You may find it helpful to simulate actual testing conditions, giving yourself 90 minutes to work on the questions. You can cut out and use the answer sheet provided if you wish.

When you have finished the practice questions, you can score your answers and read the explanations for the best answer choices in chapter 6.

The listening section for this practice test is found on the French CD included with this study guide. Tracks 1-5 refer to the *French: Content Knowledge* test. (Note that tracks 6-13 refer to the *French: Productive Language Skills* test; you will not need to listen to this section of the CD unless you are planning to take that test as well.) As you listen to the CD, you will notice that pauses have been included in the narration. During the pauses, you may bubble in your answers on the provided answer sheet.

To simulate actual testing conditions, do not stop your CD player during the practice test.

Keep in mind that the test you take at an actual administration will have different questions, although the proportion of questions in each area and major subarea will be approximately the same. You should not expect the percentage of questions you answer correctly on this practice test to be exactly the same as when you take the test at an actual administration, since numerous factors affect a person's performance in any given testing situation.

THE PRAXIS
S E R I E S
Professional Assessments for Beginning Teachers ®

TEST NAME:

French: Content Knowledge (0173)

90 Practice Questions

Time—90 minutes

(**Note:** At the official test administration, there will be 120 questions, and you will be allowed 120 minutes to complete the test.)

Answer Sheet L

(ETS)

THE PRAXIS SERIES
Professional Assessments for Beginning Teachers®

DO NOT USE INK

Use only a pencil with soft black lead (No. 2 or HB) to complete this answer sheet.
Be sure to fill in completely the oval that corresponds to the proper letter or number.
Completely erase any errors or stray marks.

1. NAME

Enter your last name and first initial.
Omit spaces, hyphens, apostrophes, etc.

Last Name (first 6 letters) / F I

(Grid of letter ovals A–Z for name)

2.

YOUR NAME: (Print)
Last Name (Family or Surname) — First Name (Given) — M. I.

MAILING ADDRESS: (Print)
P.O. Box or Street Address — Apt. # (If any)

City — State or Province

Country — Zip or Postal Code

TELEPHONE NUMBER: ( ) Home — ( ) Business

SIGNATURE: _____ **TEST DATE:** _____

3. DATE OF BIRTH

Month	Day
Jan.	
Feb.	
Mar.	
April	
May	
June	
July	
Aug.	
Sept.	
Oct.	
Nov.	
Dec.	

(Day ovals: 0–9)

4. SOCIAL SECURITY NUMBER

(Grid of number ovals 0–9)

5. CANDIDATE ID NUMBER

(Grid of number ovals 0–9)

6. TEST CENTER / REPORTING LOCATION

Center Number — Room Number

Center Name

City — State or Province

Country

7. TEST CODE / FORM CODE

(Grid of number ovals 0–9)

8. TEST BOOK SERIAL NUMBER

9. TEST FORM

0
1

10. TEST NAME

Educational Testing Service, ETS, the ETS logo and THE PRAXIS SERIES: PROFESSIONAL ASSESSMENTS FOR BEGINNING TEACHERS are registered trademarks of Educational Testing Service. The Praxis Series is a trademark of Educational Testing Service.

Copyright © 2004 by Educational Testing Service, Princeton, NJ 08541-0001.
All rights reserved. Printed in U.S.A.

51055 • 14725 • TF24E50 • printed in U.S.A.

MH04023   I.N. 202984   Q3032-06,07

1   2   3   4

PAGE 2

BE SURE EACH MARK IS DARK AND COMPLETELY FILLS THE INTENDED SPACE AS ILLUSTRATED HERE: ● .

1 Ⓐ Ⓑ Ⓒ Ⓓ	31 Ⓐ Ⓑ Ⓒ Ⓓ	61 Ⓐ Ⓑ Ⓒ Ⓓ	91 Ⓐ Ⓑ Ⓒ Ⓓ
2 Ⓐ Ⓑ Ⓒ Ⓓ	32 Ⓐ Ⓑ Ⓒ Ⓓ	62 Ⓐ Ⓑ Ⓒ Ⓓ	92 Ⓐ Ⓑ Ⓒ Ⓓ
3 Ⓐ Ⓑ Ⓒ Ⓓ	33 Ⓐ Ⓑ Ⓒ Ⓓ	63 Ⓐ Ⓑ Ⓒ Ⓓ	93 Ⓐ Ⓑ Ⓒ Ⓓ
4 Ⓐ Ⓑ Ⓒ Ⓓ	34 Ⓐ Ⓑ Ⓒ Ⓓ	64 Ⓐ Ⓑ Ⓒ Ⓓ	94 Ⓐ Ⓑ Ⓒ Ⓓ
5 Ⓐ Ⓑ Ⓒ Ⓓ	35 Ⓐ Ⓑ Ⓒ Ⓓ	65 Ⓐ Ⓑ Ⓒ Ⓓ	95 Ⓐ Ⓑ Ⓒ Ⓓ
6 Ⓐ Ⓑ Ⓒ Ⓓ	36 Ⓐ Ⓑ Ⓒ Ⓓ	66 Ⓐ Ⓑ Ⓒ Ⓓ	96 Ⓐ Ⓑ Ⓒ Ⓓ
7 Ⓐ Ⓑ Ⓒ Ⓓ	37 Ⓐ Ⓑ Ⓒ Ⓓ	67 Ⓐ Ⓑ Ⓒ Ⓓ	97 Ⓐ Ⓑ Ⓒ Ⓓ
8 Ⓐ Ⓑ Ⓒ Ⓓ	38 Ⓐ Ⓑ Ⓒ Ⓓ	68 Ⓐ Ⓑ Ⓒ Ⓓ	98 Ⓐ Ⓑ Ⓒ Ⓓ
9 Ⓐ Ⓑ Ⓒ Ⓓ	39 Ⓐ Ⓑ Ⓒ Ⓓ	69 Ⓐ Ⓑ Ⓒ Ⓓ	99 Ⓐ Ⓑ Ⓒ Ⓓ
10 Ⓐ Ⓑ Ⓒ Ⓓ	40 Ⓐ Ⓑ Ⓒ Ⓓ	70 Ⓐ Ⓑ Ⓒ Ⓓ	100 Ⓐ Ⓑ Ⓒ Ⓓ
11 Ⓐ Ⓑ Ⓒ Ⓓ	41 Ⓐ Ⓑ Ⓒ Ⓓ	71 Ⓐ Ⓑ Ⓒ Ⓓ	101 Ⓐ Ⓑ Ⓒ Ⓓ
12 Ⓐ Ⓑ Ⓒ Ⓓ	42 Ⓐ Ⓑ Ⓒ Ⓓ	72 Ⓐ Ⓑ Ⓒ Ⓓ	102 Ⓐ Ⓑ Ⓒ Ⓓ
13 Ⓐ Ⓑ Ⓒ Ⓓ	43 Ⓐ Ⓑ Ⓒ Ⓓ	73 Ⓐ Ⓑ Ⓒ Ⓓ	103 Ⓐ Ⓑ Ⓒ Ⓓ
14 Ⓐ Ⓑ Ⓒ Ⓓ	44 Ⓐ Ⓑ Ⓒ Ⓓ	74 Ⓐ Ⓑ Ⓒ Ⓓ	104 Ⓐ Ⓑ Ⓒ Ⓓ
15 Ⓐ Ⓑ Ⓒ Ⓓ	45 Ⓐ Ⓑ Ⓒ Ⓓ	75 Ⓐ Ⓑ Ⓒ Ⓓ	105 Ⓐ Ⓑ Ⓒ Ⓓ
16 Ⓐ Ⓑ Ⓒ Ⓓ	46 Ⓐ Ⓑ Ⓒ Ⓓ	76 Ⓐ Ⓑ Ⓒ Ⓓ	106 Ⓐ Ⓑ Ⓒ Ⓓ
17 Ⓐ Ⓑ Ⓒ Ⓓ	47 Ⓐ Ⓑ Ⓒ Ⓓ	77 Ⓐ Ⓑ Ⓒ Ⓓ	107 Ⓐ Ⓑ Ⓒ Ⓓ
18 Ⓐ Ⓑ Ⓒ Ⓓ	48 Ⓐ Ⓑ Ⓒ Ⓓ	78 Ⓐ Ⓑ Ⓒ Ⓓ	108 Ⓐ Ⓑ Ⓒ Ⓓ
19 Ⓐ Ⓑ Ⓒ Ⓓ	49 Ⓐ Ⓑ Ⓒ Ⓓ	79 Ⓐ Ⓑ Ⓒ Ⓓ	109 Ⓐ Ⓑ Ⓒ Ⓓ
20 Ⓐ Ⓑ Ⓒ Ⓓ	50 Ⓐ Ⓑ Ⓒ Ⓓ	80 Ⓐ Ⓑ Ⓒ Ⓓ	110 Ⓐ Ⓑ Ⓒ Ⓓ
21 Ⓐ Ⓑ Ⓒ Ⓓ	51 Ⓐ Ⓑ Ⓒ Ⓓ	81 Ⓐ Ⓑ Ⓒ Ⓓ	111 Ⓐ Ⓑ Ⓒ Ⓓ
22 Ⓐ Ⓑ Ⓒ Ⓓ	52 Ⓐ Ⓑ Ⓒ Ⓓ	82 Ⓐ Ⓑ Ⓒ Ⓓ	112 Ⓐ Ⓑ Ⓒ Ⓓ
23 Ⓐ Ⓑ Ⓒ Ⓓ	53 Ⓐ Ⓑ Ⓒ Ⓓ	83 Ⓐ Ⓑ Ⓒ Ⓓ	113 Ⓐ Ⓑ Ⓒ Ⓓ
24 Ⓐ Ⓑ Ⓒ Ⓓ	54 Ⓐ Ⓑ Ⓒ Ⓓ	84 Ⓐ Ⓑ Ⓒ Ⓓ	114 Ⓐ Ⓑ Ⓒ Ⓓ
25 Ⓐ Ⓑ Ⓒ Ⓓ	55 Ⓐ Ⓑ Ⓒ Ⓓ	85 Ⓐ Ⓑ Ⓒ Ⓓ	115 Ⓐ Ⓑ Ⓒ Ⓓ
26 Ⓐ Ⓑ Ⓒ Ⓓ	56 Ⓐ Ⓑ Ⓒ Ⓓ	86 Ⓐ Ⓑ Ⓒ Ⓓ	116 Ⓐ Ⓑ Ⓒ Ⓓ
27 Ⓐ Ⓑ Ⓒ Ⓓ	57 Ⓐ Ⓑ Ⓒ Ⓓ	87 Ⓐ Ⓑ Ⓒ Ⓓ	117 Ⓐ Ⓑ Ⓒ Ⓓ
28 Ⓐ Ⓑ Ⓒ Ⓓ	58 Ⓐ Ⓑ Ⓒ Ⓓ	88 Ⓐ Ⓑ Ⓒ Ⓓ	118 Ⓐ Ⓑ Ⓒ Ⓓ
29 Ⓐ Ⓑ Ⓒ Ⓓ	59 Ⓐ Ⓑ Ⓒ Ⓓ	89 Ⓐ Ⓑ Ⓒ Ⓓ	119 Ⓐ Ⓑ Ⓒ Ⓓ
30 Ⓐ Ⓑ Ⓒ Ⓓ	60 Ⓐ Ⓑ Ⓒ Ⓓ	90 Ⓐ Ⓑ Ⓒ Ⓓ	120 Ⓐ Ⓑ Ⓒ Ⓓ

PRAXIS FRENCH: CONTENT KNOWLEDGE

90 Multiple-Choice Questions
(Time—90 minutes)

RECORDED PORTION OF THE TEST

Section I	Interpretive Listening	Parts A, B, C
Section II	Structure of the Language (Grammatical Accuracy)	Part A

[The following directions will be heard on the CD.]

This is the recorded portion of the study guide for the Praxis *French: Content Knowledge* test. All the directions you will hear for this portion of the test are also printed in your test book.

In a moment, you will hear an introductory statement by two of the people who recorded this test. The purpose of this introduction is to familiarize you with the speakers' voices. Listen to the following passage.

> *Les élèves doivent aller en classe du lundi au vendredi, sauf les jours de congé. Cette année, tous les élèves sortiront tôt de l'école le 20 et le 27 janvier à cause des réunions auxquelles assisteront les professeurs du lycée.*

[Heard twice]

GO ON TO THE NEXT PAGE

SECTION I

INTERPRETIVE LISTENING

Approximate time—23 minutes

Section I is designed to measure how well you understand spoken French.

Part A: Questions 1–6

Directions: In Part A you will hear short conversations between two people. After each conversation you will hear one or more questions. The conversations and questions are not printed in the test book.

During the pause after each question, read the four answer choices printed in your test book and choose the <u>one</u> most appropriate answer. Indicate your choice on your answer sheet.

For example, you will hear:

[Recorded conversation and question]

In your test book you will read:

(A) De la construction d'un bâtiment.
(B) D'une maladie subite.
(C) D'une sortie remise.
(D) D'une prédiction astrologique.

SAMPLE ANSWER
Ⓐ Ⓑ ● Ⓓ

Of the four answer choices, (C) is the most appropriate answer. Therefore, you would fill in space (C) on your answer sheet.

You may take notes, but <u>only</u> in your test book.

Now we will begin Part A with the conversation for question number 1.

1. (A) Dans un magasin de chaussures.
   (B) Dans un magasin de vêtements.
   (C) Dans une droguerie.
   (D) Dans une boulangerie.

   _____

2. (A) Un rendez-vous manqué.
   (B) Le mauvais temps.
   (C) Des problèmes de circulation.
   (D) La fin des congés d'été.

Les questions 3 et 4 se rapportent à la conversation suivante.

3. (A) Son amie n'a pas rangé sa chambre récemment.
   (B) Marlène n'est pas très heureuse de le voir.
   (C) Son amie a de nouveaux meubles.
   (D) Marlène est en train d'étudier pour un examen.

4. (A) Ils vont se préparer pour une intervention qu'ils feront en classe.
   (B) Ils vont discuter d'une lecture que Paul n'a pas tout à fait comprise.
   (C) Ils vont regarder une cassette vidéo faite en classe la semaine dernière.
   (D) Ils vont voir une exposition de peintres surréalistes.

Les questions 5 et 6 se rapportent à la conversation téléphonique suivante.

5. (A) Il demande des renseignements concernant un emploi.
   (B) Il veut avoir l'occasion de louer une voiture.
   (C) Il veut placer une annonce dans un journal.
   (D) Il prend rendez-vous pour voir une voiture.

6. (A) A midi.
   (B) A trois heures de l'après-midi.
   (C) Dans une quinzaine de minutes.
   (D) Dans une heure.

GO ON TO THE NEXT PAGE

Part B: Questions 7–12

Directions: In Part B you will hear short narrations. The narrations are not printed in your test book. After each narration you will hear one or more questions, which are printed in your test book.

During the pause after each question, read the four answer choices printed in your test book and choose the one most appropriate answer. Indicate your choice on your answer sheet.

For example, you will hear:

[Recorded narration and question]

In your test book you will read:

La question se rapporte à l'information suivante.

De quoi s'agit-il ?

(A) D'une semaine de camping.
(B) D'une aventure hasardeuse.
(C) D'une partie de ski.
(D) D'une avalanche dans les Alpes.

SAMPLE ANSWER

Ⓐ ● Ⓒ Ⓓ

Of the four answer choices, (B) is the most appropriate answer. Therefore, you would fill in space (B) on your answer sheet.

You may take notes, but only in your test book.

Now we will begin Part B with the narration for questions 7 and 8.

Les questions 7 et 8 se rapportent au monologue suivant.

7. Qu'est-ce que cette jeune femme a l'intention de faire maintenant ?

   (A) De trouver du travail à Marseille.
   (B) De continuer ses études à Genève.
   (C) De devenir professeur.
   (D) De démarrer sa propre entreprise.

8. Comment pourrait-on caractériser la jeune femme qui parle ?

   (A) Elle est malheureuse.
   (B) Elle est plutôt optimiste.
   (C) Elle est très fâchée.
   (D) Elle est plutôt sensible.

Les questions 9 et 10 se rapportent à l'anecdote suivante.

9. Qu'est-ce que Jean-Pierre a fait avant d'aller au Louvre ?

   (A) Il s'est arrêté à la banque.
   (B) Il a nettoyé ses chaussures.
   (C) Il est allé chez le coiffeur.
   (D) Il a repassé ses vêtements.

10. Pourquoi est-ce que Françoise n'était pas au rendez-vous ?

   (A) Françoise ne voulait pas venir.
   (B) Jean-Pierre est arrivé trop tard.
   (C) Jean-Pierre s'est trompé de jour.
   (D) Françoise a eu un empêchement.

Les questions 11 et 12 se rapportent à l'explication suivante.

11. D'après ce texte, dans quel endroit peut-on acheter une télécarte ?

   (A) A l'intérieur d'une cabine téléphonique.
   (B) Dans les magasins d'électroménager.
   (C) Dans les bureaux de poste.
   (D) Au marché aux puces.

12. Qu'est-ce qu'on peut déduire de ce passage ?

   (A) Les cartes peuvent avoir de la valeur pour des collectionneurs.
   (B) Les télécartes existent depuis plus de vingt ans en France.
   (C) Certaines télécartes peuvent être renouvelées tous les mois.
   (D) Les télécartes vont remplacer les timbres-poste en France.

GO ON TO THE NEXT PAGE

Part C: Questions 13–24

Directions: In Part C you will hear narrations and conversations that are longer than those in Parts A and B. The narrations and conversations are not printed in your test book. After each narration or conversation, you will hear several questions, which are printed in your test book.

During the pause after each question, read the four answer choices printed in your test book and choose the one most appropriate answer. Indicate your choice on your answer sheet.

There is no sample question for this part.

You may take notes, but only in your test book.

Now we will begin Part C with the conversation for questions 13 and 14.

Les questions 13 et 14 se rapportent à la conversation suivante entre deux amis qui passent la soirée ensemble.

13. Que peut-on dire des interlocuteurs ?

    (A) Ils viennent de terminer leur repas.
    (B) Ils viennent de voir un film.
    (C) Ils vont commander des sandwichs.
    (D) Ils vont rendre visite à leur famille.

14. Laquelle des affirmations suivantes est vraie ?

    (A) L'homme n'aime pas les films d'horreur.
    (B) La femme n'a pas d'argent sur elle.
    (C) L'homme et la femme se disputent.
    (D) La femme est très critique.

Les questions 15 à 18 se rapportent au monologue suivant, dans lequel Jacques parle de sa carrière.

15. Pourquoi est-ce que Jacques n'arrivait pas à trouver un emploi après sa sortie du lycée ?

    (A) Il n'avait pas obtenu de diplôme.
    (B) Il ne trouvait pas d'emploi dans sa profession.
    (C) Il n'avait pas fait son service militaire.
    (D) Il n'aimait pas le sport.

16. Quel métier Jacques aurait-il souhaité faire ?

    (A) Ouvrier.
    (B) Chauffeur de bus.
    (C) Professeur d'éducation physique.
    (D) Cuisinier.

17. Comment est-ce que Jacques a trouvé son emploi actuel ?

    (A) En regardant les petites annonces.
    (B) Tout à fait par hasard.
    (C) Grâce à ses connaissances.
    (D) Avec l'aide d'une agence.

18. Quel est le métier actuel de Jacques ?

    (A) Acteur.
    (B) Metteur en scène.
    (C) Agent.
    (D) Cascadeur.

Les questions 19 à 22 se rapportent à la conversation suivante entre deux amis qui parlent d'un événement récent dans leur ville.

19. Comment est-ce que la femme a appris la nouvelle ?

   (A)   Elle a lu un journal.
   (B)   Elle a consulté Internet.
   (C)   Elle a regardé la télé.
   (D)   Elle l'a apprise par un voisin.

20. Comment est-ce qu'on pourrait caractériser la cérémonie d'ouverture du musée ?

   (A)   C'était une cérémonie qui a attiré les gens du quartier.
   (B)   C'était une formalité sombre et sérieuse.
   (C)   C'était une affaire qui a fait venir des personnes importantes.
   (D)   C'était une petite célébration intime.

21. Qu'est-ce qu'on apprend du musée dans ce dialogue ?

   (A)   Le musée est financé par des donateurs privés.
   (B)   Le musée abrite des œuvres d'art de plusieurs époques.
   (C)   Le musée abrite des souvenirs d'une famille royale.
   (D)   Le musée offre des tarifs réduits pour les étudiants.

22. Quel commentaire a fait un des interlocuteurs ?

   (A)   L'homme veut attendre la prochaine exposition pour aller au musée.
   (B)   La femme pense que le musée présente une image limitée de la ville.
   (C)   La femme pense que les collections sont peu importantes.
   (D)   L'homme est un peu surpris que le musée soit déjà ouvert.

Les questions 23 et 24 se rapportent au discours suivant.

23. Quel est le but principal de ce discours ?

   (A)   Faire de la publicité pour un nouveau cru de vins alsaciens.
   (B)   Proposer une visite de la région des vignobles alsaciens.
   (C)   Décrire les sites touristiques les plus visités en Alsace.
   (D)   Parler d'une course d'automobiles qui aura lieu en Alsace.

24. Selon le monologue, pour vraiment connaître l'Alsace, il faut

   (A)   chercher ses trésors cachés.
   (B)   y passer au moins une semaine.
   (C)   comprendre que les Alsaciens sont des gens très secrets.
   (D)   visiter les châteaux les plus célèbres.

GO ON TO THE NEXT PAGE

SECTION II

STRUCTURE OF THE LANGUAGE (Grammatical Accuracy)

Approximate time—26 minutes

Part A (recorded portion)—3 minutes
Parts B, C, and D—23 minutes

Section II is designed to measure your knowledge of the structure of the French language.

Part A: Questions 25–30

Directions: In Part A you will hear selections spoken by students who are learning French and who make errors in their speech. The selections are not printed in your test book. After hearing a selection, you will hear one or more excerpts from the selection. Each excerpt contains only <u>one</u> error. You will be asked to identify, correct, or describe the type of error in the excerpt. When answering each question, consider the error in the context of the entire selection. The questions are printed in your test book.

During the pause after each question, read the four answer choices printed in your test book and choose the <u>one</u> most appropriate answer. Indicate your choice on your answer sheet.

For example, you will hear:

[Recorded selection and question]

Then you will hear again:

[Recorded excerpt]

In your test book you will read:

The question refers to the following selection about a student's school and vacation.

Correct the error in the following excerpt.

(A) Change *Dans* to *En.*
(B) Change *je* to *nous.*
(C) Change *voyage* to *voyagé.*
(D) Change *mes* to *ma.*

SAMPLE ANSWER
● Ⓑ Ⓒ Ⓓ

Of the four answer choices, (A) is the most appropriate answer. Therefore, you would fill in space (A) on your answer sheet.

You may take notes, but <u>only</u> in your test book.

Now we will begin Part A with the selection for questions 25 and 26.

Questions 25 and 26 refer to the following comments by a student.

25. Describe the type of error in the following excerpt.

   (A)   Incorrect use of preposition
   (B)   Incorrect number of possessive adjective
   (C)   Incorrect past participle
   (D)   Incorrect auxiliary verb

26. Identify the error in the following excerpt.

   (A)   *Sur samedi*
   (B)   *j'ai passé*
   (C)   *à jouer*
   (D)   *au football*

Questions 27 and 28 refer to the following selection about a student's family.

27. Describe the type of error in the following excerpt.

   (A)   Incorrect pronunciation of verb
   (B)   Incorrect possessive adjective
   (C)   Incorrect object pronoun
   (D)   Incorrect placement of adverb

28. Describe the type of error in the following excerpt.

   (A)   Incorrect object pronoun
   (B)   Incorrect agreement between subject and verb
   (C)   Incorrect verb tense in subordinate clause
   (D)   Incorrect partitive

Questions 29 and 30 refer to the following comments about chocolates.

29. Describe the type of error in the following excerpt.

   (A)   Incorrect comparative
   (B)   Incorrect verb tense
   (C)   Incorrect use of reflexive verb
   (D)   Incorrect use of preposition

30. Identify the error in the following excerpt.

   (A)   *avons*
   (B)   *achetés*
   (C)   *pendant*
   (D)   *dans la*

STOP.

THIS IS THE END OF THE RECORDED PORTION OF THE TEST.

AT THE ACTUAL TEST ADMINISTRATION, YOU MUST NOT TURN THE PAGE UNTIL YOU ARE TOLD TO DO SO.

END OF RECORDING.

Part B: Questions 31–36

Directions: In Part B you will read paragraphs written by students who are learning French. Each paragraph contains errors. You will be asked to identify the error, correct the error, or describe the type of error in some of the sentences from each paragraph; each of those sentences contains only <u>one</u> error. When answering each question, consider the error in the context of the entire paragraph.

For each question, choose the one most appropriate answer from the four answer choices printed in your test book. Indicate your choice on your answer sheet.

For example:

The question refers to the following selection about a birthday.

(1) Mon anniversaire est samedi prochain; c'est le premier de juin. (2) J'espère recevoir beaucoup de cadeaux.

Correct the error in sentence 1.

(A) Change *Mon* to *Ma.*
(B) Change *prochain* to *prochaine.*
(C) Change *le premier* to *la première.*
(D) Change *de juin* to *juin.*

SAMPLE ANSWER

Ⓐ Ⓑ Ⓒ ●

Of the four answer choices, (D) is the most appropriate answer. Therefore, you would fill in space (D) on your answer sheet.

You may take notes, but <u>only</u> in your test book.

Questions 31–33 refer to the following paragraph about a ring.

(1) Hier, mon amie Mélanie a perdu sa bague préféré. (2) C'était un cadeau que sa grand-mère l'avait offert pour son anniversaire. (3) Nous avons cherché pour la bague partout, mais nous n'avons rien trouvé.

31. Describe the type of error in sentence 1.

    (A) Lack of agreement between possessive and noun
    (B) Lack of agreement between adjective and noun
    (C) Incorrect verb tense
    (D) Incorrect word order

32. Correct the error in sentence 2.

    (A) Change *l'* to *lui.*
    (B) Change *avait* to *a.*
    (C) Change *offert* to *offerte.*
    (D) Change *son* to *sa.*

33. Describe the type of error in sentence 3.

    (A) Incorrect word order
    (B) Incorrect conjunction
    (C) Incorrect use of preposition
    (D) Incorrect use of tense

Question 34 refers to the following sentence about swimming.

Après avoir nagé dans la piscine, je me lave mes cheveux.

34. Correct the error in the sentence.

    (A) Change *avoir* to *être.*
    (B) Change *dans* to *en.*
    (C) Change *me* to *se.*
    (D) Change *mes* to *les.*

Question 35 refers to the following sentence about a letter.

Voilà une lettre que j'ai écrit hier à ma tante.

35. Correct the error in the sentence.

    (A) Replace *j'ai* with *je suis.*
    (B) Replace *que* with *qui.*
    (C) Change *écrit* to *écrite.*
    (D) Change *ma* to *mon.*

Question 36 refers to the following sentence written by a student.

Si j'étais toi, je ne penserai pas à ce problème.

36. Correct the error in the sentence.

    (A) Change *penserai* to *penserais.*
    (B) Change *toi* to *tu.*
    (C) Change *à* to *de.*
    (D) Change *j'étais* to *je serais.*

Part C: Questions 37–43

Directions: In Part C you will read questions about the structure of the French language. For each question, choose the <u>one</u> most appropriate answer from the four answer choices printed in your test book. Indicate your choice on your answer sheet.

For example:

A *liaison* occurs in

(A) *des heures*
(B) *des Hollandais*
(C) *des haut-parleurs*
(D) *des hors-d'oeuvre*

SAMPLE ANSWER

● Ⓑ Ⓒ Ⓓ

Of the four answer choices, (A) is the most appropriate answer. Therefore, you would fill in space (A) on your answer sheet.

You may take notes, but <u>only</u> in your test book.

37. Which of the following pronouns can be used appropriately as the object of the preposition *pour* ?

   (A) *te*
   (B) *lui*
   (C) *me*
   (D) *ils*

38. Which of the following adjectives always follows the noun it modifies?

   (A) *rond*
   (B) *bon*
   (C) *grand*
   (D) *vieux*

39. Which of the following verbs is followed by an indirect object?

   (A) *regarder*
   (B) *téléphoner*
   (C) *chercher*
   (D) *écouter*

40. Which of the following words does NOT have the same meaning as its English cognate?

   (A) *attendre*
   (B) *copier*
   (C) *abandonner*
   (D) *investir*

41. Which of the following expressions requires the use of the subjunctive in the clause that follows?

   (A) *Je veux que*
   (B) *Il me semble que*
   (C) *Je pense que*
   (D) *J'espère que*

42. In which of the following words is the letter combination *ille* pronounced differently from the others?

   (A) *gentille*
   (B) *fille*
   (C) *tranquille*
   (D) *coquille*

43. Which of the following requires past participle agreement when changed to the *passé composé* ?

   (A) *Isabelle se brosse les dents.*
   (B) *Marie se parle tout bas.*
   (C) *Lucie se couche très tard.*
   (D) *Florence se pose des questions.*

Part D: Questions 44–50

Directions: In Part D you will read sentences or paragraphs from which words or phrases have been omitted. Each sentence is followed by four possibilities for completing the sentence. For each blank, choose the <u>one</u> answer that results in the best sentence or paragraph in written French. When choosing your answer, consider it in the context of the entire sentence or paragraph. Indicate your choice on your answer sheet.

For example:

Je me souviens de cette histoire avec _____ précision que
je pourrais vous la raconter en détail.

(A) tant
(B) tant de
(C) tant que
(D) autant que

SAMPLE ANSWER

Ⓐ ● Ⓒ Ⓓ

Of the four answer choices, (B) is the most appropriate answer. Therefore, you would fill in space (B) on your answer sheet.

You may take notes, but <u>only</u> in your test book.

Autrefois, __(44)__ souvent mes vacances au bord de la mer, mais une année, je suis allée à la montagne. Avant __(45)__ ma destination cette année-là, j'ai consulté Internet. J'ai trouvé un très joli endroit __(46)__ Suisse. J'ai demandé __(47)__ si elle voulait venir avec moi. Nous avons décidé __(48)__ du camping. Nous avons fait la connaissance de deux garçons __(49)__ . Tous ensemble, nous nous __(50)__ .

44. (A) j'ai passé
    (B) je passais
    (C) je passerais
    (D) je passerai

45. (A) de choisir
    (B) avoir choisi
    (C) choisir
    (D) j'ai choisi

46. (A) dans
    (B) au
    (C) en
    (D) à la

47. (A) à une amie
    (B) d'une amie
    (C) une amie
    (D) pour une amie

48. (A) à faire
    (B) de faire
    (C) faire
    (D) en faire

49. (A) bons
    (B) sympathiques
    (C) grands
    (D) beaux

50. (A) avons amusé
    (B) avons amusés
    (C) sommes amusés
    (D) sommes amusées

SECTION III

INTERPRETIVE READING

(Suggested time—26 minutes)

Section III is designed to measure how well you can understand written French.

Section III: Questions 51–74

Directions: In Section III you will read several selections or passages in French. Each selection or passage is followed by questions. For each question, choose the <u>one</u> most appropriate answer from the four answer choices printed in your test book. Indicate your choice on your answer sheet.

When answering the questions, consider them in the context of the entire selection or passage. Base each answer <u>only</u> on what is stated or implied in the selection or passage.

For example:

La question se rapporte à l'extrait suivant d'une lettre en réponse à la critique d'une pièce de théâtre.

Puis-je vous affirmer, Madame, qu'on ne gagne aucun argent au théâtre en attaquant la religion et que si le but de ma vie était de gagner de l'argent, je crois que j'aurais depuis longtemps changé de métier ? Vous faites erreur sur ma personne et sur mes intentions.

On peut déduire que la dame à qui ces remarques
sont adressées

SAMPLE ANSWER

(A) (B) ● (D)

(A) connaît bien le théâtre
(B) est antireligieuse
(C) a accusé l'auteur de matérialisme
(D) a compris les intentions de l'auteur

Of the four answer choices, (C) is the most appropriate answer. Therefore, you would fill in space (C) on your answer sheet.

You may take notes, but <u>only</u> in your test book.

Les questions 51 et 52 se rapportent à l'annonce suivante.

La Seine.

Le 1er avril 1999, on y recense 30 espèces de poissons de plus qu'il y a 30 ans. Sans blague.

La Seine, c'est la vie.
Elle s'y développe et drôlement bien.
C'est pour cela que la SEPA la protège.
Un beau geste pour l'environnement.
Tous les jours les habitants de l'Ile-de-France rejettent de l'eau usée dans les égouts.
Tous les jours la SEPA lave cette eau
avant de la redonner à la Seine.
Pour que les poissons puissent continuer
à faire de plus en plus de bébés,
pour que la Seine continue de vivre sa vie,
la SEPA œuvre sans relâche.

LA SEINE : VOUS L'AIMEZ,
NOUS LA PROTÉGEONS

51. Que fait la SEPA principalement ?

(A) Elle représente les gens qui habitent près de la Seine.
(B) Elle assure la protection des animaux typiques de l'Ile de France.
(C) Elle assainit l'eau que l'on utilise et la renvoie au fleuve.
(D) Elle fait de la recherche sur les fleuves de France.

52. Laquelle des affirmations suivantes est vraie ?

(A) La Seine est polluée à cause des Parisiens qui y jettent leurs ordures.
(B) La SEPA promet qu'il y aura plus de poissons dans la Seine d'ici 30 ans.
(C) La SEPA visite la Seine une fois par mois pour contrôler l'eau.
(D) La Seine abrite plus de variétés de poissons maintenant qu'avant.

Les questions 53 à 56 se rapportent à l'extrait suivant d'une œuvre littéraire.

Ligne   La Comtesse de Lamarre allait de pièce en pièce, cherchant les meubles qui lui rappelaient des événements, ces meubles amis qui font partie de notre vie, presque de notre être, connus
5 depuis la jeunesse et auxquels sont attachés des souvenirs de joies ou de tristesses, des dates de notre histoire, qui ont été les compagnons muets de nos heures douces ou sombres, qui ont vieilli, qui se sont usés à côté de nous, dont l'étoffe est
10 crevée par places et la doublure déchirée, dont les articulations branlent, dont la couleur s'est effacée.
    Elle les choisissait un à un, hésitant souvent, troublée comme avant de prendre des
15 déterminations capitales, revenant à tout instant sur sa décision, balançant les mérites de deux fauteuils ou de quelque vieux secrétaire comparé à une ancienne table à ouvrage.
    Elle ouvrait les tiroirs, cherchait à se
20 rappeler les faits, puis quand elle s'était bien dit : « Oui, je prendrai ceci », on descendait l'objet dans la salle à manger. Elle voulut garder tout le mobilier de sa chambre, son lit, ses tapisseries, sa pendule, tout.
25   Puis en rôdant par tous les coins de cette demeure qu'elle allait abandonner, elle monta un jour dans le grenier.
    Elle demeura saisie d'étonnement ; c'était un fouillis d'objets de toute nature, les uns brisés,
30 les autres salis seulement, les autres montés là on ne sait pourquoi, parce qu'ils ne plaisaient plus, parce qu'ils avaient été remplacés. Elle apercevait mille bibelots connus jadis, et disparus tout à coup, sans qu'elle y eût songé,
35 des riens qu'elle avait maniés, ces vieux petits objets insignifiants qui avaient traîné quinze ans à côté d'elle, qu'elle avait vus chaque jour sans les remarquer et qui, tout à coup, retrouvés là, dans ce grenier, à côté d'autres plus anciens dont
40 elle se rappelait parfaitement les places aux premiers temps de son arrivée, prenaient une importance soudaine de témoins oubliés, d'amis retrouvés.

53. Quelle valeur ces meubles ont-ils pour la Comtesse ?

(A)   Une valeur sentimentale
(B)   Une valeur monétaire
(C)   Une valeur utilitaire
(D)   Une valeur sociale

54. Qu'est-ce qui trouble la Comtesse ?

(A)   Elle ne peut pas s'offrir des meubles neufs.
(B)   Elle doit prendre des décisions financières difficiles.
(C)   Elle ne peut pas garder toutes ses affaires.
(D)   Elle doit trouver un remplaçant pour son ancien secrétaire.

55. Quelle a été la réaction de la Comtesse quand elle a vu le contenu du grenier ?

(A)   Elle était mécontente parce que tout était en désordre.
(B)   Elle était déçue parce que tous les objets semblaient cassés.
(C)   Elle était surprise de retrouver des objets qu'elle avait oubliés.
(D)   Elle était heureuse de retrouver des objets qu'elle avait recherchés.

56. La Comtesse semble être en proie à quelle émotion ?

(A)   Le courage
(B)   La nostalgie
(C)   La colère
(D)   La crainte

Les questions 57 à 59 se rapportent à l'article suivant sur certains aspects de la ville de Montréal.

Une ville sous la ville

Ligne Bien que les Montréalais le surnomment « la ville souterraine » ou encore « le souterrain », il s'agit plutôt d'un vaste réseau piétonnier qui s'étend sous la ville. Plus
5 précisément, c'est sous le centre-ville que ce réseau déploie ses 30 kilomètres de corridors, de places centrales et de carrefours.

  Plus de 500 000 personnes y passent chaque jour occupées à trouver la bonne affaire dans les
10 quelque 1 700 boutiques, ou affairées à se rendre au travail ou à l'université. On l'emprunte aussi pour les loisirs puisque le réseau, parfois via le métro, est relié à environ 40 salles de spectacles, de théâtre ou de cinéma sans compter les
15 restaurants, les attraits touristiques et les musées.

  C'est en 1962 que le souterrain commence à prendre forme et la galerie marchande du premier gratte-ciel montréalais, la Place Ville Marie, en constitue le premier élément. Ensuite,
20 la venue de l'Exposition universelle à Montréal en 1967 a fait aboutir le projet de métro dont les Montréalais rêvaient depuis longtemps.

  Par la suite, le souterrain a connu plusieurs phases de développement dont la plus
25 spectaculaire fut certes la mise sur pilotis de la cathédrale Christ Church pour permettre de creuser ses fondations et y installer un centre commercial.

  Depuis mars 2003, de nouveaux corridors
30 allongent le réseau existant et forment un quadrilatère dans le tout nouveau Quartier international. On profite de l'absence d'activités commerciales pour promouvoir l'art et la culture. Des niches et vitrines abritent des témoins de la
35 richesse des collections des musées montréalais. À l'abri des intempéries, des froides journées d'hiver ou des canicules de juillet, les Montréalais s'y pressent et les touristes s'y « perdent ».

57. On va au « souterrain » pour toutes les activités suivantes SAUF pour

 (A) faire des achats
 (B) faire du tourisme
 (C) faire un tour en voiture
 (D) voir un film

58. Quel a été l'effet de l'Exposition universelle de 1967 sur le métro ?

 (A) Les rails du métro ont été détruits.
 (B) Le métro du « souterrain » a été achevé.
 (C) Les travaux pour le métro ont été ralentis.
 (D) Le service du métro a été interrompu.

59. Selon l'article, qu'est-ce que l'on peut dire au sujet des nouvelles parties du « souterrain » ?

 (A) Elles ne sont pas reliées aux autres corridors.
 (B) Elles sont quatre fois plus grandes que le reste du « souterrain ».
 (C) Elles sont consacrées à la culture plutôt qu'à l'achat.
 (D) Elles ne sont pas rentables parce que l'on s'y perd.

Les questions 60 à 63 se rapportent au texte suivant qui définit des catégories de crèches enfantines.

Ligne   La crèche collective : elle accueille les enfants dans une structure adaptée aux bébés comme aux plus grands, répartis en section de bébés, moyens et grands. Les capacités d'accueil

5   varient entre 30 et 65 places. Les enfants sont pris en charge par des personnels spécialisés et bénéficient d'activités organisées sur place par une éducatrice de jeunes enfants.

     La crèche familiale : les enfants sont

10   accueillis au domicile des assistantes maternelles recrutées par la Ville de Paris. Les enfants participent plusieurs fois par semaine à des ateliers dans les locaux de la crèche familiale, ils sont pris en charge par une éducatrice de jeunes

15   enfants. Les assistantes maternelles sont sous l'autorité d'une directrice.

     La crèche parentale : il s'agit d'une structure adaptée aux enfants, leur garde est assurée conjointement par du personnel spécialisé et des

20   parents.

     Les assistantes maternelles privées : elles accueillent à leur domicile un à trois enfants et doivent être agréées par la Mairie. Elles sont contrôlées par le service de protection maternelle

25   et infantile.

     L'accès à ces crèches est soumis :

     ■ à l'acceptation d'un dossier d'inscription établi auprès du Bureau de la Petite Enfance.

30   ■ à la décision prise par les commissions* d'attribution des places en crèches.

   * Deux commissions sont organisées chaque année, l'une fin mai, l'autre à la fin du mois d'octobre pour des entrées respectives en septembre et janvier. Le nombre de places disponibles est beaucoup plus important à la rentrée de septembre qu'en janvier. Il est lié au fait que les enfants quittent la crèche le plus souvent l'été pour une rentrée à l'école maternelle dès le début de l'année scolaire.

60. Qu'est-ce qui caractérise la crèche collective ?

(A)   Les enfants sont gardés par groupes d'âges mélangés.

(B)   Le personnel a bénéficié d'une formation particulière.

(C)   Les enfants participent souvent à des activités à l'extérieur.

(D)   Les places sont attribuées exclusivement aux tout-petits.

61. En quoi est-ce que « les assistantes maternelles privées » sont différentes de tous les autres modes de garde décrits ?

(A)   Elles viennent garder les enfants à domicile.

(B)   Les bébés ne peuvent pas leur être confiés.

(C)   Le nombre d'enfants qu'elles peuvent garder est limité.

(D)   Elles ne sont pas reconnues par les services publics.

62. Que faut-il faire pour obtenir une place dans une crèche ?

(A)   Faire une demande auprès des autorités.

(B)   Avoir au moins trois enfants à la maison.

(C)   Déposer son dossier un an à l'avance.

(D)   Aller inscrire son enfant sur place.

63. A quel moment y a-t-il le plus de places libres dans les crèches ?

(A)   En septembre
(B)   En janvier
(C)   Fin mai
(D)   Fin octobre

Les questions 64 à 67 se rapportent à l'extrait suivant d'une œuvre d'Alphonse Daudet.

Ligne

. . . Deux fois par semaine, le dimanche et le jeudi, il fallait mener les enfants en promenade. Cette promenade était un supplice pour moi.

D'habitude nous allions à la Prairie, une
5 grande pelouse qui s'étend comme un tapis au pied de la montagne, à une demi-lieue de la ville. Quelques gros châtaigniers, trois ou quatre guinguettes* peintes en jaune, une source vive courant dans le vert, faisaient l'endroit charmant
10 et gai pour l'œil. Les trois études s'y rendaient séparément ; une fois là, on les réunissait sous la surveillance d'un seul maître qui était toujours moi. Mes deux collègues allaient se faire régaler par des grands dans les guinguettes voisines, et,
15 comme on ne m'invitait jamais, je restais pour garder les élèves. Un dur métier dans ce bel endroit !

Il aurait fait si bon s'étendre sur cette herbe verte, dans l'ombre des châtaigniers, en écoutant
20 chanter la petite source ! Au lieu de cela, il fallait surveiller, crier, punir. J'avais tout le collège sur les bras. C'était terrible.

Mais le plus terrible encore, ce n'était pas de surveiller les élèves à la Prairie, c'était de
25 traverser la ville avec ma division, la division des petits. Les autres divisions emboîtaient le pas à merveille et sonnaient des talons comme de vieux grognards. Cela sentait la discipline et le tambour. Mes petits, eux, n'entendaient rien à
30 toutes ces belles choses. Ils n'allaient pas en rang, se tenaient par la main et jacassaient le long de la route. J'avais beau leur crier « Gardez vos distances ! » ils ne me comprenaient pas et marchaient tout de travers.

* guinguette : petit café

64. Qu'est-ce que les promenades représentaient pour le narrateur ?

(A) C'était une occasion de profiter des espaces verts.
(B) C'était un moment particulièrement difficile.
(C) C'était un moment où il souffrait de la chaleur.
(D) C'était une occasion de faire de l' exercice.

65. Qu'est-ce que le narrateur faisait, une fois arrivé à la Prairie ?

(A) Il s'étendait sur la pelouse.
(B) Il recherchait l'ombre.
(C) Il surveillait tous les élèves.
(D) Il allait au café avec ses collègues.

66. Que peut-on dire à propos des petits ?

(A) Ils avaient du mal à entendre le surveillant.
(B) Ils étaient attirés par les belles choses.
(C) Ils ne s'entendaient pas avec les grands.
(D) Ils ne suivaient pas bien les directives.

67. Dans le dernier paragraphe, le narrateur compare les grands élèves à

(A) un régiment de soldats
(B) un troupeau d'animaux
(C) une fanfare municipale
(D) un vol d'oiseaux

Les questions 68 à 71 se rapportent aux Journées du Patrimoine.

Ligne

Les Journées du Patrimoine constituent chaque année le grand rendez-vous culturel de l'automne. À travers les ouvertures et manifestations, un large public peut découvrir,
5 ou mieux connaître, la richesse historique et culturelle du patrimoine proche de son environnement quotidien. L'ouverture des édifices et terrains protégés et d'autres sites qui sont d'ordinaire fermés au public, offre un rare
10 accès matériel et intellectuel à la profondeur de l'environnement patrimonial. Les Journées du Patrimoine servent à sensibiliser chacun au patrimoine, à ses subtilités et ses profondeurs historiques et culturelles.
15 Depuis 1991, les Journées du Patrimoine ont pris une dimension européenne. Aujourd'hui on célèbre le patrimoine commun dans toute l'Europe car plus de 46 pays européens contribuent aux Journées. Elles sont donc
20 devenues à la fois un instrument de découverte et de compréhension mutuelle pour de nombreuses communautés culturelles européennes et une ressource de développement. On peut découvrir par exemple, le patrimoine culinaire en
25 Languedoc-Roussillon avec des ateliers de cuisine catalane, observer un chantier de renaturation d'une zone naturelle en Suisse et faire la visite guidée d'un mausolée en Italie.
En France, le grand nombre de sites et
30 d'animations offerts à la visite, à cette occasion, témoigne de la richesse et du dynamisme du patrimoine national : châteaux et demeures privés côtoient pigeonniers et fermes typiques du patrimoine rural. Toutes les époques sont
35 représentées, du village mérovingien de Blangy-sur-Bresle aux constructions du XXᵉ siècle de Rouen et du Havre. Le patrimoine religieux est fortement présent, de même que le civil et le militaire. Les élégants parcs et jardins prennent
40 activement part à la manifestation, ainsi que les jardins ouvriers et familiaux.

68. Quel est le but des Journées du Patrimoine ?

(A) Faire connaître au public son héritage culturel et historique
(B) Assurer la défense de l'environnement quotidien
(C) Mettre en valeur les actions gouvernementales dans le domaine récréatif
(D) Sensibiliser les gens à la beauté du paysage de leur région

69. Selon le texte, comment l'esprit des Journées du Patrimoine s'est-il récemment élargi ?

(A) Chaque ville a présenté un aspect différent du patrimoine.
(B) Chaque site a fait référence à son écologie.
(C) On fête les contributions de plusieurs pays européens.
(D) On y a ajouté d'autres éléments, y compris les dessins animés.

70. Quel aspect du patrimoine français est mis en relief dans le troisième paragraphe ?

(A) Sa diversité
(B) Son côté rural
(C) Son académisme
(D) Sa richesse historique

71. Parmi les affirmations suivantes, laquelle représente le mieux la réalité des Journées du Patrimoine ?

(A) Elles permettent de voir des lieux qui ne sont pas accessibles habituellement.
(B) Il faut payer un droit d'entrée modéré pour participer aux activités.
(C) Les jardins, monuments et parcs d'attraction sont fermés aux groupes.
(D) Il y a des manifestations quotidiennes pour protéger l'environnement.

Les questions 72 à 74 se rapportent à l'article suivant au sujet de l'équipe française de rugby.

Ligne

Bernard Laporte, l'entraîneur de l'équipe française de rugby, aime ménager les surprises, et la liste de joueurs appelés à disputer la prochaine Coupe du monde, que Laporte vient

5 de rendre publique, en contient une : Brian Liebenberg, joueur sud-africain du Stade français, fera désormais partie de l'équipe nationale.

Liebenberg, athlète solide, n'a encore jamais

10 porté le maillot de l'équipe de France, et pour cause : les règlements de l'IRB (la Fédération Internationale de Rugby) exigent qu'avant de jouer pour une équipe nationale, tout joueur étranger aie résidé dans le pays en question

15 pendant trois ans sans interruption. Liebenberg est arrivé en France il y a seulement trois ans pour jouer avec l'équipe du FC Grenoble. Bien qu'il ait toujours souhaité faire partie de l'équipe de France, il n'a eu le droit de jouer avec

20 l'équipe nationale que depuis le mois dernier, date anniversaire de son arrivée dans l'hexagone.

Doté d'un jeu au pied particulièrement efficace, Liebenberg a profité du fait que, jusqu'à présent, l'équipe avait peu de joueurs qui

25 puissent mener le ballon aussi bien que lui. Bernard Laporte dit qu'il cherchait quelqu'un qui soit capable de s'imposer sur le terrain par son jeu au pied.

Les réactions au sein de la famille du rugby

30 français à l'arrivée d'un troisième joueur étranger à l'équipe (qui comprend déjà un Néo-Zélandais et un autre Sud-Africain) sont loin de faire l'unanimité : beaucoup, tout en reconnaissant le talent de Liebenberg, craignent

35 que ce choix n'encourage simplement les clubs à recruter davantage de joueurs étrangers.

72. Qu'est-ce qu'on apprend au sujet de Bernard Laporte ?

(A) Il ne supporte pas bien les surprises.
(B) Il pense que les joueurs de rugby se disputent trop.
(C) Il compte rendre la Coupe du monde au public français.
(D) Il ne fait pas toujours ce que l'on attend de lui.

73. Pourquoi Liebenberg n'a-t-il pas été sélectionné pour l'équipe jusqu'ici ?

(A) Il n'avait pas habité assez longtemps en France.
(B) Il lui fallait améliorer son jeu.
(C) Il voulait d'abord jouer pour l'Afrique du Sud.
(D) Il ne voulait pas suivre les règlements de l'IRB.

74. Selon Bernard Laporte, qu'est-ce qui l'a décidé à choisir Liebenberg ?

(A) Liebenberg pourra bien organiser les membres de son équipe.
(B) Liebenberg a une compétence dont l'équipe a bien besoin.
(C) Liebenberg peut intimider les autres équipes à cause de sa grande taille.
(D) Liebenberg a profité du fait qu'on cherchait des joueurs étrangers.

SECTION IV

CULTURAL PERSPECTIVES

(Suggested time—15 minutes)

Section IV is designed to measure your knowledge of the cultures of France and French-speaking countries and regions. The questions in this section are in French.

Section IV: Questions 75–90

Directions: For each question in Section IV, choose the <u>one</u> most appropriate answer from the four answer choices printed in your test book. Indicate your choice on your answer sheet.

For example:

À quelle heure les gens ont-ils le plus de chances de dîner en France ?

(A) 15h30
(B) 16h30
(C) 20h00
(D) 23h00

SAMPLE ANSWER

Ⓐ Ⓑ ● Ⓓ

Of the four answer choices, (C) is the most appropriate answer. Therefore, you would fill in space (C) on your answer sheet.

You may take notes, but <u>only</u> in your test book.

75. Qui a fait construire le château de Versailles ?

(A) Louis XVI
(B) Charlemagne
(C) Louis XIV
(D) Charles V

76. Lequel des pays suivants NE fait PAS partie du Maghreb ?

(A) La Tunisie
(B) L'Algérie
(C) La Côte d'Ivoire
(D) Le Maroc

77. La choucroute est un plat typique de quelle région française ?

(A) La Bretagne
(B) La Provence
(C) L'Alsace
(D) La Corse

78. Quelle expression veut dire à la fois « Bonjour » et « Au revoir » pour les Français ?

(A) Salut
(B) Enchanté
(C) Adieu
(D) Bonne journée

79. Laquelle des pièces suivantes N'est PAS une pièce de Molière ?

(A) *Dom Juan*
(B) *L'École des femmes*
(C) *Le Bourgeois gentilhomme*
(D) *Cyrano de Bergerac*

80. Parmi ces journaux français, lequel est un quotidien ?

(A) *L'Express*
(B) *Paris-Match*
(C) *Libération*
(D) *Le Point*

81. Qui a écrit « Il faut cultiver notre jardin » ?

(A) Marivaux
(B) Rousseau
(C) Voltaire
(D) Sade

82. Lequel des personnages suivants N'est PAS un héros de bande dessinée en français ?

(A) Tintin
(B) Astérix
(C) Lucky Luke
(D) Rastignac

83. La Côte d'Azur est surtout connue pour

(A) ses vins et ses vignobles
(B) ses plages et son beau temps
(C) ses vaches et ses produits laitiers
(D) ses belles rivières et ses châteaux historiques

84. Parmi les mots suivants, lequel N'a JAMAIS désigné la France ?

(A) L'Hexagone
(B) La Gaule
(C) La Métropole
(D) Le pays de Galles

85. Lequel des pays francophones suivants est divisé en cantons ?

   (A) Le Luxembourg
   (B) La Suisse
   (C) Le Canada
   (D) La Belgique

86. Lequel des écrivains suivants a participé à la rédaction de *l'Encyclopédie* ?

   (A) Stendhal
   (B) Racine
   (C) Diderot
   (D) Balzac

87. Que veut dire le proverbe « Petit à petit l'oiseau fait son nid » ?

   (A) Quand on travaille lentement, on risque de manquer son coup.
   (B) Avec de la volonté et à force de persévérance, on atteint son but.
   (C) Même si on est petit, on peut construire quelque chose d'important.
   (D) Les choses qui exigent le plus de temps sont les choses qui en valent la peine.

88. Le bras de mer formé par l'Atlantique entre la France et l'Angleterre s'appelle

   (A) la mer d'Iroise
   (B) la mer du Nord
   (C) le golfe de Gascogne
   (D) la Manche

89. En France, les pharmacies sont faciles à trouver grâce à leur enseigne représentant

   (A) une plume bleue
   (B) une flasque jaune
   (C) une carotte rouge
   (D) une croix verte

90. Lequel des hommes politiques suivants N'a PAS été Président de la République française ?

   (A) Charles de Gaulle
   (B) Raymond Poincaré
   (C) Jules Ferry
   (D) Georges Pompidou

Chapter 6

Right Answers and Explanations for the Practice Questions—*French: Content Knowledge*

►   ►   ►   ►   ►   ►   ►   ►   ►   ►   ►   ►

Now that you have answered all of the practice questions, you can check your work. Compare your answers to the multiple-choice questions with the correct answers in the table below.

Question Number	Correct Answer	Content Category	Question Number	Correct Answer	Content Category
1	A	Interpretive Listening - Short Conversation	40	A	Structure of the Language - Language Analysis
2	C	Interpretive Listening - Short Conversation	41	A	Structure of the Language - Language Analysis
3	A	Interpretive Listening - Short Conversation	42	C	Structure of the Language - Language Analysis
4	B	Interpretive Listening - Short Conversation	43	C	Structure of the Language - Language Analysis
5	D	Interpretive Listening - Short Conversation	44	B	Structure of the Language - Grammar
6	C	Interpretive Listening - Short Conversation	45	A	Structure of the Language - Grammar
7	A	Interpretive Listening - Short Narration	46	C	Structure of the Language - Grammar
8	B	Interpretive Listening - Short Narration	47	A	Structure of the Language - Grammar
9	B	Interpretive Listening - Short Narration	48	B	Structure of the Language - Grammar
10	C	Interpretive Listening - Short Narration	49	B	Structure of the Language - Grammar
11	C	Interpretive Listening - Short Narration	50	C	Structure of the Language - Grammar
12	A	Interpretive Listening - Short Narration	51	C	Interpretive Reading - Content and Organization
13	A	Interpretive Listening - Long Conversation	52	D	Interpretive Reading - Content and Organization
14	B	Interpretive Listening - Long Conversation			
15	A	Interpretive Listening - Long Narration	53	A	Interpretive Reading - Content and Organization
16	C	Interpretive Listening - Long Narration	54	C	Interpretive Reading - Content and Organization
17	B	Interpretive Listening - Long Narration			
18	D	Interpretive Listening - Long Narration	55	C	Interpretive Reading - Content and Organization
19	C	Interpretive Listening - Long Conversation			
20	C	Interpretive Listening - Long Conversation	56	B	Interpretive Reading - Implied Content
21	B	Interpretive Listening - Long Conversation	57	C	Interpretive Reading - Content and Organization
22	D	Interpretive Listening - Long Conversation			
23	B	Interpretive Listening - Long Narration	58	B	Interpretive Reading - Content and Organization
24	A	Interpretive Listening - Long Narration			
25	D	Structure of the Language - Speech	59	C	Interpretive Reading - Implied Content
26	A	Structure of the Language - Speech	60	B	Interpretive Reading - Content and Organization
27	A	Structure of the Language - Speech			
28	D	Structure of the Language - Speech	61	C	Interpretive Reading - Content and Organization
29	A	Structure of the Language - Speech			
30	D	Structure of the Language - Speech	62	A	Interpretive Reading - Content and Organization
31	B	Structure of the Language - Writing			
32	A	Structure of the Language - Writing	63	A	Interpretive Reading - Content and Organization
33	C	Structure of the Language - Writing			
34	D	Structure of the Language - Writing	64	B	Interpretive Reading - Content and Organization
35	C	Structure of the Language - Writing			
36	A	Structure of the Language - Writing	65	C	Interpretive Reading - Content and Organization
37	B	Structure of the Language - Language Analysis			
38	A	Structure of the Language - Language Analysis	66	D	Interpretive Reading - Implied Content
39	B	Structure of the Language - Language Analysis	67	A	Interpretive Reading - Content and Organization

Question Number	Correct Answer	Content Category	Question Number	Correct Answer	Content Category
68	A	Interpretive Reading - Content and Organization	78	A	Cultural Perspectives - Sociolinguistic Elements
69	C	Interpretive Reading - Content and Organization	79	D	Cultural Perspectives - Literature and the Arts
70	A	Interpretive Reading - Content and Organization	80	C	Cultural Perspectives - Lifestyles and Societies
71	A	Interpretive Reading - Implied Content	81	C	Cultural Perspectives - Literature and the Arts
72	D	Interpretive Reading - Content and Organization	82	D	Cultural Perspectives - Literature and the Arts
73	A	Interpretive Reading- Content and Organization	83	B	Cultural Perspectives - Geography
74	B	Interpretive Reading - Content and Organization	84	D	Cultural Perspectives - History
75	C	Cultural Perspectives - History	85	B	Cultural Perspectives - Geography
76	C	Cultural Perspectives - Geography	86	C	Cultural Perspectives - Literature and the Arts
77	C	Cultural Perspectives - Lifestyles and Societies	87	B	Cultural Perspectives - Sociolinguistic Elements
			88	D	Cultural Perspectives - Geography
			89	D	Cultural Perspectives - Lifestyles and Societies
			90	C	Cultural Perspectives - Lifestyles and Societies

Explanations of Right Answers

1. This question tests your understanding of spoken French. The dialogue takes place in a shoe store. The man wants to buy slippers (*pantoufles*), and he gives his shoe size (*pointure*) to the clerk. Answers (B), (C), and (D) refer to stores that sell clothes, (B), household products, (C), and bread, (D). Therefore, the correct answer is (A)—a shoe store.

2. This question tests your understanding of spoken French. The conversation takes place in a taxi, and the taxi driver explains to his client why there is likely to be a lot of traffic on the road. School vacation is starting, not ending, as in (D). There is no mention in the dialogue of a missed appointment, (A), or bad weather, (B). Therefore, the correct answer is (C)—traffic problems.

3. This question tests your understanding of the first part of the dialogue on contemporary French life. Keys leading to the correct answer include *épouvantable* ("horrible"), used by Paul to describe Marlene's room, and Paul's questioning how his friend finds room to study. Paul does not address Marlene's state of mind, (B), her choice of furnishings, (C), or what she has been doing, (D). The correct answer, therefore, is (A)—his friend has not cleaned her room recently.

4. This question tests your understanding of Paul's answer to Marlene's question: "What shall we talk about today?" Key phrases leading to the correct answer include Paul's statement that he wants to review what was done in class last week. Additionally, Paul states that he didn't follow the literature lesson. Therefore, the correct answer is (B).

5. This question tests your understanding of spoken French. In this conversation, the man is calling to get information about a used car he would like to see and eventually buy. (A) is not the correct choice because he is not calling about a job. (B) is not the correct answer because he is not calling to rent a car. (C) is not the correct answer because he is not calling to place an advertisement, but rather is calling about an advertisement. At the end of the dialogue, the man makes an appointment to see the car. The correct answer, therefore, is (D).

6. This question tests your understanding of time expressions in French. The question asks you to indicate when the man will be meeting the woman. (A) is not the correct answer because the man says that noon is the current time. (B) is not the correct answer because the woman says she will be at the address until 3:00 p.m. (D) is not the correct answer because the man says he will be arriving in approximately one quarter of an hour, not in one hour. The correct answer, therefore, is (C).

7. This question asks what the young woman, who has just finished her degree in economics at the University of Geneva, intends to do. She does not plan to continue her studies in Geneva, (B), to become a professor, (C), or to start her own company, (D). The young woman intends to return to her hometown of Marseilles to find a job, and, therefore, (A) is the correct answer.

8. This question asks how one would characterize the young woman. Since she speaks to the fact that she is not troubled by the high rate of unemployment because her professors prepared her well and because she knows people who work for large companies in Marseilles, (B)— she is somewhat optimistic—is the correct answer.

9. This question asks what Jean-Pierre did before leaving for his date. The story says that he dressed with care but not that he ironed his clothes, (D); that he paid special attention to his hair but not that he went to the barber, (C). There is no mention of his stopping at the bank, as in (A). The narration says that he polished his shoes to make them shiny. Therefore, the correct answer is (B)—he cleaned his shoes.

10. This question asks why Jean-Pierre's friend Françoise did not show up for their date. Jean-Pierre wonders whether she did not feel like coming, (A), or whether she had a problem, (D). But these are not the reasons why

Françoise did not show up for the date. Jean-Pierre did not arrive late, (B). The reason is that Jean-Pierre made a mistake. He was supposed to meet Françoise the day after *(le lendemain)*. Therefore, the correct answer is (C)—Jean-Pierre mixed up the date.

11. This question asks where one can buy a French telephone card. In the monologue, it is mentioned that such cards are for sale at the post office, tobacco shops, and newsstands. Therefore, (C) is the correct answer.

12. This question asks the listener to draw a conclusion about the narrative. Since the narrative ends by saying that French telephone cards have become "objects of collection," (A) is the correct answer, because it states that the cards can have some value for collectors.

13. This question requires that you indicate what can be said about the people who are talking. Even though they are talking about a movie, they have not yet seen it, (B). The woman asks the man how much she owes him for the food she already ordered, but (C) indicates a future action and therefore is not correct. The woman mentions that her parents are going to visit her, but there is no mention that she and the man are going to visit their families, (D). Since the woman asks the man how much she owes him for the food, it is understood that they have just finished eating. The correct answer, therefore, is (A).

14. This question asks you to choose the statement that is correct about the dialogue. Since the man says that a horror movie is playing but does not mention that he does not like horror movies, (A) is not correct. The man and woman do not argue, (C). The woman does not criticize anything during the conversation, (D). The woman mentions that she forgot to withdraw money from the bank machine and asks if she can use a credit card to pay. This means that she does not have any cash with her. The correct answer, therefore, is (B).

15. This question asks why Jacques was not successful in finding a job after leaving high school. The reason why Jacques had no profession, (B), and decided to perform his

military service, (C), was precisely that he had not obtained his diploma, (A). (D) is contrary to Jacques's insistence on his love of sports. Therefore, the correct answer is (A).

16. This question tests your understanding of the main idea in the central portion of the monologue and your understanding of the verb *souhaiter*. Having explained in the beginning how much he loved sports in school, Jacques says that he wanted to become a physical-education teacher, (C). However, this was impossible without having obtained his diploma. (A), (B), and (D) describe jobs that Jacques had to do because he could not become a physical-education teacher. Therefore, the correct answer is (C).

17. This question tests your understanding of the last part of the monologue and of the expression *par hasard* in the correct answer, (B). In the beginning, Jacques stated that he had looked at the newspaper advertisements *(les petits annonces)*, (A), and could not find work. He does not mention having used contacts to find work, (C), or having visited an agency, (D). However, he emphasizes his luck at the outset of the last part of the monologue and then describes how fortunate he was to have found this work in such an unforeseen manner. The correct answer, therefore, is (B).

18. This question tests your understanding of the last portion of the monologue and of the word *métier* ("profession") in the question. Although Jacques spoke with the director *(metteur en scène)*, (B), and knows many actors, (A), he is not a member of either profession. He does not mention an agent, (C). The correct answer, therefore, is (D).

19. This question asks how the woman learned about the opening of the museum. She asks her friend if he has watched the morning news *(Est-ce que tu as vu les infos ce matin?)* and goes on to say that the opening of the museum was announced; therefore (C)—*Elle a regardé la télé* ("she watched television")—is the correct answer.

20. This question asks you to characterize the opening ceremony of the museum. There is no

mention in the narration of the neighborhood people coming to the ceremony, (A). Nothing is said about the atmosphere of the event, (B), or how intimate it was, (D). However, the woman mentions that the mayor and his wife, as well as other officials *(fonctionnaires),* attended the event. Therefore, the correct answer is (C).

21. This question asks what one learns about the museum in this dialogue. Since the woman describes the museum's collections as containing drawings of the city made by a variety of artists from different centuries, (B) is the correct answer.

22. This question tests your understanding of an observation made by one of the speakers. Since the man does not say anything about waiting for the next exhibit to go to the museum, (A) is not true. (B) and (C) are false because the woman feels that the museum offers a comprehensive historical view of the city and that the collection is complete. The man does mention that he didn't expect the museum to open so soon. The correct answer, therefore, is (D).

23. This question tests your understanding of spoken French. The monologue deals with the wine region of Alsace. The purpose of the narration is to invite people to visit the wine-producing area in Alsace, (B). It does not advertise a new production of local wine, (A). There is no mention of an automobile race, (D). Even though the text mentions local architecture, its purpose is not to describe the most visited tourist sites, (C). Therefore, the correct answer is (B).

24. This question asks what the visitor to Alsace needs to do to gain real knowledge of the region. Even though the text mentions the chateaus and the people, it does not expressly say that they are the key to understanding the region, (C) and (D). It does not specify, either, the amount of time the visitor should spend there, (B). But it suggests that the inquisitive traveler leave the most traveled pathways *(les sentiers battus)* in order to find the hidden treasures of the region *(les trésors cachés).* Therefore, the correct answer is (A).

25. This question tests your knowledge of the choice of auxiliary verbs in compound past tenses. The *passé composé* in French is composed of an auxiliary verb and a past participle. A number of intransitive verbs, such as *sortir,* require the use of *être* as an auxiliary verb in compound past tenses. In the question, the verb *avoir* was used as an auxiliary verb with *sortir.* Therefore, the correct answer is (D).

26. This question tests the correct use and meaning of the preposition *sur.* The preposition *sur* indicates a physical relationship. The question, however, refers to a temporal relationship. *Sur samedi* is a direct literal translation from English to French. Therefore, the correct answer is (A).

27. This question tests your ability to recognize incorrect pronunciation in French. Even though the usual pronunciation for *-ent* is [/ã/], *-ent* is not pronounced when it is used as a verb ending, as in *parlent.* Therefore, the correct answer is (A).

28. This question tests your knowledge of the *partitif* in French. Most adverbs of quantity are followed by *de* without the article. The speaker should say *les gens avaient peu d' argent.* Therefore, the correct answer is (D).

29. This question asks you to apply your understanding of comparative adjectives. (A) indicates the mistake in this sentence. The comparative form of *bons* is irregular and becomes *meilleurs.* Therefore, (A) is the correct answer.

30. This question asks you to apply your understanding of the use of prepositions with names of countries. (D) is the correct answer. *Dans* is never used with names of countries. *La France* is a country that is feminine in gender. Thus the sentence should read *en France.*

31. This question tests your knowledge of the agreement between adjective and noun. *Bague* is a feminine word, and *préféré* should be written with an *-e (préférée).* Therefore, the correct answer is (B).

32. This question tests your knowledge of indirect object pronouns. In line 3, *l'* functions as a direct object pronoun. However, an indirect object pronoun *(lui),* rather than a direct object pronoun, is required to replace the prepositional phrase *à Mélanie.* The correct answer, therefore, is (A).

33. This question tests your knowledge of structure. *Chercher* is a verb that is not followed by the preposition *pour,* which is a frequent error of English speakers. The correct answer, therefore, is (C).

34. This question tests your understanding of pronominal verbs, or more specifically, of reflexive verbs. In French, the use of a reflexive verb indicates an action performed by and on the subject. Consequently, the use of a possessive adjective such as *mes* is redundant. The correct answer, therefore, is (D).

35. This question asks you to apply your understanding of the agreement of the past participle with the preceding direct object when the *passé composé* is used with *avoir.* (C) is the correct answer because the past participle *écrit* must agree with the relative pronoun *que,* which refers to *une lettre.*

36. This question asks you apply your understanding of sentences in which *si* clauses are used. (A) is the correct answer because the conditional must be used in the main clause when the imperfect is used in a *si* clause.

37. This question tests your knowledge of pronouns. Prepositions in French are followed by stress pronouns. The only answer containing a stress pronoun is (B)—*lui.* The correct answer, therefore, is (B).

38. This question tests your knowledge of the placement of adjectives in French. Most French adjectives are placed after the noun. A small number of very common adjectives referring to beauty, goodness, age, and size are placed before the noun. This is the case with *bon, grand,* and *vieux. Rond* refers to shape and is placed after the noun. Therefore, the correct answer is (A).

39. This question asks you to identify a verb that is followed by an indirect object. An indirect object in French is introduced by a preposition. The verb *téléphoner* is followed by the preposition *à,* so it will be followed by an indirect object. The other three choices are verbs that are followed by direct objects. The correct answer, therefore, is (B).

40. This question tests your knowledge of French vocabulary and asks you to be aware of false cognates. *Attendre* means "to wait" and not "to attend." Therefore, the correct answer is (A).

41. This question asks you to apply your understanding of the use of the subjunctive in contrast to the use of the indicative in a subordinate clause. For example, verbs of doubt, willingness, and emotion require the use of the subjunctive in the subordinate clause. (B), *Il me semble que,* is not to be confused with *Il semble que,* which expresses doubt and requires the subjunctive. (C), *Je pense que,* expresses certainty and demands the indicative in the dependent clause. (D), *J'espère que,* expresses emotion but is an exception to the rule. (A) is the correct answer as it is an expression of will that necessitates the subjunctive.

42. This question asks you to be aware of the different French pronunciations. Most words with the letters *ille* are pronounced [ij]. *Tranquille* is an exception; the letters *ille* in *tranquille* are pronounced [il]. Therefore, the correct answer is (C).

43. This question asks you to apply your understanding of the use of agreement of the past participle in the conjugation of pronominal verbs. The past participle agrees only with the preceding direct object. In answer (A), the direct object, *les dents,* and in answer (D), the direct object, *des questions,* follow the verb. In (B), *se* is an indirect object ("she talks to herself"). Therefore, (C) is the correct answer.

44. This question asks you to draw on your knowledge of past tenses. When the description of past habitual action is made in French, the imperfect tense is used. (A) is a past tense, the *passé composé,* but is not appropriate in this

context because of the repetition of the action. (C) is the conditional and (D) is the future, neither of which make sense in this passage. It should be noted as well that certain words and expressions typically accompany the imperfect tense. For example, *autrefois, tous les étés,* etc., suggest habitual action in the past. Therefore, (B) is the correct answer.

45. This question tests your knowledge of verb forms that follow prepositions. The preposition *avant* must be followed by *de* and an infinitive if the subject is the same in both parts of the sentence. (C) is incorrect because it does not include the *de.* (B) and (D) are forms that typically follow the preposition *après* or *après que.* Therefore, (A) is the correct response.

46. This question tests your knowledge of how prepositions are used with names of countries. Because *Suisse* is feminine, it is necessary to use the preposition *en.* In (B), *au* is used to refer to masculine countries. The preposition *dans,* (A), would not be used with countries. In (D), the preposition *à la* would be used in certain cases to refer to a city or a country with *la* in its name (e.g., *à La Martinique*). The correct answer is therefore (C).

47. This question tests your knowledge of a particular verb. The verb *demander* is followed by the preposition *à* if a question is being addressed to someone. It is possible for the verb *demander* to be followed by *de,* but only when an infinitive follows *(demander à quelqu'un de faire quelque chose).* The other two choices are not appropriate to use with the verb *demander.* Therefore, (A) is the correct response.

48. Again, this question tests your knowledge of a particular verb. *Décider,* when followed by an infinitive, requires the use of the preposition *de.* Therefore, (A) and (D), which use *à* and *en,* are not correct; neither is (C). (B) is the correct answer.

49. This question tests your knowledge of the position of the adjective in French. Most French adjectives are placed after the noun. A small number of common adjectives expressing beauty (as *beaux*), size (as *grand*), and

goodness (as *bons*) are placed before the noun. This is not the case with *sympathiques.* Therefore, the correct answer is (B).

50. This question tests your knowledge of the conjugations of the pronominal verbs in the *passé composé.* In the past tense, pronominal verbs are conjugated with the auxiliary verb *être.* Therefore, (A) and (B) are wrong. The past participle has to be in agreement with the preceding direct object, *nous,* which refers to *ensemble,* which is masculine and plural. Therefore, the correct answer is (C).

51. This question asks what the principal task of SEPA is. Since it is clearly stated in the text that SEPA cleans the water used by Parisians before putting it back into the Seine *(la renvoie au fleuve),* (C) is the correct answer.

52. This question asks which statement is true. Lines 1 and 2 explain that a recent survey of the Seine showed 30 more species of fish than 30 years ago. Therefore, answer (D), on how the Seine shelters more varieties of fish than before, is correct.

53. This question tests your comprehension of the general idea of the text. The *comtesse* thinks of her furniture as friends *(ces meubles amis,* line 3) that have been witnesses to many essential moments of her life (lines 4–8, lines 43–44). There is no mention in the text of the furniture having any monetary, (B), social, (D), or utilitarian, (C), value. Therefore, the correct answer is (A).

54. This question tests your comprehension of the second and third paragraphs. The *comtesse* does indeed have to make a difficult decision, but it is not a financial decision, (B). She is not trying to get new furniture or to replace some old piece, (A) and (D), but she has to decide whether to keep an object or get rid of it, because she cannot keep everything *(choisissait,* line 13; *oui, je prendrai ceci,* lines 21–22, etc.). Therefore, the correct answer is (C).

55. This question tests your understanding of the last paragraph. When the *comtesse* goes up to the attic, she is very surprised to find objects that she had forgotten *(Elle demeura saisie*

d'étonnement, line 28). She does not mind the mess, (A), or the fact that some of the objects are in poor condition, (B). There is no mention of her being happy to find some objects she had been looking for. Therefore, the correct answer is (C).

56. This question tests your comprehension of the general idea of the text. When looking at all her belongings, the *comtesse* reminisces about old times. The text does not describe her as feeling anger, (C), or fear, (D), or showing courage, (A). Therefore, the correct answer is (B), *La nostalgie.*

57. This question tests your comprehension of the first and second paragraphs of the text and the word *SAUF* ("EXCEPT") in the question. The first paragraph confirms to the reader that this is a vast pedestrian complex. The second paragraph lists many of the amenities that can be found in the complex, including approximately 1,700 shops, (A), and numerous movie theaters, (D). Although not described, tourist attractions, (B), are specifically listed in paragraph two. Therefore, the correct answer is (C).

58. This question tests your comprehension of paragraph three of the text and the verb *achever* ("to complete") in the question. Presenting a historical overview of the evolving construction of this underground city, paragraph two notes that the 1967 World's Fair brought about completion of the *métro,* the underground public-transportation system needed to service the complex, (B). It would be contrary to the text to say that the subway rails were destroyed or that subway service was interrupted during the 1967 World's Fair. Finally, the text does not state that the 1967 World's Fair slowed work on the subway, (C). The correct answer, therefore, is (B).

59. This question tests your comprehension of paragraph five, the final paragraph of the text. The topic sentence of paragraph five informs the reader that the newest part of the underground complex opened in 2003. The next sentence specifies that the city has made the most of the absence of commerical enterprises in this new section by using the

space to promote art and culture, which makes (C) the correct answer. The first sentence of paragraph five notes that with the new construction, the entire complex forms a quadrangle, thus eliminating (A). The size of the new section, (B), is not addressed. Local residents flock to this new section in the cold of winter and the boiling heat of summer, and tourists "lose" themselves in it, though figuratively, not literally, (D). The correct answer, therefore, is (C).

60. This question asks you to identify what characterizes a *crèche collective,* or group day care. Children are not grouped in mixed-age groups, (A). There is no mention of outdoor activities, (C), and the text states that the child care is not restricted to very young children, (D). In line 6, the personnel are referred to as *spécialisés,* meaning that they have had some training. Therefore, (B) is the correct answer.

61. This question asks how the *assistantes maternelles privées* are different from the other day-care options described. It is stated that children come to the homes of these registered babysitters, so (A) is incorrect. The text does not state that babies cannot be left with the babysitters, (B), and the text explicitly states that these caregivers are registered and overseen by child services, so (D) is also incorrect. The text does state that this type of babysitter takes care of one to three children; therefore, (C) is the correct answer. (NB: The word *limité* in French means limited to a SMALL number.)

62. This question refers to the necessary steps for registering a baby in a day-care center. The answer is in lines 26–31 of the text. It is not necessary to have at least three children at home, (B), to apply a year ahead of time, (C), or to go in person to register the child, (D). The parent needs to fill out a registration form with the local authority; therefore, the correct answer is (A).

63. This question refers to the last paragraph of the text (after the *). It asks you to tell when the number of places available in day care is the largest. The text mentions specifically that this

occurs in the month of September; therefore, the correct answer is (A).

64. This question asks you to tell how the narrator felt about his outings with the students. He would have been happy to enjoy the outdoors (lines 16–17). But he could not do that, (A); neither could he exercise, (D). There is no mention of the heat in the text, (C). However in several instances the narrator talks about how difficult this moment was for him (line 16, *Un dur métier;* line 22, *terrible;* line 3, *un supplice*). Therefore, the correct answer is (B).

65. This question tests your understanding of what the narrator had to do once he reached his final destination with his students. According to lines 18–19, he would have enjoyed lying down on the grass, (A), and in the shade, (B). His colleagues went to the local outdoor café, but he did not, (D). He had to stay and watch all the students (lines 15–16). Therefore, the correct answer is (C).

66. This question refers to the behavior of the youngest students, as described in the last paragraph. In answers (A) and (C), there is a play on the verb *entendre* (lines 29–30 of the text, *Mes petits, eux, n'entendaient rien à toutes ces belles choses*). The meaning of *entendre* in this context is "to understand." There is no mention of the fact that the little ones could not hear what the narrator was saying, (A), or that they did not get along with the older children, (C). They were not especially attracted by beautiful things, (B). But they had a hard time following instructions that they did not understand. Therefore, the correct answer is (D).

67. This question asks you to pay attention to words used by the narrator in the last paragraph to describe the older students. The narrator uses military vocabulary (*emboîtaient le pas, sonnaient des talons, vieux grognards, discipline,* etc.). The author does not compare the students to animals, (B), a local music band, (C), or a flock of birds, (D). Therefore, the correct answer is (A).

68. This question asks you to identify the goal of the *Journées du Patrimoine* in France. The last

sentence of the first paragraph (lines 11–14) clearly states that the *Journées du Patrimoine* serve to sensitize citizens to their historical and cultural heritage, (A). There is mention of the cultural environment, but the text does not discuss the preservation of the physical/natural environment, (B). While the text does state that the *Journées du Patrimoine* have taken on a more European flavor since 1991 (lines 15–16), there is no specific reference to government actions, French or otherwise, (C). Even though the text suggests in the third paragraph that appreciation of the region's countryside may be a result of the *Journées du Patrimoine,* (D), it is not the sole or principal goal of these days. Therefore, (A) is the correct answer.

69. This question asks how the *Journées du Patrimoine* have recently been expanded. The second paragraph describes the new European dimension of this cultural event (lines 15–16), making (C) the correct response. While some cities are mentioned in the third paragraph, it is not stated that every city presented a different cultural aspect during the event, (A). There are some references to nature and ecology (lines 26–27), but it is not stated that every site focused on its ecology, (B). There is no mention of cartoons, (D); therefore, the correct answer is (C).

70. This question tests your understanding of the main idea of the third paragraph. While both the rural, (B), and historical richness, (D), of the *Journées du Patrimoine* are mentioned in the paragraph, it is the diversity of the event that is important, (A). Grand chateaus and small farms are included in the event (lines 32–34); several eras are represented (lines 34–37); religious, military, and civilian aspects of life are all represented (lines 37–39); and elegant parks and gardens are juxtaposed with more practical family gardens (lines 39–41). There is no mention of the academic interest of the *Journées du Patrimoine,* (C), in the paragraph. Therefore, the correct response is (A).

71. This question asks you to identify which statement most accurately describes the *Journées du Patrimoine.* There is no mention in the text of the price of admission, (B), or of the

event being closed to groups, (C). While the word *manifestations* is used in the text (line 4), it is not referring to protests, (D); *manifestations* as used in the text means "event". The answer to this question lies in lines 8–9: *sites qui sont d'ordinaire fermés au public* ("sites usually closed to the public"). Therefore, (A) is the correct answer.

72. This question tests your comprehension of the first sentence of the passage. The text does not say anything about Bernard Laporte not liking surprises, (A), or about his intentions to give back the World Cup to the French public, (C). It does not say anywhere that the coach thinks that the players fight too much, (B). But Bernard Laporte likes to surprise people (in line 2, *aime ménager les surprises*). Therefore, he does not always do what is expected of him. The correct answer is (D).

73. This question asks you the reason why the South African rugby player was not selected earlier for the team. The answer is in the second paragraph, and more specifically in lines 11–15. The rules stipulate that a player has to have lived in a country for three years before he is eligible to join the national team. Liebenberg arrived in France only three years ago (lines 15–16). He is a good player, so he did not need to improve his game, (B). He did not express the desire to play for South Africa first, (C), and there is certainly no mention of his refusing to follow the rules of the International Federation, (D). Therefore, the correct answer is (A): He had not lived in France long enough.

74. This question tests your comprehension of the third paragraph. The text does mention that the South African is a solid athlete (line 9), but the reason why Bernard Laporte selected him is not because he is very tall and could intimidate the other teams, (C). The coach did not select him because of his talents as an organizer, (A). Neither was there a tendency in French rugby to choose foreign players, (D). On the contrary, there is a general fear that more foreign players will be recruited (end of the passage). The reason Liebenberg was selected is that he has talents that the team can use (third paragraph). Therefore, the correct answer is (B).

75. This question tests your knowledge of French history. The correct answer is (C)—Louis XIV. Louis XIV, the "Sun King," was known for his love of symbolic prestige, represented most famously in his construction of Versailles.

76. This question tests your knowledge of French-speaking countries in North Africa. *Le Maghreb* is located in northwest Africa and includes Morocco, Algeria, and Tunisia. *La Côte d'Ivoire* ("Ivory Coast") is in western Africa. Therefore, the correct answer is (C), *La Côte d'Ivoire.*

77. This question asks you to apply your knowledge of French regional cusine. Alsace is a region in France near the German border, and *choucroute* is a dish that is of German origin ("sauerkraut"). The correct answer, therefore is (C)—*L'Alsace.*

78. This question tests your knowledge of French expressions relating to greetings and introductions. The correct answer is (A), as it means both *Bonjour* ("Hello") and *Au revoir* ("Good-bye"). (B), *Enchanté,* means "Pleased to meet you." (C), *Adieu,* means only "Farewell." (D), *Bonne journée,* means "Have a nice day." Therefore, (A), *Salut,* is the correct answer.

79. This question tests your knowledge of classical French theater. *Cyrano de Bergerac* was written by Edmond Rostand, a nineteenth-century author. The correct answer, therefore, is (D).

80. This question tests your knowledge of the contemporary French press. Of the four publications listed, only *Libération* appears daily *(un quotidien). L'Express, Le Point,* and *Paris-Match* are weekly magazines. The correct answer, therefore, is (C).

81. This question tests your knowledge of French literature. This famous quotation is taken from Voltaire's *Candide.* The correct answer, therefore, is (C).

82. This question tests your knowledge of popular culture. Tintin, Astérix, and Lucky Luke are comic-book heroes. Rastignac is a character in Balzac's novels. Therefore, the correct answer is (D), Rastignac.

83. This question asks you to apply your knowledge of French regions. *La Côte d'Azur* is a popular vacation spot in southern France on the Mediterranean Sea. Therefore, (B) is the correct answer.

84. This question asks you to apply your knowledge of French culture. (A), (B), and (C) are all names referring to France. (A), *L'Hexagone,* is derived from the shape of the country. (B), *La Gaule,* is a historical name for France. (C), *La Métropole,* refers to continental France as opposed to its overseas departments. However, (D), *Le pays de Galles,* is the name of Wales in French. The correct answer, therefore, is (D).

85. This question asks you to apply your knowledge of francophone countries. Answers (A), (C), and (D)—Luxembourg, Canada, and Belgium—are divided administratively into regions or provinces. Only Switzerland, (B), is divided into *cantons.* The correct answer, therefore, is (B).

86. This question tests your knowledge of French literature. *L'Encyclopédie* was written by a group of scientists and philosophers in the eighteenth-century, the age of "Enlightenment." Stendhal and Balzac are nineteenth-century novelists; Racine is a seventeenth-century playwright. Therefore, the correct answer is (C), Diderot.

87. This question tests your knowledge and understanding of French proverbs. The correct answer is (B), since the proverb literally means, "Bit by bit, the bird makes his nest." (B) states that with good will and hard work, one can achieve one's goals. (A) is incorrect in that it implies that if one works slowly, one will miss one's chance. (C) is incorrect since it says that even if one is small, one can construct something important. (D) is incorrect because it suggests that things that require the most time are those that are worth the effort. Therefore, the correct answer is (B).

88. This question tests your knowledge of geography. The English Channel is known as *La Manche* and is the stretch of the Atlantic Ocean that separates England from France. Therefore, the correct answer is (D).

89. This question tests your knowledge of daily French life. Some French stores have signs showing what their specialties are. The red carrot shows the location of a tobacco shop. The green cross indicates a pharmacy. Therefore, the correct answer is (D), *une croix verte.*

90. This question tests your knowledge of French history. The correct answer is (C), Jules Ferry. Although Jules Ferry did much for the French educational system, he did not serve as president of France. The correct answer, therefore, is (C).

Chapter 7

Preparing for *French: Productive Language Skills*

▶   ▶   ▶   ▶   ▶   ▶   ▶   ▶   ▶   ▶   ▶   ▶

The purpose of this chapter is to provide you with strategies for listening to, reading carefully, and understanding the questions on the Praxis *French: Productive Language Skills (PLS)* test in order for you to be able to provide proficient oral and written responses in French.

Introduction to the Test

The test is designed for candidates applying for licenses/credentials to teach French in grades K-12. The *PLS* test in French measures the speaking and writing proficiency of prospective teachers of French. The test questions elicit samples of speaking and writing skills that a teacher of French needs in order to demonstrate the language in the classroom clearly and accurately and to develop and improve students' performance in all four language skills: listening, speaking, reading, and writing. This test is designed to gather evidence about your knowledge of the French language and your ability to use it.

The test contains a total of nine questions.

- Six questions consist of stimuli or situations to which you must provide spoken responses in French.

- Three questions consist of stimuli or situations to which you must provide written responses in French.

In all nine questions, you will have to demonstrate that you can correctly use various verb tenses and moods, express ideas, and describe situations accurately and fluently. Your response must demonstrate an appropriate range of vocabulary and idioms for the task presented in each question.

What to Study

Success on this test is not simply a matter of learning more about how to respond to the question types of this *PLS* test; it also takes real knowledge of French language and culture. You must show the ability to produce comprehensible and proficient oral or written responses to each question. It must be obvious that your ability in all four language skills (reading, listening, speaking, and writing) in French is strong enough to serve as a solid, desirable model in guiding your students in the classroom to develop and improve their own capabilities in the French language.

Therefore, it would serve you well to consider the following areas for review prior to taking the test.

1. Familiarize yourself with the test content and format by reviewing this chapter and answering the practice questions included in this study guide.

2. Review the chapter containing sample responses to the practice questions and explanations for how the responses were scored. Compare your responses to the high-scoring responses in this chapter to develop a sense of areas in which you need further review and practice. Then, refer to additional resources to help you brush up on those areas.

Based on your French-language skills, you may find the following materials helpful.

L'essentiel de la grammaire. Hoffmann, Prentice Hall, 1995.

Facile à dire—Les sons du française. Duménil, Prentice Hall, 2003.

Traitements de textes—Une introduction à l'expression écrite. New & Scott, Prentice Hall, 2000.

Sans détour—A complete reference manual for French grammar. Gac-Artigas, Prentice Hall, 2000.

Une fois pour toutes. Sturges & Hale, Pearson Prentice Hall, 1993.

Longman's AP Guide—French language

You may also wish to consult available tape/CD/CD-ROM/video materials that complement French language texts, as well as separate computer software and online Internet resources that focus on developing and improving all four language skills in French. A good place to start would be Tennessee Bob's Famous French Links at www.utm.edu/departments/french.

The above-mentioned materials are particularly relevant to the types of knowledge, topics, and skills covered on the test. Note, however, that the test is not based on these resources. Instead, the list of works is intended to help you revisit topics you have already covered in your French courses.

Understanding What the Questions Are Asking

It is impossible to produce orally, or in written form, a successful response to a question unless you thoroughly understand the question. Test takers often jump into their responses without taking enough time to understand exactly what the question is asking, how different parts of the question need to be addressed, and how the information in the written prompts and picture stimuli need to be approached and used. The appropriate time and attention you invest in making sure you understand what the question is asking will definitely pay off in a better performance.

Examine the overall question closely; then identify what specific information and details your responses must contain. In the preparation time allotted for each question, mentally organize your response and take notes in the space provided in your test book. Write down key words and outline your answer. Leave yourself plenty of time to speak or write your answer.

Question Types Used in the Speaking Section

To illustrate the importance of understanding the question before you begin answering, let's look at the question types for the Presentational Speaking section.

1. Role-playing/phone message

This question type describes a situation that requires you to request a favor from someone in order to solve a problem. Listen to and carefully read the description of the situation. You should outline your answer by writing down key words and brief notes to guide your spoken response. Make sure that you clearly and precisely address each of the information items you are required to include in your answer.

2. Picture description

This question type presents a picture of an everyday scene, which usually shows an incident in progress. For a good response you should demonstrate the ability to use different verb tenses and moods, such as present, past, future, and conditional. Make sure that, once again, you clearly address each of the prompts or tasks that accompany the picture. Someone who cannot see the picture must be able to visualize it from the detailed description of your response.

Prior to taking the test, you might want to practice key verbs in major tenses by describing an interesting picture from a magazine. Within a two-minute period, explain in French what has just happened, what is happening now, what people would probably say, what will most likely happen next, and how the incident could have been avoided.

3. Giving instructions or giving a narration for a series of pictures

In the question, you are required to give instructions (using the imperative) or tell a story (using past tenses) describing a progression of activities. A sequence of six to nine pictures is provided to assist you in formulating your response. The necessary vocabulary can be fairly specific. It is imperative that you say something about each picture in the logical sequence. Do not try to lump two or more pictures together in your description. Don't forget that you are speaking to someone who cannot see the pictures you are describing. Scorers advise that candidates use appropriate verb tenses and do not elaborate into areas that are not illustrated in the pictures. Stay on task.

4. Stating and defending an opinion

In this question type, you must carefully use the allotted preparation time to take notes and outline the presentation of your opinion. Jot down key vocabulary words that you will use to support as many specific examples as possible in defense of your opinion. Clarity in stating your point of view is critical and should be immediately apparent in the introduction of your response. You then should give, in an orderly fashion, detailed examples that clearly address and support the objectives of your answer, for or against the idea.

5. Oral paraphrase

First, it is assumed by scorers that you fully understand what "paraphrase" means. If you are uncertain, the *New Oxford American Dictionary* definition is "Rewording or restating the meaning of a spoken or written passage using different words (if possible) to achieve greater clarity." In this question, you will hear a passage read twice, during which time you have the opportunity to take notes while listening. You will be required to retell the story in French in your own words. You must demonstrate your listening comprehension skills in order to produce an accurate recreation of the passage with appropriate vocabulary. You do not translate, analyze, or critique the passage; you simply restate the contents of the passage. It need not be word for word; it can be in your own words, but your paraphrase must contain all the essential points of the story, including the ending, which at times may reveal a surprise conclusion. The keys to a good response are accuracy and completion.

6. Brief talk

This question type requires that you prepare and deliver a short, formal talk to a particular gathering of people. The directions establish the premise of a determined situation. The prompts for this question usually have two parts: (1) greetings, thanks, and acknowledgement of the situation and (2) substantial, detailed information about the purpose or intended results of the situation. This second part should make up the greater portion of your response. Listen to and read very carefully what specific information is expected in the content of your speech. Outline your talk with key words and details so that your delivery will flow smoothly, with a minimum of hesitation and the proper degree of formality.

Question Types Used in the Writing Section

It is obvious and quite natural that errors will show up much more clearly in a written response than in a spoken one. Inappropriate or limited vocabulary and idiomatic expressions, wrong word order, accent marks, spelling, and, most of all, poor grammatical control are all quickly exposed in written responses. Common errors in standard written French are shown on the opposite page.

- Missing contractions for *à* and *de* + a definite article

- Subject-verb agreement errors

- Misuse of past tenses, particularly the *passé composé* and *imparfait*

- Misusing and confusing direct and indirect object pronouns

- Poor use of, or missing, connectors and prepositions

- Wrong gender

- Wrong word order

- Missing accents

- "Anglicisms": American syntax, vocabulary, and idiomatic expressions transcribed into French word for word

To illustrate the importance of understanding the question before you begin answering, let's look at the question types for the Presentational Writing section.

7. Picture narration

This question type presents a series of pictures (usually six) for which you must write a continuous narrative. There is always a lead-in prompt that clearly suggests the use of past tenses. *"La semaine dernière..."* is a common example. Therefore, scorers will expect at least the appropriate, simultaneous use of the *passé composé* and *imparfait* tenses. Do not deviate from what is in the pictures. Make sure to write something about each picture and keep the narrative flowing. Do not assume that the reader can see the pictures.

8. Writing a letter or e-mail

You may wish to practice writing a formal letter or e-mail at home before taking the actual test. Check out samples of formal or business letters in a university-level grammar/composition textbook. Possibilities are a business letter to a store or company concerning purchase of merchandise, or a cover letter for a job application. Be aware of the specific types of opening and closing salutations in French. The directions and prompts for this type of question are very specific. Include information requested in each of the prompt items in the order provided. These prompts will very likely suggest the use of various verb tenses (e.g., past, future, conditional, subjunctive) and specialized vocabulary. Communicating formally in writing requires that you not use the *tu* form in addressing people, but rather *vous*.

9. Writing questions

Here, in response to a particular situation described in the test book, you are required to write four questions addressed to one or more persons. The situation could relate to one person you are expected to interview, for example. The four questions should be very clear and deal only with the subject presented in the prompt. One can be a short-answer question; the other three questions should extract longer answers, such as an opinion, a description, or a narration. You may ask a two-part question; but do not combine several questions into one question. Do not ask silly, personal, or insensitive questions, such as "What is your name?" or "Are you divorced/ married?" Maintain a proper degree of politeness and formality. Never use the *tu* form; always use *vous*. Your complete written response will involve a relatively small amount of text, so individual errors may be costly; your grammar, sentence-construction, and spelling mistakes will count a great deal in determining your score. Check your questions carefully after you have finished. You may wish to practice at home prior to taking the *PLS* test. For example, assume that you are writing four questions that you will ask an exchange French teacher who has just arrived at your school.

How the Test Scorers Evaluate Your Responses

Even if you feel confident about your language skills and knowledge of the content to be tested, you still may want to know how the scorers evaluate your answers. The fact is that you can find out what the test scorers want by looking carefully at the questions themselves. The Praxis *French: PLS* questions are worded as clearly as possible regarding the specific tasks you are expected to do. The French educators who evaluate your responses base your score on two considerations:

1. Whether you do all the tasks that the question requests

2. How well you do them using the French language skills you possess

The *French: PLS* tests are scored by expert teachers of French from high schools, community colleges, and universities; educators who have many years of experience scoring Praxis French tests. The team of scorers/readers is made up of both native and nonnative speakers of French, representative of diverse personal backgrounds. Scorers follow strict procedures to ensure that scoring is fair and consistent. Scores are based on carefully established criteria in the scoring guide. They do not reflect the scorers' personal opinions or preferences. At the readings, or scoring sessions, the process involves a number of critical steps to confirm the quality of the scoring process.

- All scorers, whether they are long-experienced readers or not, undergo rigorous training before and during the scoring session.

- The scoring guide is completely reviewed and studied so that everyone clearly understands the criteria for each score (ranging from 0 to 4).

- Old benchmark responses are used prior to the actual scoring to illustrate how the criteria determine the score for each question.

- During the actual scoring of your test, each question is scored twice, once each by two different readers working independently. The two scores for a given question must never be more than one point apart. Scores that are more than one point apart represent a discrepancy, which is immediately resolved by the scoring leader, who scores the response a third time. This step reinforces strict adherence to the criteria set in the scoring guide.

- The scorers' performances are continuously monitored by the scoring leader in order to keep everyone focused on the consistent and accurate application of the scoring criteria.

- The *PLS* exams are scored holistically. Scorers first assess the quality and overall comprehensibility of the response. The four key factors in the criteria that make a difference between one score and another (e.g., between 2 and 3) are as follows:

  1. *Comprehensibility.* How much of an effort does the scorer have to make to understand what is being said or written?

  2. *Accuracy of content.* Each task of every question must be addressed appropriately and accurately.

  3. *Grammatical control.* Strong grammatical control of basic structures that are used with high frequency by speakers and writers in ordinary situations, or by teachers of French in a classroom, is essential for scores of 3 and 4.

  4. *Fluency.* Spoken and written fluency should demonstrate control of complex sentences, connectors, and transition words, and some elaboration to give substance to a response. A response made up of single words or short, choppy phrases, poorly formulated sentences, limited vocabulary with little or no idiomatic constructions, and no elaboration will very likely score a 2.

Sample Questions

To answer more specifically the question "How do the scorers evaluate your responses?" we should look at sample questions much like the ones you will encounter on the test.

Sample Question 1: Picture Description—Speaking

Directions: In this question, you are asked to describe in French the picture in your test book. Do <u>not</u> assume that the person listening can see the picture. In your description, include <u>all</u> of the following details:

- A description of where this incident is taking place

- What has just occurred

- What the woman probably would say to the man in this situation

- What is probably going to happen next

- How this situation could have been avoided

Before you are asked to speak, you will have <u>2 minutes</u> to study the picture and think about your response. Then you will have <u>2 minutes</u> to give your response.

Reading the Question—Key Components of the Question

Focus on understanding the question: what are the parts of the question, and what does each part ask? Here, you are to give a description of the picture and provide *details for each of the five tasks,* which tell you in general terms what your response should address.

Organizing Your Response

Successful responses start with successful planning, either with an outline or with another form of notes. By planning your response, you greatly decrease the chances that you will forget to answer any part of the question. You increase the chances of creating a well-organized response, which is something the scorers look for.

To illustrate a possible strategy for planning a response, let us focus again on this sample picture-description question. By analyzing the question, we find that it asks for five tasks to be addressed. You might begin by numbering those parts on your notes page, leaving space under each. This will ensure that you address each part when you begin speaking.

First, look at the picture carefully and remember that you are to describe what is happening, not what the people were doing before, or your opinion of their personal relationship. Then jot down key vocabulary words for the objects and actions involved in this incident. Decide which verb tenses you are expected to use for each of the five tasks required.

Sample Notes

Here you start by identifying each part of the question and quickly writing down the main vocabulary and verb tenses you want to address in each part. Your notes could include some of the following:

1. salon, salle de séjour, homme et femme, étagère, livres, bibelots, plantes, fauteuil [présent]
2. prendre [ou remettre] un livre sur l'étagère, basculer, glisser [passé récent]
3. femme, probablement, dire, faire attention, maladroit [conditionel présent, impératif]
4. livres, tomber, bibelots, casser, par terre, plancher, être surpris [futur proche]
5. éviter, fixer, clouer, mur, équilibrer [conditionel passé, plus-que-parfait]

You have now created the skeleton of your oral response and have enough vocabulary to choose from to provide information for each task.

Speaking Your Response

Now the important step of *speaking* your response begins. The scorers will **not** consider your notes when they score your response, so it is crucial that you integrate all the important ideas from your notes into your actual oral response.

Sample Response (Transcribed with Mistakes) That Earned a Score of 4

Keep in mind that a response need not be perfect to earn a score of 4. There may be some small mistakes, but your oral response must be completely comprehensible, even to a native speaker of French who is not accustomed to dealing with nonnative learners of the language. It must be completely accurate, with appropriate elaboration, strong grammatical control, and broad, precise vocabulary. Your overall fluency should rarely be hesitant and your pronunciation may be slightly nonnative, but always easily comprehensible. *Speak clearly and loudly into your microphone.*

> Cet incident se passe à la maison, dans la salle de séjour de Monsieur et Madame Dupont. Madame Dupont est assise dans un fauteuil et lit un livre et M. Dupont est debout devant un meuble et une étagère de livres. Il y a aussi des plantes et des autres choses comme un petit cheval et une photo.
>
> M. Dupont vient de prendre un livre au bout de l'étagère en haut, à droite. Les livres commencent de glisser à droite parce que M. Dupont vient de basculer l'étagère.
>
> La femme probablement dirait à son mari: "Fais attention, tu vas faire tomber l'étagère, tu as mis trop de livres à droite."
>
> Probablement, tous les livres vont tomber sur le plancher et aussi sur M. Dupont. Peut-être l'étagère va se casser et aussi le petit cheval et les plantes. Et après, il faudra nettoyer toutes les choses cassées sur le plancher.
>
> On aurait pu éviter cette situation si M. Dupont avait fait attention avant de prendre un livre, si on avait placé les livres au milieu de l'étagère et si on avait réparé l'étagère.

Commentary on Sample Response that Earned a Score of 4

The response is complete and very comprehensible. All five parts of the prompt have been addressed with some elaboration. It would be quite easy to recreate this picture from the description given. The verb tenses are correctly used and show very good grammatical control. The minor mistakes involve a few details that could be more precise. In part one, we could say *des étagère* since there is more than one shelf. For knickknacks like the little horse, the word *bibelots* could be used. In part two, it would be more precise to say *du haut,* which refers to the top shelf, instead of *en haut,* which usually means "upstairs" or "above." The preposition *à*—not *de*—should be used after the verb *commencer.* Overall, the response demonstrates an excellent knowledge of the language and a full understanding of all parts of the question.

Sample Question 2: Picture Narration—Writing

Directions: In this question, you are asked to write a <u>continuous</u> story in French, based only on the six pictures below. In your story, tell what happened in <u>each</u> of the six pictures. Do not assume that the reader of the story can see the pictures.

Start the story with the words *"La semaine dernière . . . "*

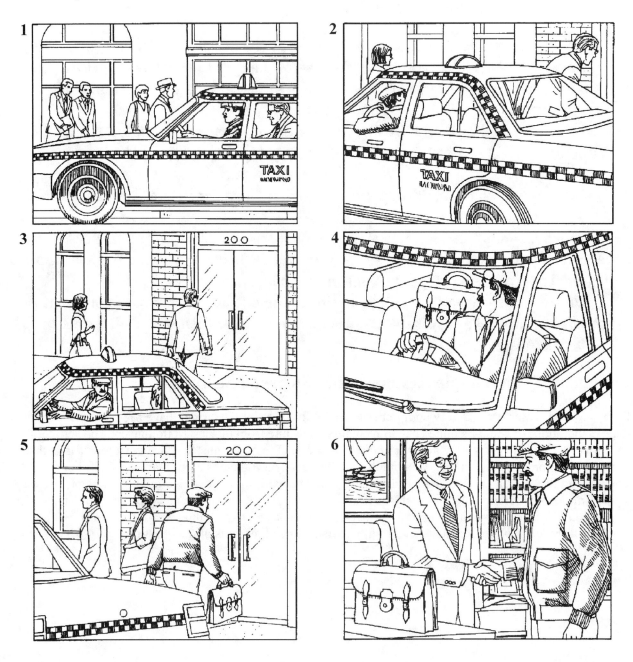

Reading the Question—Key Components of the Question

Focus on the content of the six pictures for which you will have to write a story. Your story should be written in the past tenses because the prompt tells you to start with *"La semaine dernière . . . "* ("Last week . . . ").

Organizing Your Response

First, look at the pictures carefully. Remember that you are to tell something about each picture in order to describe an event that happened "last week." In your notes, jot down key vocabulary words for the objects and actions involved in this story. The French verb tenses you are likely to use are *passé composé, imparfait,* and *plus-que-parfait.*

Sample Notes

Your notes for each of the six pictures might include some of the following words and verbs, depending on your knowledge of the French language:

1. taxi, chauffeur de taxi, homme d'affaires, s'arrêter, bâtiment, piétons
2. homme d'affaires, descendre du taxi
3. bâtiment, numéro 200, regarder à gauche, démarrer la voiture serviette siege arrière, laisser, homme d'affaires, se diriger
4. chauffeur de taxi, regarder derrière, remarquer, avoir oublié, serviette
5. arrêter le taxi, descendre, prendre, rapporter la serviette
6. trouver le bureau de l'homme d'affaires, rendre la serviette, remercier, serrer la main, être content, honnête, sourire

Writing Your Response

Now the important step of writing your response begins. The scorers will not consider your notes in determining your score, so it is crucial that you integrate all the details of the pictures from your notes into your actual written response.

Sample Response That Earned a Score of 4

Keep in mind that a response need not be perfect to earn a score of 4. There may be some small mistakes (e.g., spelling and accents), but your written response must be completely comprehensible, even to a native speaker of French who is not accustomed to dealing with nonnative learners of the language. It must be completely accurate, with appropriate elaboration, strong grammatical control, and broad, precise vocabulary. Your word choice should be generally idiomatic, rarely awkward, and easily comprehensible.

1. La semaine dernière, un homme d'affaires, M. Martin, a pris un taxi pour aller à son bureau. Le taxi s'arrête devant un bâtiment et il y avait des gens qui marchent sur le trottoir.
2. M. Martin est descendu du taxi.

3. L'homme d'affaires est allé au numéro 200. Il portait des papiers à la main. Le chauffeur de taxi a regardé à gauche pour partir. Sur le siège arrière, il y avait la serviette de M. Martin.

4. En allant, le chauffeur a regardé derrière lui et a remarqué que son client avait oublié sa serviette sur le siège arrière.

5. Le chauffeur a stationné son taxi devant le numéro 200 du grand bâtiment. Il portait la serviette de M. Martin.

6. Le chauffeur de taxi a trouvé le bureau de M. Martin et il lui a rendu sa serviette. M. Martin était très content et il souriait. Il a remercié le chauffeur pour être honnête et il lui a serré la main. Peut-être que l'homme d'affaires lui a donné un autre pourboire.

Commentary on Sample Response that Earned a Score of 4

The response is complete and very comprehensible. All six pictures have been described with some elaboration. It would be quite easy to recreate these pictures from the description given. The verb tenses are correctly used and show very good grammatical control. The mistakes are minor: Two of the verbs in the second sentence of picture 1 are written in the present tense—*s'arrête* should be *s'est arrêté* and *marchent* should be *marchaient*. In picture 4, the beginning of the description should be *En partant* or *En démarrant, le chauffeur...*. Overall, the response demonstrates an excellent knowledge of the language and a full understanding of the sequence of events in the six pictures, resulting in an accurate story.

Sample Response That Earned a Score of 2

A score of 2 definitely suggests lack of proficiency. Even a sympathetic reader must make an effort to understand and interpret the intended meaning of the response. The grammar and vocabulary are limited, and word choice is often unidiomatic. The response, which is often missing some of the tasks, is poorly organized and not very coherent.

1. La semaine dernière, monsieur Martin a prendu le taxi à le travail. Le homme du taxi arête devant l'office de M. Martin.

2/3. M. Martin va a l'office a la porte 200.

4. Le homme du taxi a regardé le sac derrière le taxi.

5. M. Martin oubliait le sac et le homme lui porte le sac.

6. A l'office M. Martin prend le sac et merci l'homme du taxi.

Commentary on Sample Response that Earned a Score of 2

This response is poorly written. There are grammatical and spelling errors in every sentence. There is no consistency in the use of the past tenses; vocabulary is indeed limited, some of which involves direct transposition of English words, such as "office" for *bureau*. Missing accents and contractions also contribute to a weak response. The pictures are poorly described, and it would be somewhat difficult to recreate them just from this written effort.

In Conclusion

The important thing is that your answers be clearly comprehensible, complete, and detailed. You need to be certain to do the following:

- Answer all parts of the question.

- Select appropriate vocabulary and grammatical constructions.

- Demonstrate language-specific knowledge and proficiency in your answer.

- Refer to the data in the stimulus: pictures, written prompts, and directions.

Even though you may be teaching first-year French now, your daily experiences in teaching beginning students are not enough to prepare you adequately to take this test. You need to practice and be exposed to a more advanced level than first-year French. Facility with basic verb tenses is critical not only in teaching students to speak and write French, but also in successfully demonstrating in this test that you have a thorough knowledge of basic and advanced French verb forms. Develop your vocabulary by reading different types of materials, both fiction and nonfiction. Talk to French-speaking friends whenever you can; listen to the language in films and on cable television, if possible.

It is highly recommended that you use the practice questions provided in chapter 9 to help you develop a plan for taking the Praxis *French: PLS* test on the actual testing day.

Chapter 8
Succeeding on Constructed-Response Questions—
French: Productive Language Skills

▶   ▶   ▶   ▶   ▶   ▶   ▶   ▶   ▶   ▶   ▶   ▶

This chapter provides advice for maximizing your success on the *French: Productive Language Skills* test, with special focus on the scoring guides and procedures used by the scorers. Chapter 7 offers step-by-step strategies for working through questions, lists of the topics covered, and lists of sources you can use to prepare.

TIP Advice from the Experts

Scorers who have scored hundreds of real tests were asked to give advice to teacher candidates planning to take the *French: Productive Language Skills* test. The scorers' advice boiled down to the practical suggestions given below.

1. *Read and answer the question accurately.*

   Be sure to dissect the parts of the question and analyze what each part is asking you to do. If the question asks you to *describe* or *discuss,* keep those requirements in mind when composing your response—do not just give a list.

2. *Answer everything that is asked in the question.*

   This seems simple, but many test takers fail to provide a complete response. If a question asks you to do three distinct things in your response, don't give a response to just two of those things. No matter how well you speak or write about those two things, the scorers will not award you full credit.

3. *Give a thorough and detailed response.*

   Your response must indicate to the scorers that you have a thorough command of the French language. The scorers will not read into your response any information that is not specifically stated. If something is not spoken or written, they do not know that you know it and will not give you credit for it.

   A word of caution: Superfluous speaking or writing will obscure your points and will make it difficult for the scorers to be confident of your full understanding of the material. Be straightforward in your response. Do not try to impress the scorers. If you do not know the answer, you cannot receive full credit, but if you do know the answer, provide enough information to convince the scorers that you have a full understanding of what is being asked.

4. *Do not change the question or challenge the basis of the question.*

   Stay focused on the question that is asked. You will receive no credit or, at best, a low score if you choose to answer another question or if you state, for example, that there is no possible answer. Answer the question by addressing the fundamental topic at hand. Do not venture off topic, for example, to demonstrate your command of vocabulary that is not specifically related to the question. This undermines the impression that you understand the topic adequately.

5. *Reread your written response, both to improve your writing and to check that you have written what you thought you wrote.*

   Frequently, sentences are left unfinished or clarifying information is omitted.

General Scoring Guides for the *French: Productive Language Skills* Test

The scorers' advice above corresponds with the official scoring criteria used at scoring sessions. It is a good idea to be familiar with the scoring rubrics so you can maximize your success and spend your time on things that matter (e.g., demonstrating understanding of the prompts providing good examples) rather than spending time on things that don't matter (e.g., writing a very long narration or letter).

The following scoring rubrics provide the overarching framework for scoring the questions in the *French: Productive Language Skills* test.

Each question on the test is scored on a scale from 0 to 4. The response is considered in its entirety when the scorer assigns the score. The following general scoring guides are used.

Presentational Speaking Section

This scoring guide is used to evaluate responses in the Presentational Speaking section. The score range is 0 to 4.

4
- Is completely and easily comprehensible, even to an unsympathetic listener[1]

- Gives a complete and entirely accurate, relevant response, with appropriate elaboration, to all (or almost all) parts of the question

- May make sporadic errors, but they rarely or never interfere with communication

    — has strong grammatical control (no errors in basic, high-frequency structures; few errors in complex, low-frequency structures; no marked error patterns)

    — employs a broad, precise vocabulary adequate for almost all topics, with word choice that is generally idiomatic and varied and rarely awkward

    — has overall fluency: speech is occasionally or rarely hesitant, with frequent use of complex sentences and "connectors" when appropriate or required

    — may have a slightly nonnative pronunciation, with few or no phonological errors and no error patterns, but is always comprehensible

3
- Is generally comprehensible, even to an unsympathetic listener, but occasionally requires the listener's effort and interpretation of the intended meaning

- Gives a mostly accurate, relevant response to most parts of the question

- Is likely to make errors and/or produce error patterns, but they only occasionally interfere with communication

    — has moderate grammatical control (few errors in basic, high-frequency structures; some errors and/or error patterns in complex, low-frequency structures)

    — employs vocabulary adequate for most general topics, with word choice that is often idiomatic but occasionally awkward

---

[1] "Unsympathetic listener" refers to a native speaker of the language who is NOT accustomed to dealing with nonnative learners of the language. An unsympathetic listener does not make any special effort to understand the examinee.

— has considerable fluency: speech is sometimes hesitant, with some use of complex sentences and "connectors" when appropriate or required

— may have a markedly nonnative pronunciation with some phonological errors and/or error patterns, but is always or nearly always comprehensible

2
■ Is somewhat comprehensible to a sympathetic listener,[2] but often requires the listener's effort and interpretation of the intended meaning

■ Gives a somewhat accurate, relevant response to some parts of the question

■ Produces errors and/or error patterns that may often interfere with communication

— has limited grammatical control (many errors and/or error patterns in basic, high-frequency structures; no control of complex, low-frequency structures)

— employs a limited vocabulary, with word choice that is often unidiomatic and awkward

— has limited fluency, with halting speech and mostly short, simple sentences; suggests inability to use complex sentences and "connectors" when appropriate or required

— has a markedly nonnative pronunciation, with many phonological errors and/or error patterns, and is sometimes incomprehensible

1
■ Is generally incomprehensible, even to a sympathetic listener, despite the listener's constant effort to interpret the intended meaning

■ Gives an incomplete and/or mostly inaccurate and/or irrelevant response

■ Produces errors and/or error patterns that very often interfere with communication

— has very little grammatical control (many serious errors and/or error patterns in virtually all structures)

— employs very little vocabulary, with some "formulaic speech" (memorized phrases, fixed expressions) used inappropriately

— has virtually no fluency: speech is fragmentary and halting, interrupted often by long pauses and repetitions, and consists only of isolated words, memorized phrases, and fixed expressions

— has a markedly nonnative pronunciation, with many serious phonological errors and/or error patterns, and is very often incomprehensible

0
■ Is completely incomprehensible, even to a sympathetic listener, despite the listener's constant effort to interpret the intended meaning

■ Gives an entirely inaccurate, irrelevant response or fails to respond at all

■ Produces errors and/or error patterns that always interfere with communication

— has no grammatical control (many serious errors and/or error patterns in all structures)

— employs no vocabulary, not even "formulaic speech" (memorized phrases and fixed expressions)

---

[2] "Sympathetic listener" refers to a native speaker of the language who is accustomed to dealing with nonnative learners of the language. A sympathetic listener tends to make a conscious effort to understand the examinee, interpreting his or her speech for its intended meaning.

— has no fluency

— has a markedly nonnative pronunciation and is always incomprehensible

Presentational Writing Section

This scoring guide is used to evaluate responses in the Presentational Writing section. The score range is 0 to 4.

4
- Is completely and easily comprehensible, even to an unsympathetic reader[3]

- Gives a complete and entirely accurate, relevant response, with appropriate elaboration, to all (or almost all) parts of the question

- May make sporadic errors, but they rarely or never interfere with communication

  — has strong grammatical control (no errors in basic, high-frequency structures; few errors in complex, low-frequency structures; no marked error patterns)

  — employs a broad, precise vocabulary adequate for almost all topics, with word choice that is generally idiomatic and varied and rarely awkward

  — has very few or no errors in mechanics, which rarely or never interfere with meaning

  — is completely coherent and well organized, with frequent use of complex sentences and "connectors" when appropriate or required

  — uses language that is appropriate for the intended task and/or audience

3
- Is generally comprehensible, even to an unsympathetic reader, but occasionally requires the reader's effort and interpretation of the intended meaning

- Gives a mostly accurate, relevant response to most parts of the question

- Is likely to produce errors and/or error patterns, but they only occasionally interfere with communication

  — has moderate grammatical control (few errors in basic, high-frequency structures; some errors and/or error patterns in complex, low-frequency structures)

  — employs a vocabulary adequate for most general topics, with word choice that is often idiomatic but occasionally awkward

  — makes some errors in mechanics (spelling, punctuation, etc.), but they only occasionally interfere with meaning

  — is generally coherent and organized, with some complex sentences and "connectors" when appropriate or required

  — is likely to use language that is appropriate for the intended task and/or audience

---

[3] "Unsympathetic reader" refers to a native speaker of the language who is NOT accustomed to dealing with nonnative learners of the language. An unsympathetic reader does not make any special effort to understand the examinee.

2
- Is somewhat comprehensible to a sympathetic reader,[4] but often requires the reader's effort and interpretation of the intended meaning
- Gives a somewhat accurate, relevant response to some parts of the question
- Produces errors and/or error patterns that may often interfere with communication
  - has limited grammatical control (many errors and/or error patterns in basic, high-frequency structures; no control of complex, low-frequency structures)
  - employs a limited vocabulary, with word choice that is often unidiomatic and awkward
  - makes several errors in mechanics (spelling, punctuation, etc.), which may often interfere with meaning
  - is partly or often incoherent, with little evidence of organization; suggests inability to use complex sentences and "connectors" when appropriate or required
  - is likely to use language that is inappropriate for the intended task and/or audience

1
- Is generally incomprehensible, even to a sympathetic reader, despite the reader's constant effort to interpret the intended meaning
- Gives an incomplete, mostly inaccurate, and/or irrelevant response
- Produces errors and/or error patterns that very often interfere with communication
  - has very little grammatical control (many serious errors and/or error patterns in virtually all structures)
  - employs very little vocabulary, with some "formulaic language" (memorized phrases, fixed expressions) used inappropriately
  - makes many serious errors in mechanics (spelling, punctuation, etc.) in virtually all structures, which very often interfere with meaning
  - is mostly incoherent, with very little or no evidence of organization
  - uses language that is inappropriate for the intended task and/or audience

0
- Is completely incomprehensible, even to a sympathetic reader, despite the reader's constant effort to interpret the intended meaning
- Gives an entirely inaccurate, irrelevant response or fails to respond at all
- Produces errors and/or error patterns that always interfere with communication
  - has no grammatical control (many serious errors and/or error patterns in all structures)
  - employs no vocabulary, not even "formulaic language" (memorized phrases and fixed expressions)
  - makes many serious errors in mechanics (spelling, punctuation, etc.) in all structures, which always interfere with meaning
  - is completely incoherent

---

[4] "Sympathetic reader" refers to a native speaker of the language who is accustomed to dealing with nonnative learners of the language. A sympathetic reader tends to make a conscious effort to understand the examinee, interpreting his or her writing for its intended meaning.

Examples of Responses to the *French: Productive Language Skills* Test and the Scores They Received

In this question from the Presentational Speaking section, you are asked to give instructions to a young French-speaking friend who will be staying at your apartment. Explain how to enter your apartment in case your friend arrives while you are out. Based only on what you see in the pictures in your test book, give clear, step-by-step instructions, in French. In your instructions, include the information presented in all of the pictures, but do not assume that the people listening can see the pictures.

Before you are asked to speak, you have one minute to study the pictures and think about your instructions. You have two minutes to speak. Start your instructions with the words *"D'abord, va à l'appartement numéro 209 . . ."*

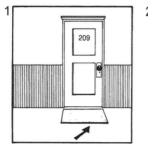 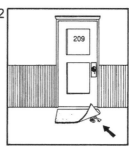 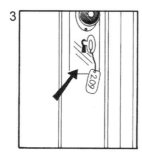 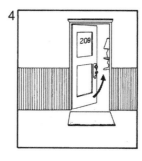

The following responses have been transcribed from the taped responses of test takers. Ellipses (. . .) are used to indicate pauses in the test takers' responses. Mispronunciations are written as they were produced.

Sample Response That Received a Score of 3

> *D'abord, va à l'appartement numéro deux cent neuf. Il y a un tapis devant la porte, et sous le tapis, ahhh, ehhh, est la clef. Ahhh, mette la clef . . . dans la porte, tourne, et ouvre la porte. Entre dans l'appartement.*

Sample Response That Received a Score of 1

> *D'abord, va à l'appartement mmm . . . two oh nine [in English]. Secondement, le clef est sous le mat [in English]. Troisième, and [in English], sous le clef est le . . . .*
> *Finalement, ouvrez la porte, et voilà . . . .*
> *Devant la porte . . . le . . . le clef est ehhh, ehhh, élevez le chose avant de la porte et vous . . . trouverez le clef . . . c'est fou de placer le clef . . . est un peu . . . à une place . . . ça est criminel pour le trouver . . . Le premier part n'est pas assez long.*

What You Should Know About How the *French: Productive Language Skills* Test Is Scored

As you build your skills in answering constructed-response questions, it is important to have in mind the process used to score the test. If you understand the process by which experts determine your scores, you may have a better context in which to think about your strategies for success.

How the Test Is Scored

After each test administration, test books and recorded responses are returned to ETS. The test books in which constructed-response answers are written and the recordings of the spoken responses are sent to the location of the scoring session.

The scoring sessions usually take place over two days. The sessions are led by scoring leaders, highly qualified French teachers who have many years of experience scoring test questions. All of the remaining scorers are experienced French teachers and French teacher-educators. An effort is made to balance experienced scorers with newer scorers at each session; the experienced scorers provide continuity with past sessions, and the new scorers ensure that new ideas and perspectives are considered and that the pool of scorers remains large enough to cover the test's needs throughout the year.

Preparing to Train the Scorers

The scoring leaders meet several days before the scoring session to assemble the materials for the training portions of the main session. Training scorers is a rigorous process, and it is designed to ensure that each response gets a score that is consistent both with the scores given to other responses and with the overall scoring philosophy and criteria established for the test when it was designed.

The scoring leaders first review the "General Scoring Guide," which contains the overall criteria for awarding the appropriate score.

To begin identifying appropriate training materials for an individual question, the scoring leaders first listen to and read through many responses to get a sense of the range of answers. They then choose a set of benchmarks, one response at each score level. These benchmarks serve as solid representative examples of the kind of response that meets the scoring criteria at each score level and are considered the foundation for score standards throughout the session.

The scoring leaders then choose a larger set of test takers' responses to serve as sample responses. These sample responses represent the wide variety of possible responses that the scorers might see. The sample responses serve as the basis for practice scoring at the scoring session, so the scorers can rehearse how they will apply the scoring criteria before they begin.

The process of choosing a set of benchmark responses and a set of sample responses is followed systematically for each question to be scored at the session.

Training at the Main Scoring Session

At the scoring session, the scorers are placed into groups according to the question they are assigned to score. New scorers are distributed equally across all groups. One of the scoring leaders is placed with each group. The "chief scorer" is the person who has overall authority over the scoring session and plays a variety of key roles in training and in ensuring consistent and fair scores.

For each question, the training session proceeds in the same way:

1. All scorers carefully listen to or read through the question they will be scoring.

2. All scorers review the "General Scoring Guides."

3. For each question, the leader guides the scorers through the set of benchmark responses, explaining in detail why each response received the score it did. Scorers are encouraged to ask questions and share their perspectives.

4. Scorers then practice on the set of sample responses chosen by the leader. The leader polls the scorers on what scores they would award and then leads a discussion to ensure that there is consensus about the scoring criteria and how they are to be applied.

5. When the leader is confident that the scorers will apply the criteria consistently and accurately, the actual scoring begins.

Quality-Control Processes

A number of procedures are followed to ensure that accuracy of scoring is maintained during the scoring session. Most importantly, each response is scored twice, with the first scorer's decision hidden from the second scorer. If the two scores for a response are the same or differ by only one point, the scoring for that response is considered complete, and the test taker will be awarded the sum of the two scores. If the two scores differ by more than one point, the response is scored by a scoring leader who has not seen the decisions made by the other two scorers. If this third score is midway between the first two scores, the test taker's score for the question is the sum of the first two scores; otherwise, it is the sum of the third score and whichever of the first two scores is closer to it.

Another way of maintaining scoring accuracy is through back-reading. Throughout the session, the leader for each question checks random samples of scores awarded by all the scorers. If the leader finds that a scorer is not applying the scoring criteria appropriately, that scorer is given more training.

At the beginning of the second day of scoring, additional sets of responses are scored using the consensus method described above. This helps ensure that the scorers are refreshed on the scoring criteria and are applying them consistently.

Finally, the scoring session is designed so that several different scorers (usually four) contribute to any single test taker's total score. This minimizes the effects of a scorer who might score slightly more stringently or generously than other scorers.

The entire scoring process—general scoring guides, standardized benchmarks and samples, consensus scoring, adjudication procedures, back-reading, and rotation of test questions to a variety of scorers—is applied consistently and systematically at every scoring session to ensure comparable scores for each administration and across all administrations of the test.

Given the information above about how constructed responses are scored and what the scorers are looking for in successful responses, you are now ready to look at specific questions, suggestions of how to approach the questions, and sample responses and the scores given to those responses.

Chapter 9
Practice Questions—*French: Productive Language Skills*

▶ ▶ ▶ ▶ ▶ ▶ ▶ ▶ ▶ ▶ ▶ ▶

Now that you have worked through preparation and strategies for taking the *French: Productive Language Skills* test, you should respond to the following practice questions. The practice questions are from actual Praxis tests, now retired. You will probably find it helpful to simulate actual testing conditions, giving yourself 60 minutes to work on the questions. You can use the lined answer pages provided if you wish.

When you have finished the practice questions, you can read through the sample responses with scorer annotations in chapter 10.

The speaking and listening sections for these practice questions are found on the *French* CD included with this study guide. Tracks 6–13 refer to the *French: Productive Language Skills* test. (Note that tracks 1–5 refer to the *French: Content Knowledge* test; you will not need to listen to that section of the CD unless you are planning to take that test as well.)

To simulate actual testing conditions, you might find it helpful to use your own tape recorder to record your responses to the questions presented on this CD. As you listen to the CD, you will notice that pauses have been included in the narration. During the pauses, you may prepare your responses and record your responses on your tape recorder.

Keep in mind that the test you take at an actual administration will have different questions. You should not expect your level of performance to be exactly the same as when you take the test at an actual administration, since numerous factors affect a person's performance in any given testing situation.

THE PRAXIS SERIES
Professional Assessments for Beginning Teachers®

TEST NAME:

French: Productive Language Skills (0171)
9 Practice Questions

Time—60 minutes

Note that for questions 1 through 6, you must answer the question in the time allotted on the CD. For questions 7–9, you will be allotted 35 minutes to answer the questions. If you finish before time is called, you may go back and review your responses to questions 7–9 only.

PRESENTATIONAL SPEAKING SECTION

Questions 1–6
Time—25 Minutes

General Directions

These questions are designed to elicit responses that demonstrate how well you speak French. There are six different questions, and special directions will be given for each one. You will be told how long you have for answering the questions. Although you need not speak for the entire time period, you should give as complete an answer as possible within the time allotted.

As you speak, your voice will be recorded. Your score for these questions will be based *only* on what is on the recording. Be sure to speak loudly enough for the recording device to record clearly what you say. You are not expected to know all the words you may feel you need. If you do not know specific vocabulary, try to express yourself as well as you can, using circumlocution if necessary. You may take notes in your test book.

Your speaking will be evaluated on the following:

- Overall comprehensibility to a native speaker of French who is not accustomed to dealing with nonnative speakers

- Accuracy and appropriateness of the content

- Presentation of ideas in a related and logical manner, supported by relevant reasons, examples, and details

- Appropriateness of vocabulary

- Accuracy of grammar and pronunciation

- Fluency of delivery and cohesiveness (including use of varied sentence structure and transitional expressions where appropriate)

- Appropriateness for a given task and/or listener

- The extent to which all of the assigned tasks are completed

If you make a mistake and correct it soon afterward, it will not be considered a mistake.

Speaking Section Directions

[The following directions will be heard on the recording.]

This is the Presentational Speaking section of the *French: Productive Language Skills* practice test.

The practice test questions contained on this CD are similar to the kinds of questions you will encounter during an actual test. The test questions you will hear are also printed in the "Practice Questions" chapter of the study guide.

To simulate actual testing conditions, you might find it helpful to use your own tape recorder to record your responses to the questions presented on this CD. As you listen to the CD, you will notice that pauses have been included in the narration. During the pauses, you may prepare your responses and record your responses on your tape recorder.

To simulate actual testing conditions, do not stop your CD player or your tape recorder during the practice test.

In a moment, you will hear an introductory statement by the person who recorded the French portions of questions one through six. The purpose of this introduction is to familiarize you with the speaker's voice. Listen to the following passage.

> *Les élèves doivent aller en classe du lundi au vendredi, sauf les jours de congé. Cette année, tous les élèves sortiront tôt de l'école le 20 et le 27 janvier à cause des réunions auxquelles assisteront les professeurs du lycée.*

For each speaking question in the test, you will be given time to prepare your response and time to record your response.

Listen for the voice on the CD to direct you to answer the question; begin speaking <u>only</u> after you have been told to start your response. You will <u>not</u> be given credit for anything recorded during the preparation time.

GO ON TO THE NEXT PAGE

Practice Questions

In this part of the test, you are asked to answer in French two warm-up questions that will not be scored. Listen to the directions for each question.

Practice Question A

Directions: Answer the following question in French. You will have <u>20 seconds</u> to prepare your response. Then you will have <u>20 seconds</u> to record your response. Remember, do <u>not</u> begin speaking until you hear the words "Answer practice question A now."

> *Décrivez ce que vous faites pendant une fin de semaine typique.*

Practice Question B

Directions: Read aloud the following passage in French. Before you are asked to speak, you will have <u>1 minute</u> to read the passage silently. Then you will have <u>1 minute</u> to record your reading of the passage.

> *Un clochard passe devant un restaurant. Il lit le menu distraitement, car il sait bien qu'il ne peut pas payer. Et tout d'un coup, il s'arrête devant une petite pancarte : « Entrez et mangez ce que vous voulez, c'est votre petit-fils qui paiera ! »*
> *—Ça, par exemple ! Se dit-il. Mon petit-fils ? Mais je n'ai pas de petit-fils ! Profitons-en !*
>
> *Il entre dans le restaurant, il commande un repas complet avec du bon champagne. Quand il a assez mangé, il se lève pour sortir et alors le garçon l'arrête :*
> *—Et l'addition, Monsieur ?*
> *—Comment ça, l'addition ? Dit-il étonné. Vous savez bien que c'est mon petit-fils qui paiera !*
> *—D'accord, Monsieur. Mais il faut régler l'addition de votre grand-père . . . .*

NOTES

GO ON TO THE NEXT PAGE

Question 1

Directions: In this question, you are asked to persuade someone to help you out of a difficult situation by leaving a message in French on a telephone answering machine.

Pretend that you are Daniel(le) DuFour and that you are spending a semester in Québec. You have just picked up your best suit from the cleaners; you need it for an important meeting tomorrow morning. However, you notice that two buttons are missing and one of the pockets has been torn. You think the cleaners should repair the suit, at no extra cost, but the shop is scheduled to close soon. You call the shop and are connected to the telephone answering machine. Record a message in French in which you

- explain the situation

- describe in detail the damage to your suit

- tell why it is important that the suit be ready by tomorrow

- tell what you think the cleaners should do, and

- try to persuade someone in the shop to help you.

You will have 1½ minutes to review the situation and to prepare your message. Then you will have 1 minute to record your message.

NOTES

GO ON TO THE NEXT PAGE

Question 2

Directions: In this question, you are asked to describe in French the picture in your test book. Do <u>not</u> assume that the person listening can see the picture. In your description, include <u>all</u> of the following details:

- a description of where this incident is taking place

- what has just occurred

- what the woman probably would say to the man in this situation

- what is probably going to happen next

- how this situation could have been avoided

Before you are asked to speak, you will have <u>2 minutes</u> to study the picture and think about your response. Then you will have <u>2 minutes</u> to give your response.

NOTES

GO ON TO THE NEXT PAGE

Question 3

Directions: In this question, you are asked to give instructions to Marcel, a young French-speaking friend who is visiting your hometown. Pretend that you have a post office box but are unable to pick up your mail today. You have asked Marcel to get the mail for you. Based <u>only</u> on what you see in the pictures in your test book, give clear, step-by-step instructions in French. In your instructions, include the information presented in <u>each</u> of the nine pictures, but do <u>not</u> assume that the person listening can see the pictures.

Before you are asked to speak, you will have 1½ minutes to study the pictures and think about your instructions. Then you will have <u>2 minutes</u> to give your instructions. Start your instructions with the words *"D'abord, attends l'autobus . . ."*

NOTES

GO ON TO THE NEXT PAGE

Question 4

Directions: In this question, you are asked to give your opinion in French on the following subject:

Should calculators be permitted in the elementary mathematics classroom?

- State and defend your opinion.
- Use specific examples to support your ideas.

You will have <u>1 minute</u> to prepare your response before you are asked to speak. Then you will have <u>2 minutes</u> to give your response.

NOTES

GO ON TO THE NEXT PAGE

Question 5

Directions: In this question, you are asked to paraphrase in French a passage after you have heard it read twice in French. You may take notes in your test book during the readings. Before you are asked to speak, you will have 1 minute to review any notes you may have taken and to prepare your response. Then you will have 1½ minutes to paraphrase the passage.

NOTES

GO ON TO THE NEXT PAGE

Question 6

Directions: In this question, you are asked to give a brief talk in French based on the following situation.

Pretend that a group of French secondary school teachers is attending a conference on exchange programs that is being held near your hometown. You host a special dinner for the teachers to propose an exchange program between students from their *lycée* and your local high school. At the dinner, you give a brief talk in French in which you

- welcome the visiting teachers, and

- explain how you think the French students would benefit from being exchange students in your town.

Be sure to observe the appropriate degree of formality for such a talk.

You will have <u>2 minutes</u> to prepare your talk. Then you will have <u>1½ minutes</u> to give your talk.

NOTES

THIS IS THE END OF THE PRESENTATIONAL SPEAKING SECTION.

AT THE ACTUAL TEST ADMINISTRATION, YOU MUST NOT TURN THE PAGE UNTIL YOU ARE TOLD TO DO SO.

END OF RECORDING.

PRESENTATIONAL WRITING SECTION

Questions 7–9
Time—35 minutes

General Directions

There are three questions in this section. Be sure to answer each question completely. For each question, there is a <u>suggested</u> time limit so that you can pace yourself as you work.

Write your answers in French as clearly and neatly as possible on the lined pages provided. Your written French should be acceptable to a wide range of educated native speakers.

You may use the area marked "NOTES" to plan and take notes on each question. These notes will not be used in evaluating your response.

Your writing will be evaluated on the following:

- Overall comprehensibility to a native speaker of French who is not accustomed to dealing with the writing of nonnative learners

- Accuracy and appropriateness of content

- Presentation of ideas in a related and logical manner, supported by relevant reasons, examples, and details

- Appropriateness of vocabulary

- Accuracy of grammar and mechanics (including spelling and accent marks)

- Cohesiveness (including use of varied sentence structure and transitional expressions where appropriate)

- Appropriateness for a given task and/or reader

- The extent to which all the assigned tasks are completed

Use only the lined pages provided for your response. Although you need not use all of the space on the lined pages provided, you should give as complete a response as possible.

Question 7
(Suggested time—10 minutes)

Directions: In this question, you are asked to write a <u>continuous</u> story in French, based <u>only</u> on the six pictures below. In your story, tell what happened in <u>each</u> of the six pictures. Do <u>not</u> assume that the reader of the story can see the pictures.

Start the story with the words *"La semaine dernière . . ."*

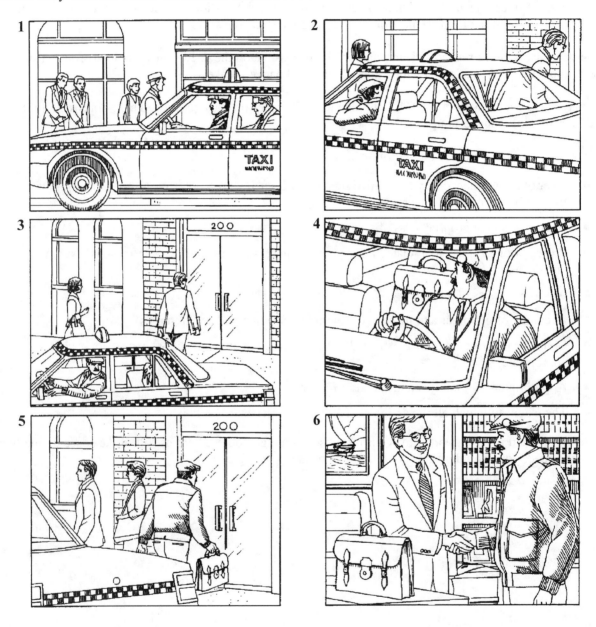

NOTES

Begin your response here.

_____

_____

_____

_____

_____

_____

_____

_____

_____

_____

_____

_____

_____

_____

_____

_____

_____

_____

_____

_____

_____

_____

Question 8
(Suggested time—15 minutes)

Directions: In this question, you are asked to write a formal letter in French based on the following situation.

While you were on vacation in Limoges, France, you bought a beautiful hand-painted porcelain plate and arranged for it to be shipped to your home. After you returned home, the plate arrived broken. Write a letter to the store explaining the situation and persuading the store to resolve the problem promptly. Include all the following information:

- when and where you bought the plate
- a description of the plate
- how you paid for the plate
- what the problem is
- what you want the store to do

Be sure to observe the appropriate degree of formality for such a letter.

NOTES

Begin your response here.

_____

_____

_____

_____

_____

_____

_____

_____

_____

_____

_____

_____

_____

_____

_____

_____

_____

_____

_____

_____

_____

_____

Question 9
(Suggested time—10 minutes)

Directions: In this question, you are asked to write four questions in French based on the following situation.

Pretend that you are working for an exchange program that places student visitors from the United States with host families in France. You are designing a questionnaire in French to help you select the French families who will receive the students.

In the lined space provided on the next page, write in complete French sentences the four questions that you wish to ask of the potential host families.

Include a variety of question types. Ask

- one question that requires only a <u>short</u> answer, and

- three questions that require a <u>longer</u> answer, such as an opinion, a description, a comparison, or a narration.

Be sure to observe the appropriate degree of formality for the purpose of your questionnaire.

NOTES

Begin your response here.

First Question:

_____

_____

_____

_____

_____

Second Question:

_____

_____

_____

_____

_____

Third Question:

_____

_____

_____

_____

_____

Fourth Question:

_____

_____

_____

_____

_____

STOP.

THIS IS THE END OF THE TEST.

If you finish before time is called, you may go back and review your responses to Questions 7–9 only.

Chapter 10

Sample Responses and How They Were Scored—
French: Productive Language Skills

▶   ▶   ▶   ▶   ▶   ▶   ▶   ▶   ▶   ▶   ▶   ▶

This chapter presents transcriptions of actual sample responses to the practice questions in chapter 9 and explanations for the scores the responses received. The sample responses are transcribed with errors. After you have finished answering the practice questions in chapter 9, review your answers in light of the scored sample responses. If you find it difficult to evaluate your answers and assign them scores, ask a colleague, a professor, or a practicing teacher for help.

As discussed in chapter 8, each constructed-response question on the *French: Productive Language Skills* test is scored on a scale from 0 to 4. The scoring guides used to score these questions are reprinted here for your convenience.

General Scoring Guides for the *French: Productive Language Skills* Test

Presentational Speaking Section

This scoring guide is used to evaluate responses in the Presentational Speaking section. The score range is 0 to 4.

4
- Is completely and easily comprehensible, even to an unsympathetic listener[1]
- Gives a complete and entirely accurate, relevant response, with appropriate elaboration, to all (or almost all) parts of the question
- May make sporadic errors, but they rarely or never interfere with communication
  - has strong grammatical control (no errors in basic, high-frequency structures; few errors in complex, low-frequency structures; no marked error patterns)
  - employs a broad, precise vocabulary adequate for almost all topics, with word choice that is generally idiomatic and varied and rarely awkward
  - has overall fluency: speech is occasionally or rarely hesitant, with frequent use of complex sentences and "connectors" when appropriate or required
  - may have a slightly nonnative pronunciation, with few or no phonological errors and no error patterns, but is always comprehensible

3
- Is generally comprehensible, even to an unsympathetic listener, but occasionally requires the listener's effort and interpretation of the intended meaning
- Gives a mostly accurate, relevant response to most parts of the question
- Is likely to make errors and/or produce error patterns, but they only occasionally interfere with communication
  - has moderate grammatical control (few errors in basic, high-frequency structures; some errors and/or error patterns in complex, low-frequency structures)
  - employs vocabulary adequate for most general topics, with word choice that is often idiomatic but occasionally awkward
  - has considerable fluency: speech is sometimes hesitant, with some use of complex sentences and "connectors" when appropriate or required
  - may have a markedly nonnative pronunciation with some phonological errors and/or error patterns, but is always or nearly always comprehensible

---

[1] "Unsympathetic listener" refers to a native speaker of the language who is NOT accustomed to dealing with nonnative learners of the language. An unsympathetic listener does not make any special effort to understand the examinee.

2
- Is somewhat comprehensible to a sympathetic listener,[2] but often requires the listener's effort and interpretation of the intended meaning
- Gives a somewhat accurate, relevant response to some parts of the question
- Produces errors and/or error patterns that may often interfere with communication
  - has limited grammatical control (many errors and/or error patterns in basic, high-frequency structures; no control of complex, low-frequency structures)
  - employs a limited vocabulary, with word choice that is often unidiomatic and awkward
  - has limited fluency, with halting speech and mostly short, simple sentences; suggests inability to use complex sentences and "connectors" when appropriate or required
  - has a markedly nonnative pronunciation, with many phonological errors and/or error patterns, and is sometimes incomprehensible

1
- Is generally incomprehensible, even to a sympathetic listener, despite the listener's constant effort to interpret the intended meaning
- Gives an incomplete and/or mostly inaccurate and/or irrelevant response
- Produces errors and/or error patterns that very often interfere with communication
  - has very little grammatical control (many serious errors and/or error patterns in virtually all structures)
  - employs very little vocabulary, with some "formulaic speech" (memorized phrases, fixed expressions) used inappropriately
  - has virtually no fluency: speech is fragmentary and halting, interrupted often by long pauses and repetitions, and consists only of isolated words, memorized phrases, and fixed expressions
  - has a markedly nonnative pronunciation, with many serious phonological errors and/or error patterns, and is very often incomprehensible

0
- Is completely incomprehensible, even to a sympathetic listener, despite the listener's constant effort to interpret the intended meaning
- Gives an entirely inaccurate, irrelevant response or fails to respond at all
- Produces errors and/or error patterns that always interfere with communication
  - has no grammatical control (many serious errors and/or error patterns in all structures)
  - employs no vocabulary, not even "formulaic speech" (memorized phrases and fixed expressions)
  - has no fluency
  - has a markedly nonnative pronunciation and is always incomprehensible

---

[2] "Sympathetic listener" refers to a native speaker of the language who is accustomed to dealing with nonnative learners of the language. A sympathetic listener tends to make a conscious effort to understand the examinee, interpreting his or her speech for its intended meaning.

Presentational Writing Section

This scoring guide is used to evaluate responses in the Presentational Writing section. The score range is 0 to 4.

4
- Is completely and easily comprehensible, even to an unsympathetic reader[3]

- Gives a complete and entirely accurate, relevant response, with appropriate elaboration, to all (or almost all) parts of the question

- May make sporadic errors, but they rarely or never interfere with communication

  — has strong grammatical control (no errors in basic, high-frequency structures; few errors in complex, low-frequency structures; no marked error patterns)

  — employs a broad, precise vocabulary adequate for almost all topics, with word choice that is generally idiomatic and varied and rarely awkward

  — has very few or no errors in mechanics, which rarely or never interfere with meaning

  — is completely coherent and well organized, with frequent use of complex sentences and "connectors" when appropriate or required

  — uses language that is appropriate for the intended task and/or audience

3
- Is generally comprehensible, even to an unsympathetic reader, but occasionally requires the reader's effort and interpretation of the intended meaning

- Gives a mostly accurate, relevant response to most parts of the question

- Is likely to produce errors and/or error patterns, but they only occasionally interfere with communication

  — has moderate grammatical control (few errors in basic, high-frequency structures; some errors and/or error patterns in complex, low-frequency structures)

  — employs a vocabulary adequate for most general topics, with word choice that is often idiomatic but occasionally awkward

  — makes some errors in mechanics (spelling, punctuation, etc.), but they only occasionally interfere with meaning

  — is generally coherent and organized, with some complex sentences and "connectors" when appropriate or required

  — is likely to use language that is appropriate for the intended task and/or audience

2
- Is somewhat comprehensible to a sympathetic reader,[4] but often requires the reader's effort and interpretation of the intended meaning

- Gives a somewhat accurate, relevant response to some parts of the question

- Produces errors and/or error patterns that may often interfere with communication

---

[3] "Unsympathetic reader" refers to a native speaker of the language who is NOT accustomed to dealing with nonnative learners of the language. An unsympathetic reader does not make any special effort to understand the examinee.

[4] "Sympathetic reader" refers to a native speaker of the language who is accustomed to dealing with nonnative learners of the language. A sympathetic reader tends to make a conscious effort to understand the examinee, interpreting his or her writing for its intended meaning.

— has limited grammatical control (many errors and/or error patterns in basic, high-frequency structures; no control of complex, low-frequency structures)

— employs a limited vocabulary, with word choice that is often unidiomatic and awkward

— makes several errors in mechanics (spelling, punctuation, etc.), which may often interfere with meaning

— is partly or often incoherent, with little evidence of organization; suggests inability to use complex sentences and "connectors" when appropriate or required

— is likely to use language that is inappropriate for the intended task and/or audience

1   ▪ Is generally incomprehensible, even to a sympathetic reader, despite the reader's constant effort to interpret the intended meaning

   ▪ Gives an incomplete, mostly inaccurate, and/or irrelevant response

   ▪ Produces errors and/or error patterns that very often interfere with communication

— has very little grammatical control (many serious errors and/or error patterns in virtually all structures)

— employs very little vocabulary, with some "formulaic language" (memorized phrases, fixed expressions) used inappropriately

— makes many serious errors in mechanics (spelling, punctuation, etc.) in virtually all structures, which very often interfere with meaning

— is mostly incoherent, with very little or no evidence of organization

— uses language that is inappropriate for the intended task and/or audience

0   ▪ Is completely incomprehensible, even to a sympathetic reader, despite the reader's constant effort to interpret the intended meaning

   ▪ Gives an entirely inaccurate, irrelevant response or fails to respond at all

   ▪ Produces errors and/or error patterns that always interfere with communication

— has no grammatical control (many serious errors and/or error patterns in all structures)

— employs no vocabulary, not even "formulaic language" (memorized phrases and fixed expressions)

— makes many serious errors in mechanics (spelling, punctuation, etc.) in all structures, which always interfere with meaning

— is completely incoherent

Presentational Speaking Section
Constructed-Response Question 1—Sample Responses

We will now look at four scored responses to the first constructed-response practice question ("Phone Message—Dry Cleaner") and see comments from the scoring leader about why each response received the score it did.

Sample Response 1: Score of 4

> Euh, bonjour. Je m'appelle ma…Danielle Dufour. Euh, je viens de…, de chercher mon tailleur chez vous. Euh, malheureusement j'ai remarqué que, euh, euh, mon tailleur manque deux boutons et la poche s'est, la poche est déchirée. Euh, demain j'ai un rendez-vous à Québec et il est très important que j'aie, euh, mon tailleur. Donc, j'aimerais bien que vous répariez les boutons et la poche. Je comprends que vous allez bientôt fermer, mais je paierai un frais supplémentaire si vous pouvez réparer mon tailleur ce soir. Euh, merci beaucoup pour, euh, l'aide que vous pouvez me donner. Vous pouvez, euh, m'appeler chez moi ce soir, euh, ou vous pouvez m'appeler même sur mon portable. Euh, le numéro, c'est 04 67 euh, 53, euh, 66 32. Euh, merci beaucoup et, euh…, merci au revoir.

Commentary on Sample Response That Earned a Score of 4

The response includes all tasks with appropriate details and strong grammatical control, and it demonstrates excellent use of verb tenses and moods, including subjunctive and conditional. The speech is occasionally hesitant but always comprehensible, with no phonological errors.

Sample Response 2: Score of 3

> Allo madame, c'est Danielle Dufour. Je viens de, d'avoir ma meilleure robe nettoyée à sec dans votre établissement et j'ai remarqué qu'il y a deux boutons qui manquent. Et aussi la poche, il y a la poche qui manque aussi. Alors j'ai besoin de cette robe pour un conférence importante demain et je…je voudrais vous demander si vous pouvez me répa…, la réparer aussitôt que possible. Euh, aussi madame, je n'…je pense que je ne dois pas payer pour, pour la réparation…et je comprends que vous allez fermer bientôt mais c'est très important. Je n'ai pas, je suis au Québec…

Commentary on Sample Response That Earned a Score of 3

The speech quality is generally comprehensible, with considerable fluency despite slight hesitancies. The information required in the phone message is mostly accurate and includes most of the assigned tasks. The test taker mentions *la poche qui manque* instead of *la poche déchirée* and fails to address specifically how the store can take care of the problem after closing hours. The choice of vocabulary is quite adequate and often idiomatic. The pronunciation is always comprehensible. The total response could be more complete and better organized.

Sample Response 3: Score of 2

> Bonjour monsieur. Euh, Danielle Dufour ici. Euh, j'ai une coutume que, euh, vous avez, euh, nettoyée pour moi, mais euh, et c'est une coutume, euh, très, très chère et j'ai besoin de cette coutume pour un rendez-vous très important demain. Et, mais j'ai un petit problème et j'ai besoin de votre assississtance. Euh, mon costume que vous avez, euh, nettoyé, euh, il y a deux, deux boutons qui, euh, qui se manquent de le coutume et aussi le tissu à la poche est, euh, est tiré, c'est, euh, c'est pas...parfait comme, euh, comme c'était, euh, devant vous avez, euh, nettoyé...

Commentary on Sample Response That Earned a Score of 2

The speech is quite hesitant and requires a sympathetic ear to interpret the intended meaning of the message. The response includes only some of the assigned tasks and is not always accurate—for example, *le tissu à la poche est tiré* instead of *la poche est déchirée*. The word choice and sentence structure tend to be unidiomatic: *c'est pas . . . parfait comme . . . , comme c'était devant vous avez nettoyé.* Therefore, grammatical control is limited, with basic errors like *cette coutume* instead of *ce costume* and *qui se manquent de le coutume* instead of *qui manquent du costume*. Because it contains mispronounced words like *coutume* instead of *costume,* the markedly nonnative speech is sometimes incomprehensible.

Sample Response 4: Score of 1

> Bonjour, je m'appelle Daniel Dufour. Ma costume n'est pas une bonne forme. Il n'y a pas deux boutons et la poche est en mauvaise forme. Je voudrais beaucoup si vous pourrez me donner de l'argent pour ma costume parce que...j'ai payé beaucoup d'argent pour ma costume et...je voudrais...pour vous me donner l'argent que j'ai payé pour cette costume. Merci beaucoup, et mon numéro de téléphone est 3-5-5, 1-7, 1-9. Merci beaucoup.

Commentary on Sample Response That Earned a Score of 1

The response is generally incomprehensible and constant effort is required to interpret the intended meaning of the phone message. Grammatical control is quite limited. There is no control of complex structures and verb tenses: *Je voudrais beaucoup si vous pourrez me donner,* which should be *je voudrais que vous me donniez.* There is an obvious inability to use appropriate connectors like *que*. Most of all, the vocabulary is very limited, unidiomatic, and awkward. Some constructions are obviously direct, poor translations from English: *Ma* (should be *mon*) *costume n'est pas une bonne forme . . . la poche est en mauvaise forme.* ("My suit is not a good shape.") The speech is fragmentary with phonological errors.

Constructed-Response Question 2—Sample Responses

We will now look at four scored responses to the second constructed-response practice question ("The Bookshelf") and see comments from the scoring leader about why each response received the score it did.

Sample Response 1: Score of 4

> Le monsieur dans son salon vient de mettre un livre de trop sur l'étagère supérieure et, tout de suite, il s'est rendu compte qu'il a mis un livre de trop et il a mal équilibré l'étagère supérieure, alors tous les tas de livres, tout le tas de livres...vont tomber, vont tomber par terre. Il va tout faire chavirer, euh, euh, par dessus. La femme regarde ce désastre et lui dit: "Attention, mon chéri, tu viens de mettre beaucoup trop de livres sur l'étagère supérieure. Attention aux bibelots, attention au vase, euh, que j'ai aussi, euh, aux petites statues que j' euh, que j'ai sur, euh, sur la table d'en bas. Tu vas tout, euh, laisser chavirer par terre, il faut que tu, que tu ranges les livres d'une autre façon. La situation aurait pu, aurait pu être évitée si tu avais fait plus, euh, plus d'attention, si tu avais mis les livres sur, euh, sur la table, euh, sans les mettre sur les étagères. Euh, j'espère que tu feras attention la prochaine fois et que ceci ne se répète, et que ceci ne se répète plus."

Commentary on Sample Response That Earned a Score of 4

This response immediately demonstrates a well-developed vocabulary and strong grammatical control: *étagère supérieure; équilibré; chavirer; la situation aurait pu être évitée;* etc. The delivery is very slightly hesitant, but the speech is always clearly comprehensible, with no phonological errors.

Sample Response 2: Score of 3

> Il y a un homme et une femme qui est en train de, qui sont dans un, leur salon, euh, chez eux. La dame s'est, euh, s'est assise, est en train de lire un livre et le monsieur est allé, euh, à l'étag...et l'étagère pour, euh, choisir un, un autre livre. En le faisant, il a, il a bouleversé toute l'étagère où sont rangés une douzaine de livres. Euh, le, l'étagère commence à tomber et le monsieur, euh, essayait de les rattraper. Euh, entre temps la femme dit: "Oh là là ! C'est, c'est pas possible, il faut, il faut faire attention." Euh...mais le monsieur probablement arrivera pas de...de...corriger la situation. Alors, je crois que, si il a fait attention comment il a fait sorti le livre de son choix, euh, il a peut-être pu, euh, il a évité, euh, que toute la la boulevers...tout, que que la balance, euh, ne changera pas et la, l'étagère ne bouleverse pas.

Commentary on Sample Response That Earned a Score of 3

The response shows moderate to strong grammatical control. There are a few mistakes of syntax, but they never interfere with the listener's ability to visualize the incident in the picture (*Le monsieur essayait* should be *a essayé; arrivera pas de corriger* should be *n'arrivera pas à corriger*). The last sentence, on how the situation could have been avoided, is quite awkward and should be completely reconstructed because it requires a fair amount of effort to interpret the intended meaning. Overall, the vocabulary is good and often idiomatic. The fluency is sometimes hesitant, but the pronunciation is clear, with good intonation, and is always easy to understand.

Sample Response 3: Score of 2

L'incident ici, il est dans le salon de Marie et elle voit un grand problème. S..., son marié, il va destruire tous les, détruire tous les les livres, les collections de livres que qu'elle a. Euh, c'est dans le salon, et, et, il va, il va prendre un livre, mais il est stupide peut-être et il a oublié que tous les livres sont, sont pas balanced. Ils ne, ils ne sont pas une balance entre les livres dans l'étage. Le, le femme, il va dire que il est, il est stupide, euh, il a tort ici. Tous les livres, ils sont, euh, iront tomber dans, dans l'étage, et il va peut-être détruire tous les livres ici. Euh, le, le solution de ce problème est que qu'il a demandé à elle de prendre le livre je crois.

Commentary on Sample Response That Earned a Score of 2

The response does not indicate sufficient French-language tools needed to make the response generally comprehensible. The response clearly suggests lack of proficiency; it requires continuous, sympathetic listening to interpret the intended meaning of the situation in the picture. The vocabulary is often erroneous (*marié, étage, détruire* are all misused) and at times just plain English ("balanced") as well as unidiomatic. The grammatical control is very limited and contributes to the incomprehensibility of the content: *Ils ne, ils ne sont pas une balance entre les livres dans l'étage.* Fluency is indeed limited. Some phonological errors obstruct comprehensibility of the pronunciation.

Sample Response 4: Score of 1

...Alors, l'incident euh...se passe à une bibliothèque, et les livres vient de tomber...par terre. Alors le, la femme problablement dira, euh, au au l'homme, que si tu m'as de...si tu m'as demandé pour t'aider, les livres ne tomberaient pas. ...Euh donc, je crois que...le prochain événement euh...sera que l'homme et la femme va nettoyer... euh la bibliothèque et, et, et ils mettent, ils mettent les livres, euh, dans...dans son, dans ses places.

Commentary on Sample Response That Earned a Score of 1

The response makes it almost impossible to recreate the picture without seeing it. Few of the assigned tasks are included. Though the pronunciation is fairly comprehensible, the fluency is quite halting. The grammatical control is rather erratic and demonstrates error patterns in basic constructions: *les livres vient de tomber* (should be *viennent*); *au l'homme* (should be *à l'homme*); *l'homme et la femme va nettoyer* (should be *vont nettoyer*); *ils mettent les livres dans ses places* (should be *à leur place sur l'étagère*). The word choice for the location of the incident in the picture, *à une bibliothèque* ("at a library"), instead of *dans un salon* or *une salle de séjour* ("in a living or family room") shows limited vocabulary.

Constructed-Response Question 3—Sample Responses

We will now look at four scored responses to the third constructed-response practice question ("Give Instructions—Post Office") and see comments from the scoring leader about why each response received the score it did.

Sample Response 1: Score of 4

D'abord, attends l'autobus. C'est le numéro 30 qu'il faut prendre. Eh bien, tu entres dans l'autobus et…tu pourrais peut-être demander au chauffeur de te dire où il faut descendre. Alors, tu, le, la banque est, non, c'est le bureau de poste est tout près de l'arrêt d'autobus. Tu la verrais. Il y…c'est un, c'est un grand bâtiment avec des colonnes devant et tu verras aussi des boîtes à lettres juste devant, euh, près du trottoir. Alors, tu montes trois marches et tu entres dans le bureau de poste. Euh, oui, c'est entre, c'est entre des, des colonnes. Il y a trois colonnes à gauche et trois à droite. Alors, une fois dans le, le hall central, tu, tu passes à droite et…tu verras beaucoup de, de petites boîtes à lettres. Ils sont tous marqués, ils ont tous des numéros. Alors…des, le courrier sera dans une, une petite boîte. Alors tu regardes. La boîte est au milieu mais c'est complètement au fond. C'est dans le coin à gauche au fond et au milieu. Eh bien, il faut prendre le clé. Tu, tu mets la clé dans la serrure et le numéro, écoute bien, c'est le soixante-dix-sept, soixante-dix-sept. Donc tu le mets, tu le tournes et dedans tu trouveras, euh, des lettres. Le courrier sera là.

Commentary on Sample Response That Earned a Score of 4

This is a complete response, with excellent elaboration for the description of all nine pictures. The directions given are precise and easy to follow. The vocabulary is well chosen and accurate (e.g., *tu montes trois marches; le hall central; au fond et au milieu; serrure*). There are a few gender mistakes, which do not distract at all from the high quality of the response: *les boîtes à lettres . . . Ils sont tous marqués* should be *Elles sont toutes marquées*. Also, *le clé* should be *la clé*. Fluency is very rarely hesitant, and pronunciation is always comprehensible and near native.

Sample Response 2: Score of 3

Tu peux demander à, au chauffeur de, du b…de l'autobus, euh, quand descendre, mais c'est évident parce que le bureau de po…poste, c'est un immeuble assez remarquable. Il y a des colonnes romains. C'est fait en gréco-romain et ça, ça c'est marqué sur la rue. Ok, tu des…tu descends de l'autobus trente et tu vas dans les, dans les, dans la...porte centrale du bureau de poste. Dès que vous rentrez, vous tournez à droite. Ok alors, à droite il y a un mur pleine de petites boîtes et sur le troisième carré, euh, des boîtes, en bas, tu vas trouver mon petite boîte à moi qui est marqué le numéro soixante-dix-sept. Ecris-le là, c'est soixante-dix-sept et aussi c'est marqué sur la clé que je vais te donner. Et c'est dans ce...tte boîte que tu vas trouver, j'espère, l'enveloppe qui est très chère à moi et je...j'apprécie beaucoup ce que tu vas faire, Marcel, je sais que tu connais pas bien la ville, mais ce petit voyage en ville va vous...montrer un peu de la beauté de notre petite ville américain et à bientôt, Marcel. Euh, merci encore.

Commentary on Sample Response That Earned a Score of 3

The response is generally comprehensible, but at times it requires a little effort from the listener to interpret the intended meaning. However, most of the assigned tasks are presented accurately and are easy to follow. The grammatical control is moderate, though at times erratic. The test taker constantly switches from the informal *tu* form to the formal *vous,* and some genders are wrong: *un mur pleine de petites boîtes* should be *un mur plein; mon petite boîte* should be *ma petite boîte.* The fluency is considerable, with a few hesitations, although the speech is sometimes a little hurried. The pronunciation is very nonnative on a few occasions, and some words are poorly enunciated (*colons* instead of *colonnes,* for example), but overall the response is quite comprehensible.

Sample Response 3: Score of 2

Attendre l'autobus numéro trente. Descends l'autobus à l'arrêt près du...bureau de poste. A l'entrance, au porte, allez à droit...et sur la gauche, il y avait des petites boîtes au postales. Mon boîte postal est au c...au m...milieu et c'est au-dessous des autres boîtes. C'est dans le coin et c'est numéro, ...c'est numéro soixante-dix-sept. Ici c'est le clé pour mon boîte postal. Si vous mets le clé, vous pouvez ouvrir mon petit boîte postal et vous pouvez prendre mes lettres chez moi. Merci, Marcel.

Commentary on Sample Response That Earned a Score of 2

Limited grammatical control and inadequate vocabulary necessitate much effort and a sympathetic ear to understand the partial accomplishment of the task that this response presents. The use of verb tenses is totally inaccurate. In the first two sentences, there is a mix of the infinitive, *attendre;* the imperative, *descends* and *allez;* and the imperfect, *avait.* The last one particularly baffles: *Il y avait des petites boîtes postales,* which translates as "There were mail boxes." *Si vous met le clé* should be *Si vous mettez la clé.* Genders are wrong: *mon boîte* and *le clé* should be *ma boîte* and *la clé.* The fluency is halting, and the speech is mostly in short, simple sentences, which suggests an inability to use complex sentences and connectors. Pronunciation is markedly nonnative, even falling into English, as in the use of *l'entrance.*

Sample Response 4: Score of 1

> D'abord...prendre l'autobus numéro trente devant la maison. Tu prends le numéro trente jusqu'à...à la poste. Tu sors et tu montes. Tu vas dedans la poste. Là, il y a les boîtes. Il faut aller à la petite boîte numéro soixante-sept et... dedans il y a les lettres. Tu prends les lettres dans numéro soixante-sept.

Commentary on Sample Response That Earned a Score of 1

Though what is said in the response is somewhat comprehensible, it demonstrates a lack of proficiency. The vocabulary is so limited that most of the pictures are not described at all. Fluency and pronunciation are very shaky; the test taker, on no fewer than four instances, speaks in incomprehensible phrases. This is a very abbreviated response of about 30 seconds. Some of the information given in the directions is false: *Tu sors et tu montes*. This can be translated as "You get out and you go up (or "climb")," but "Get off the bus and go up the steps" is intended. The box number is also wrong: 67 instead of 77.

Constructed-Response Question 4—Sample Responses

We will now look at four scored responses to the fourth constructed-response practice question ("Opinion—Calculators") and see comments from the scoring leader about why each response received the score it did.

Sample Response 1: Score of 4

> Les calculé...latrices ne doivent pas être permis dans les élèves, l'é...l'école primaire. Je pense non, parce que ces petits élèves doivent apprendre à faire les calculs avec les crayons et savoir la base de l'arithmétique. Ils doivent savoir les tables de multiplication, l'addition, la sustra, la substra, la soubstra, soustraction et savoir comment manipuler et...les règles de calcul. Pour cela, je crois que les calculatrices ne doivent pas être permis...aux...écoles élémentaires. Persol... personnellement, je crois que...l'élève doit savoir comment faire les petits... calculs, les petites, les petits calculs comme additionner un plus deux, deux fois deux, trois moins deux, quatre divisés par deux, avec leur crayon et non pas utiliser les calculatrices parce que les calculatrices...ne...ne la, ne l...ne va pas le s...l'aider à réussir, par exemple dans un petit examen quand il doit utiliser...il ne, il ne sera pas permis d'utiliser les calculatrices, les calculatrices dans...la...dans un endroit où il doit faire l'examen. Même dans un autre cas, si l'élève doit...va aller dans, dans un supermarché avec sa maman, il peut l'aider pour acheter les choses et fait l'addition, la, la mu...la...multiplier les choses. Alors, personnellement, je crois que les calculatrices ne doivent pas permis aux écoles élémentaires.

Commentary on Sample Response That Earned a Score of 4

The test taker's response about the use of calculators in the elementary mathematics classroom is very well stated, with sound, specific examples to support her opinion: *apprendre à faire le calcul avec le crayon, les tables de multiplication, l'addition, la soustraction,* and *dans un supermarché . . . aider [sa maman] . . . [à faire] l'addition.* The fluency is occasionally hesitant, but the continuous flow of speech is easy to follow. The pronunciation, slightly nonnative with a light accent, is always clear and comprehensible. The grammatical control is fairly strong, but there are errors with complex structures: *les calculatrices ne doivent pas être permis (permis* should be *permises).* The vocabulary is appropriate for the topic of the question.

Sample Response 2: Score of 3

> A mon avis, les calculatrices…doivent interdire…à l'école primaire parce que c'est nécessaire pour le prof enseigne…enseigner les principes des mathématiques. Je pense que les étudiants doivent mémoriser les principes comme les tables de multiplication ou d'addition. Il est nécessaire à faire beaucoup de répétitions avec ces étudiants… Je pense que…les principes de, des maths qu'on apprend à l'école primaire sont les racines des mathématiques plus avancées. Sans ces principes, on ne peut pas faire les maths plus élevées. Par exemple, il y a beaucoup d'étudiants à l'état du Nevada qui ne peuvent pas réussir à l'examen de l'état en maths parce qu'ils ne peuvent pas faire les maths sans calculatrice et il y a chaque année des étudiants que…qui ne fait p…, qui ne fait pas le diplôme à cause de…cet examen. Et je, si je suis étudiant au lycée à Nevada, je serai très déçue si j'ai…suivi beaucoup de cours de maths et je ne peux pas réussir à cet examen. A l'âge des, des élèves primaires….

Commentary on Sample Response That Earned a Score of 3

This is a generally comprehensible response. It presents an opinion that is fairly easy to follow. The grammatical control can be defined as moderate, with few high-frequency, basic errors. There are some misused verbs: *les calculatrices doivent interdire* should be *doivent être interdites; il y a des étudiants qui ne fait pas le diplôme* should be *qui ne reçoivent pas leur diplôme.* The opinion could be a bit more specific in its defense, particularly in stating why students in Nevada do not pass the state math test without a calculator. There is considerable fluency and errors are rare.

Sample Response 3: Score of 2

> Dans une classe de petit élèves, je pense qu'il n'est pas d'accord d'avoir les calculateurs pour les étudiants. Euh, c'est pas possible pour les étudiants d'apprendre les mathématiques très bien si il est possible pour eux…de utiliser une calculateur. Euh, avec une calc…calculateur, les étudiants n'a pas besoin de…travailler avec tous les numéros et tous les…les…euh, manières de manipuler les, euh, les numéros. C'est pas possible pour ils de…d'apprendre les…euh, les mathématiques, les standards des mathématiques, les

multiplications, les divisions, c'est pas possible, euh, s'il peut…simplement utiliser une calculateur. Donc je pense que c'est pas, c'est pas d'accord pour les ét…les étudiants, spécifiquement les, les petit élèves, euh, de utiliser une calculateur dans les cours de mathématiques.

Commentary on Sample Response That Earned a Score of 2

In spite of what sounds like fairly considerable fluency, this test taker shows poor grammatical control, limited vocabulary, and unidiomatic word choice: With *je pense qu'il n'est pas d'accord d'avoir des calculateurs,* the test taker is trying to say, "I don't think that it is right to have calculators" but instead says, "I think he does not agree to have calculators." There are grammatical mistakes in every sentence: *les étudiants n'a pas besoin* should be *n'ont pas besoin*; *C'est pas possible pour ils d'apprendre* should be *ce n'est pas possible pour eux.* Because of these many mistakes, the listener must be patient and very sympathetic and always make an effort to interpret the intended meaning. The pronunciation is very nonnative and sometimes incomprehensible.

Sample Response 4: Score of 1

Non, on ne peut pas penser de mathématiques avec un ordinateur. C'est très nécessaire pour prendre…parce que tu dois…tu dois u…utiliser votre propre pensée pour prendre…c…ce sujet. …Pour apprendre, c'est très nécesssaire…euh, utiliser…l'addition…avec…tes propres pensées…

Commentary on Sample Response That Earned a Score of 1

This response clearly demonstrates lack of proficiency. It includes very few of the assigned tasks, which are largely erroneously presented. The three sentences are quite nonsensical: *On ne doit pas penser de mathématiques avec un ordinateur* translates as "One cannot think of mathematics with a computer." Speech is totally fragmentary; mostly isolated words and short phrases are used; and there is no evidence of an ability to formulate a grammatically correct sentence: *C'est très necessaire pour prendre . . . parce que tu dois . . . utiliser votre propre pensée pour prendre . . . ce sujet.* This sentence cannot be interpreted.

Constructed-Response Question 5—Sample Responses

We will now look at four scored responses to the fifth constructed-response practice question ("Paraphrase—Teddy Bear") and see comments from the scoring leader about why each response received the score it did.

Sample Response 1: Score of 4

Voici l'histoire d'une enfant qui s'appelle Giselle Rochard. Elle était une petite fille de quatre ans, de quatre ans. Son jouet favori était un nounours en peluche qui ne pesait que 100 gram, qui pesait moins que 100 gram en fait qui mesurait que 25 centimètres. En regardant par les yeux bruns de son nounours, on…peut affirmer, on pouvait affirmer qu'il n'était pas du tout féroce, mais par contre tendre et affectueux. Un jour, ce nounours communiquait un besoin à Gis…a communi…pardon. Ce, un jour, ce nounours a communiqué un besoin à Giselle. Il voulait quelque chose à boire, et à manger. Giselle a répondu en allant chercher quelque chose dans le cuisine. Elle a cherché un verre de limonade, elle l'a ramené, elle l'a posé sur la table dans le…dans, dans sa chambre. Puis elle est rentrée à la cuisine pour chercher des biscuits. Cependant, certains dans sa famille s'inquiétaient et se disent: "Comment est-ce possible qu'un enfant ne peut, ne peut pas re…reconnaître le la différence entre ce qui est réel et ce qui est fantasie. Elle ne comprend pas qu'un jouet, c'est simplement comme animal, ce n'est pas du tout réel." Mais la mère, elle dit : "Ah, mais une enfant de cet âge doit, doit pouvoir se permettre quelques illusions toujours." Pendant cette conversation, François, le frère aîné de Giselle, est allé la chercher dans sa chambre…

Commentary on Sample Response That Earned a Score of 4

The test taker shows excellent, full understanding of the story and is able to paraphrase it accurately and with abundant, appropriate detail. Only the very end of the story is missing (the brother drinking the lemonade and Giselle's being surprised), but that does not detract from the obvious quality of the response. The test taker needed just another ten seconds to complete the tasks. The fluency is very good, and the speech is rarely hesitant. The pronunciation is slightly nonnative but always comprehensible. The grammatical constructions demonstrate excellent use of verb tenses.

Sample Response 2: Score of 3

Dans cette histoire, il y avait une, un enfant qui s'appelle Giselle. Elle avait quatre ans. Elle possédait un nounour qui était très petit et sympathique. Il n'avait pas…de figure féroce. Giselle aimait très fort ce nounour. …Un, une journée, elle jouait avec ce nounour et tout d'un coup, le nounour…a dit: "J'ai besoin de quelque chose à manger, de quelque chose à boire !" Et p…et puis Giselle a apporté de la limonade et après, elle est allée à la cuisine pour chercher quelque chose à manger. Elle a trouvé des biscuits et elle a apporté les biscuits au nounour, et puis elle, elle est partie du salon et la famille dit: "Pourquoi Giselle parle à nounour, pourquoi elle a dit que le nounour a besoin de quelque chose à manger? C'est une fantasie, ce n'est pas du réalité." Et puis, son frère François qui est plus aîné, cherche Giselle à sa chambre mais il a vu la limonade au salon et il a bu tout la limonade et puis il est parti et quand Giselle est retournée…

Commentary on Sample Response That Earned a Score of 3

The test taker has a fair understanding of the story but distorts some of the facts. The teddy bear does not actually speak, as the test taker states, and the quotes from the family are not altogether accurate. "The teddy bear seemed to communicate" is what the reader of the story says. Grammatical control is moderate; some verb tenses are wrong: *Dans cette histoire il y avait* (should be *il y a*) *un enfant qui s'appelle;* and *ce n'est pas du réalité* should be *ce n'est pas la réalité*. There is considerable fluency and the pronunciation, though markedly nonnative, is quite comprehensible.

Sample Response 3: Score of 2

> *C'est l'histoire d'une petite fille Giselle qui a quatre ans. Un jour elle voit…Giselle parle avec l'ours et il cherche pour quelque chose à boire et à manger. Et aussi il…un peu. Il mangeait des biscuits et il but de la limonade. Et puis…est très fâché parce que, euh, elle a peur que sa fille, elle ne comprend pas la différence entre un jouet et un vrai animaux. Euh, et puis, euh, plus tard, elle apporte, Giselle a…apporte la limonade à sa chambre et que, et quand elle retourne, la verre est vide. Alors, est-ce que l'animaux, euh, jouet est une vrai animaux? Nous ne savons pas.*

Commentary on Sample Response That Earned a Score of 2

The retelling of the teddy bear story is very fragmented, incomplete, and partially inaccurate. Some parts are unclear and mumbled, often requiring the listener's effort and sympathy to interpret the intended meaning. There are grammatical errors in almost every sentence. For example, the test taker says *Il mangeait des biscuits et il bu de la limonade*. This statement, which falsely refers to the teddy bear eating cookies and drinking lemonade, can be interpreted as "He was eating cookies, and he drank lemonade." Forgetting the inaccuracy of the statement, correct French here would be *Il a mangé des biscuits et il a bu de la limonade*. Gender and number mistakes are also evident: *un vrai animaux* instead of *un vrai animal; la verre est vide* instead of *le verre est vide*. The comprehensibility of the response is very limited. The fluency is halting, and the pronunciation is often incomprehensible.

Sample Response 4: Score of 1

> *C'est une histoire qui s'appelle, une histoire de l'enfant. Euh, c'est…il y a une, une petite fille qui s'appelle Gisalle, Giselle Richard. Euh, elle est décrit comme une, une très petite euh, fille euh, elle est très jeune et très petite, euh, dans sa physique. Euh, elle a une une amie qui elle pense est vraie, mais, mais les gens vieux comme ses parents et sa frère, euh, son frère, euh, ils ont pense que son a…sa amie est une jouet amie et non pas une vraie amie. Euh, mais elle, elle, elle parle avec son son amie, euh, et Giselle, euh, lui a apporté, euh, le limonade et les biscuits, euh, parce que son son amie c'est, euh, soif et c'est faim…euh, mais quand elle, euh, lui a porté une limonade, elle l'a laissée sur la, la cuisine et son frère a allé sur la cuisine et boit, a bu, euh, tout le limonade et quand elle rentrait à la cuisine, elle pense que son amie l'a bu donc elle pense que son, son, son amie, euh, c'est une vraie, une vraie amie, une vraie personne. Euh, elle a dit, la verre c'est vide, euh, mais les les gens pensent qu'elle ne peut pas euh…*

Commentary on Sample Response That Earned a Score of 1

There is very little evidence in this paraphrase that the test taker has an accurate understanding of the story. Instead of a teddy bear, there is a friend, supposedly real: *une amie qui elle pense est vraie* (correct French would be *une amie qu'elle...*). Not only is the paraphrase filled with inaccuracies, but the grammar is also full of many serious errors: *son amie c'est soif...et c'est faim,* instead of *son amie a soif et a faim; son frère a allé sur la cuisine* instead of *son frère est allé dans la cuisine.* There is limited fluency, but the syntax is so poor that it impedes the listener's ability to comprehend the story being retold.

Constructed-Response Question 6—Sample Responses

We will now look at four scored responses to the sixth constructed-response practice question ("Formal Talk—Exchange Program") and see comments from the scoring leader about why each response received the score it did.

Sample Response 1: Score of 4

> Bonjour collègues! J'ai le plaisir de vous accueillir chez nous et de pouvoir vous offrir ce dîner. Le sujet dont, dont je voudrais vous parler ce soir est un échange d'élèves entre votre lycée et le nôtre. Cet échange permettrait aux élèves, à vos élèves et à nos élèves, de...de profiter de plusieurs, euh, avantages. Par exemple: améliorer leur français, ou leur anglais, en pouv...en pouvant parler aux autochtones, aux personnes, euh, qui parlent le français ou l'anglais couramment comme langue maternelle. Euh...cet échange permettrait aux élèves aussi de, d'apprendre les différences culturelles qui existent. Aussi cet échange permettrait aux...aux élèves de faire de nouveaux amis, euh, dans de nouvelles cultures. Aussi il y a la cuisine. Cet échange permettrait...eh aux é...aux élèves d'apprécier de la nouvelle cuisine. Par exemple, la cuisine française, comme vous savez, est très connue dans le monde et j'aimerais bien que mes élèves puissent pouvoir en profiter. Aussi cet échange, euh, permettrait aux élèves de visiter un nouveau pays, nouveau pays, et de pouvoir voyager beaucoup et de voir, euh, du monde.

Commentary on Sample Response That Earned a Score of 4

This is a well-organized, excellent talk by a nonnative speaker. All tasks are covered carefully, and the degree of formality is most appropriate. The grammatical control is strong, and the vocabulary is broad and idiomatic. Here is a good example: *Le sujet dont je voudrais vous parler ce soir est un échange d'élèves entre votre lycée et le nôtre.* The overall fluency is occasionally hesitant, but the test taker makes frequent use of complex sentences (as above). Pronunciation is always comprehensible.

Sample Response 2: Score of 3

> Bonjour messieurs, bonjour mesdames. Enchantée. C'est un grand plaisir de vous accueillir chez moi. …Les élèves franç…les élèves français auront une grande chance, une bonne expérience de venir rester avec nos familles américaines. Les élèves seront mis dans des maisons, bien accueillis par les parents qui ont des élèves très, très bons à l'école, et ces élèves auront la chance d'être immergés avec les autres élèves de notre lycée. Ils parleront l'anglais toute la journée, il…auront la chance de visiter les musées et les places dans notre ville. Ils seront tellement bien accueillis dans notre…ville et dans notre, euh, lycée. Alors…pour cette conférence, j'…ai l'opportuni…portunité de vous parler de comment est-ce que cet échange va marcher. Au premier abord, je vais vous, je vais vous introduire tout le plan pour… vous expliquer comment ce, cet échange marchera. Alors, nous allons…

Commentary on Sample Response That Earned a Score of 3

The response, though fairly comprehensible, is poorly organized. The premise about establishing an exchange is not mentioned until the end. The talk immediately gets into the benefits for French students of staying with American families. There is nothing said of the benefits of American students staying in France; therefore, an important part of the task is missing. The degree of formality is good, and the word choice is often idiomatic. *Enchantée,* stranded by itself at the beginning, is out of place in this context. What was probably intended was *Je suis enchantée de vous accueillir.* Another awkward sentence is *j'ai l'opportunité de vous parler de comment est-ce que cet échange va marcher.* What is likely intended is *j'ai l'opportunité de vous expliquer (dire) comment cet échange va marcher.*

Sample Response 3: Score of 2

> Bonjour ! Je m'appelle Dominique Piaf…Je suis prof de français et d'histoire mondiale au lycée Centennial…à Las Vegas. Je suis très heureuse…se de faire vos connaissances. Je pense que ce sera très bénéficiel si vos élèves et mes élèves font une ex…une échange. Las Vegas, bien sûr, n'est pas de ville américaine typique parce que nous sommes un peu bizarres. Il y a beaucoup d'argent ici. Il y a bien sûr beaucoup des casinos, et d'hôtels, mais en autre sens, mon lycée est très typique. Il y a, euh, quelques étudiants chinois, quelques étudiants avec un Américain etc. Beaucoup de nos élèves habitent dans une maison avec seulement une mère ou un père. C'est typique en Amérique. Je pense que…on doit…nous, nous devons…développer de la tolérance pour les coutules, coutures…

Commentary on Sample Response That Earned a Score of 2

This formal talk is only somewhat accurate and could demonstrate a more appropriate degree of formality. *Bonjour! Je m'appelle…Je suis prof de français* is a little too casual to begin a formal talk and to welcome guest teachers from another country. The content deals mostly with the peculiarities of the city of the test taker. Nothing is really said about specific benefits of the exchange for the students of both countries. Grammatical control is very uneven, and the vocabulary tends to be unidiomatic. Here are examples: 1. *Je suis très heureuse se de faire vos connaissances. (Je suis très heureuse de faire votre connaissance.)* 2. *bénéficiel (profitable/avantageux)* 3. *développer de la tolérance pour les coutules, coutures (tolérer les cultures différentes).* The fluency is halting, and occasionally some phonological errors make pronunciation incomprehensible.

Sample Response 4: Score of 1

> Bienvenue les professeurs ! Les étudiants vont apprendre beaucoup de la culture française et la langue française. Pour avoir un exchange entre nos pays, …et aider tout le monde. Tout le monde est no…C'est très nécessaire avoir un exchange entre nos…nos pays pour aider tout le monde et notre monde. Merci. …J'espère que tu, j'espère que vous allez considérer…ma proposition.

Commentary on Sample Response That Earned a Score of 1

This is a clear demonstration of a lack of proficiency. The much-too-brief response includes very few of the assigned tasks, as well as some irrelevant information. The fluency is quite limited; the test taker speaks in simple sentences and isolated short phrases: *Tout le monde est; Merci; Pour avoir un exchange entre nos pays . . . et aider tout le monde.* These are fragmentary constructions (including the English pronunciation of "exchange" instead of *échange*) and totally incomprehensible sentences.

Presentational Writing Section
Constructed-Response Question 7—Sample Responses

We will now look at four scored responses to the seventh constructed-response practice question ("Taxi/Briefcase") and see comments from the scoring leader about why each response received the score it did.

Sample Response 1: Score of 4

> La semaine dernier un monsieur a pris un taxi pour se rendre quelque part. Le taxi est arrivé à son destination et le monsieur a reglé le prix du taxi. Il est sorti du taxi ensuite et s'est dirigé vers la porte 200, tenant en main une chemise. Pendant ce temps le taxi est reparti. En cour de route le chauffeur du taxi s'est retourné et il a constanté…que le monsieur avez oublié son sac. Il a retourné et s'arrêté devant la porte 200, où le monsieur se dirigeait quand il était descendu du taxi. Il lui a remis le sac et le monsieur, tout content d'avoir retrouvé son sac, lui a serré la main. Tout est bien qui finit bien.

Commentary on Sample Response That Earned a Score of 4

Proficiency is clearly demonstrated, and the story is easily comprehensible. The few structural errors do not take away from the good quality of the response: *son destination* should be *sa destination; avez oublié* should be *avait oublié; Il a retourné et s'arrête* should be *Il est retourné et s'est arrêté*. Overall, the grammatical control is strong and shows excellent use of past tenses. There are complex sentences, and word choice is quite idiomatic: *En cours de route le chauffeur de taxi s'est retourné et il a constaté que le monsieur avez* (sic) *oublié son sac*. The response is completely coherent and well organized.

Sample Response 2: Score of 3

> La semaine dernière j'ai amené un homme d'affaires (je crois qu'il était un avocat) dans mon taxi à son bureau au centre-ville. C'était No. 200 dans la Rue de l'Eglise. J'ai venu de partir quand j'ai remarqué que son cartable était encore dans la voiture. Je suis revenu au bureau. J'ai laissé mon taxi dans la rue devant l'immeuble à No. 200. J'ai donné le cartable à l'homme dans son bureau au deuxième étage. Il était très contente de recevoir ses papiers qui étaient essentiels pour ses affaires. Il m'a donné la main et il a eu une grande sourire.

Commentary on Sample Response That Earned a Score of 3

Most of the assigned tasks are included in this response, but it is difficult to recreate all six pictures because very little is written about pictures 2 and 3. The story is comprehensible enough and it requires little effort to understand the intended meaning of the situation. The vocabulary is adequate and fairly idiomatic. The use of *cartable* ("schoolbag") is a little off for "briefcase." There are a few basic, high-frequency grammatical errors: *J'ai venu de partir* for *Je venais de partir; Il était très contente* for *très content;* and *Il m'a donné la main et il a eu une grande sourire* for *Il m'a serré la main et il avait un grand sourire*. The story is generally coherent, and there is evidence of organization.

Sample Response 3: Score of 2

> La semaine dernière je conduisait mon taxi dans la ville. Mon client c'etait un homme de moyen âge qui avait l'aire d'un homme d'affaires. A la fin du parcour il est descendue du taxi et j'ai vue comment il rentrait dans un bâtiment avec le numéro deux cent. Avant de reprendre la route, je me suis retourné vers le siège d'arrière et je remarqué que l'homme avait oublié sa petite valise! J'ai garé mon taxi, et rentré dans le bâtiment avec la valise. On m'a guidé vers le bureau de l'homme et je lui est rendu sa propriété. Il était vraiment soulagé et il m'a remercié avec un grand sourire et un salut avec sa main.

Commentary on Sample Response That Earned a Score of 2

There is a fairly clear understanding of the pictures. However, the reader must constantly make an effort in interpreting the meaning of the events in the pictures. The limited grammatical control is evidenced by incorrect verb endings (*je conduissait* for *je consuisais*), wrong or missing auxiliary verbs (*je lui est rendu* for *je lui ai rendu; je remarqué et entré* for *j'ai remarqué et je suis entré/e*), and wrong endings of past participles (*il est descendue* for *il est descendu; j'ai vue* for *j'ai vu*). These are high-frequency, basic grammatical structures. Faulty mechanics and unidiomatic, awkward word choice are also apparent: *qui avait l'aire* for *qui avait l'air*; *le siège d'arrière* for *le siège arrière*; *homme de moyen âge* means "man of the Middle Ages," not "middle-aged man"; *rendu sa propriété* means "land property," not "personal belongings"; *un salut avec sa main* is used instead of *il m'a serré la main*; *j'ai vue comment il rentrait dans un bâtiment avec le numéro deux cent* is used instead of *j'ai vu qu'il entrait dans le bâtiment numéro 200*. All these mistakes make this response partly incoherent.

Sample Response 4: Score of 1

> La semaine dernière, je suis arrivé à ma bibliotheque dans un taxi, je suis exité le taxi et je suis entrée ma bibliotheque. Le condriveur de taxi a vu mon sac dans le taxi. Je l'ai oublié! Il a apporté mon sac à moi. J'ai eu très heureux! Je l'ai dit "Merci beaucoup, Monsieur!"

Commentary on Sample Response That Earned a Score of 1

This response contains few of the assigned tasks. The very brief story is made up of formulaic language with some memorized phrases and is full of grammar and vocabulary errors: *je suis exité le taxi* for *je suis descendu/sorti du taxi*; *je suis entrée ma bibliothèque* for *je suis entrée dans ma bibliothèque*; *Le condriveur de taxi* for *Le chauffeur de taxi*; *Il a apporté mon sac à moi* for *Il m'a apporté mon sac*; *J'ai eu très heureux* for *J'étais très heureux*; *Je l'ai dit* for *Je lui ai dit*. It clearly demonstrates a lack of proficiency, with inappropriate, limited language ability.

Constructed-Response Question 8—Sample Responses

We will now look at four scored responses to the eighth constructed-response practice question ("Letter—Broken Plate") and see comments from the scoring leader about why each response received the score it did.

Sample Response 1: Score of 4

> 7 juillet 2004
>
> Chere Monsieur LeBrun,
> Je viens de rentrer de nos vacances en France où nous avons passé quelques jours à votre ville agréable où j'ai acheté une assiette à votre petit magasin. L'assiette était blanche avec les petites fleurs bleues et jaunes. La marque s'appellait "Fleurs sauvages". Elle coutait cent-douze francs et j'ai payé avec ma carte de credit. Vous m'avez envoyé l'assiette ici aux Etats-Unis, mais elle est arrivée complètement cassée en plusieurs morceaux. J'adore cette assiette. Elle est pour moi un beau souvenir de mon séjour en France et de votre jolie ville. Je voudrais que vous m'en envoyiez une autre.
> Dans l'attente de votre bienveillante décision, je vous prie de croire, Monsieur, à l'expression de mes meilleurs sentiments.
>
> (Signature)

Commentary on Sample Response That Earned a Score of 4

This letter is clear, to the point, and polite. It is completely comprehensible and includes all the information requested. Grammar errors are few and never interfere with communication: *Chere Monsieur* for *Cher Monsieur; à votre ville* and *à votre magasin* should be *dans votre ville* and *dans votre magasin; s'appellait* should be *s'appelait*. The closing salutation is particularly good.

Sample Response 2: Score of 3

Madame, Monsieur,

J'espère que vous pouvez m'aider. Il y a trois semaines que j'ai passé mes vacances à Limoges. Chez votre boutique, j'ai acheté une magnifique assiette de porcelain, fabriqué à la main. Je l'aime beaucoup. Vous m'avez offré d'envoyer mon assiette en avion à ma maison aux Etas-Unis. Je suis certain que vous avez pris beaucoup de soin en preparant mon assiette pour voyager. Malheuresement quand j'ai reçu l'assiette aujourd'hui, j'ai trouvé qu'elle s'est cassé en route.

Je vous ai pourvu avec une copie de ma methode de paiement. Si vous pouvez replacer l'assiette je l'apprécierais vraiment. Si non je vous en prie de crediter mon Visa.

Je vous prie mes salutation distinguées.

Mme...

Commentary on Sample Response That Earned a Score of 3

The degree of formality for this letter is appropriate, and most of the tasks are completed. The description of the plate is the most important detail missing. The grammatical control is moderate, with a few errors of past participle agreement and awkward constructions: *Vous m'avez offré* should be *. . . m'avez offert; elle s'est cassé* should be *s'est cassée; une assiette . . . fabriqué* should be *. . . fabriquée; Si vous pouvez replacer l'assiette* should be *. . . remplacer l'assiette*. The closing salutation is not clear: *Je vous prie mes salutation distinguées* should be *Je vous prie de croire à mes salutations*. Vocabulary is adequate (*porcelain* should be *porcelaine*), and some accents are missing. The letter could be better organized, but it is generally coherent and comprehensible.

Sample Response 3: Score of 2

lundi, le 12 janvier

Monsieur Dubois,

Je regret que je vous ecris avec les nouvelles mauvaises. Il y a deux semaines, j'ai acheté une plat spéciale dans votre magasin. C'est plat était pour ma fille pour son anniversaire. Je suis sûr que vous comprennez l'importance de ces merchandises et que je suis très triste quand je l'ai reçu et elle était cassé !

J'ai déjà payé pour les merchandises avec mon carte de credit. Je demande que vous me donnez une autre plat de la même descritpion (rouge, avec les petits fleurs jaune), ou me payez la monnaie que je vous ai déja payez.

> S'il vous plaît, envoyez les merchandises avec la même description ou m'envoyez l'argent—a la même addresse. Je vous prie agrere (?), monsieur, l'expression de mes sentiments les plus sincères,
>
> (Signature)

Commentary on Sample Response That Earned a Score of 2

This letter immediately suggests a lack of proficiency and often requires the reader's effort in interpreting the intended meaning. Though the information is mostly relevant, error patterns often interfere with communication of the message. Grammatical control is definitely limited. Every sentence has serious mistakes, including the following: *Je regret que je vous ecris avec les nouvelles mauvaises* should be *Je regrette de vous écrire avec de mauvaises nouvelles. C'est plat était pour ma fille* should be *Ce plat était pour ma fille.* Many words are misspelled. The response (as in the first sentence of the letter) uses French words in English sentence structures and makes literal translation of English idioms.

Sample Response 4: Score of 1

> Chèr Administrateur,
>
> Pendant ma séjour au Limoges, le dernière mois, j'ai acheté en votre magazine une assiette peintre a main. Je vous ai payé 50 francs pour lui. J'ai le reçu, aujourdhui et je vois quielle est cassée. Je vouler (?) savoir si vous pouvez me changé l'assiette pour autre tant joli come cette-lui. Cette assiette a des fleurs rouges, jaunes et bleues. Je vous remercie pour m'aider

Commentary on Sample Response That Earned a Score of 1

This letter clearly demonstrates a lack of proficiency and is generally incomprehensible. The grammar and vocabulary mistakes are numerous (no fewer than twenty in five short, fractured sentences) and strongly interfere with the communication of the intended message. Here are some examples: *ma séjour* for *mon séjour; le dernière mois* for *le mois dernier; en votre magazine* for *dans votre magasin; une assiette peintre a main* for *une assiette peinte à la main; une autre tant joli come cette-lui* for *une autre aussi jolie que celle-ci.* This letter is incoherent, with little or no evidence of organization.

Constructed-Response Question 9—Sample Responses

We will now look at four scored responses to the ninth constructed-response practice question ("Questions to Host Families") and see comments from the scoring leader about why each response received the score it did.

Sample Response 1: Score of 4

First Question

> Avez-vous des enfants? Combien en avez-vous et quel âge ont-ils ?

Second Question

> La famille joue un role très important dans la vie des jeunes. Quel est votre avis ?

Third Question

> Comment vous trouvez l'adolescent américain? Est-ce que vous avez déjà rencontré des jeunes américains ? Et quelles étaient les circonstances ?

Fourth Question

> Connaissez-vous un peu les coutumes américaines ? Et avez-vous l'intention de changer des idées avec le étudiants américains ? Lesquelles ?

Commentary on Sample Response That Earned a Score of 4

The questions are intelligent, relevant, and well written. Grammatical control is very strong, and vocabulary is well chosen. Only in the last question should there be a slight adjustment: *l'intention de changer des idées avec les étudiants,* which very likely should be *l'intention d'échanger/de partager des idées.*

Sample Response 2: Score of 3

First Question

> Est-ce que vous fumez ou utilisez les boissons alcoholic ?

Second Question

> Decrivez votre famille, vos professions, enfants, votre apartement.

Third Question

> Est-ce que vous avez l'experience d'avoir un/e etudiant/e etranger/e dans le passé ? Si oui, decrivez le.

Fourth Question

> Pourquoi est-ce que vous voulez avoir en/e etudiant/e etranger/e qui va vivre avec vous ? Decrivez vos raisons pour lesquelles vous pensez que vous êtes une famille ideal pour un/e étudiant/e etranger/e.

Commentary on Sample Response That Earned a Score of 3

The questions are quite appropriate, though the first question about smoking and alcoholic beverages might be a bit personal. The written French is generally comprehensible. The grammatical control and vocabulary are moderate and provide generally coherent questions. Many accents are missing. Some of the mistakes are *boissons alcoholic* for *boissons alcooliques; une famille ideal* for *une famille idéale.* Question 3 is a little awkward and could be clearer: *Est-ce que vous avez l'experience d'avoir un/e etudiant/e etranger/e dans le passé ? Si oui, decrivez le* could be rewritten as follows: *Avez-vous déjà hébergé des étudiants étrangers chez vous ? Si oui, expliquez, s'il vous plaît.*

Sample Response 3: Score of 2

First Question

> Il y a combien de chambres de lit (dans) votre maison ? Et des salles de bain ?

Second Question

> Pourquoi avez-vous pris le decision de prendre des étudiants dans votre maison ?

Third Question

> Quels sorts de repas allez-vous préparer pour les étudiants et quel sort de cuisine est-ce que vous ferez pour le diner, et le petit déjeuner ? Le diner est-ce qu'ils consistera d'un pôtage, une sorte de viande, des legumes, et un désert ?

Fourth Question

> Comment est-ce que vous comptez diviser le temps de salle de bain pour votre famille et les étudiants pendant les fins de semaines et les soirés en générale ?

Commentary on Sample Response That Earned a Score of 2

The writing is somewhat comprehensible. The relevance and quality of the questions, which do not always observe the appropriate degree of formality, is questionable. Unidiomatic word choice and poor grammar often require the reader's effort to understand the questions. Examples include *chambres de lit* for *chambres à coucher; le decision de prendre des étudiants* for *la décision d'accepter des étudiants; Quels sorts de repas* for *Quel genre de repas* and *quel sort de cuisine* for *quelle sorte de cuisine/quel genre de cuisine; désert* for *dessert.*

Sample Response 4: Score of 1

First Question

> Pouvez-vous décrire votre vie familiale ?

Second Question

> Que pensez-vous que la vie americaine soit ?

Third Question

> Comment est-ce que vous supporterez la jeune américain si elle a peur ou a l'air dépressée ?

Fourth Question

> Où iront-les américains au lycée ?

Commentary on Sample Response That Earned a Score of 1

These questions clearly show a lack of proficiency. The response demonstrates little ability to construct sensible questions in French. There is no coherence and little evidence of organization and relevance. One example is the second question: *Que pensez-vous que la vie americaine soit?* Roughly and literally translated, it asks, rather incomprehensibly: "What do you think American life be?" Incorrect vocabulary includes *vie familliale* instead of *vie de famille* and *l'air dépressée* instead of *l'air déprimé*. The response is mostly incoherent.

Chapter 11

Study Topics—*German: Content Knowledge*

▶ ▶ ▶ ▶ ▶ ▶ ▶ ▶ ▶ ▶ ▶ ▶

Introduction to the Test

The Praxis *German: Content Knowledge* test is designed to assess the knowledge and competencies necessary for beginning or entry-level teachers of German. You will be required to answer questions based on recorded conversations and narrations. You will also be required to read, interpret, and correct written German and to identify errors and error patterns in grammar, structure, mechanics, word choice, and register. You will be asked questions about the geography, history, and culture of Germany and German-speaking countries.

The purpose of this chapter is to provide guidance on how to prepare for the test. A broad overview of the areas covered in the *German: Content Knowledge* test is followed by detailed lists of the specific topics that are covered under each broad area.

You are not expected to be an expert on all aspects of the topics that follow. However, you should understand the major characteristics or aspects of each topic and be able to recognize them in various kinds of examples or selections.

Here is an overview of the areas covered on the test, along with their subareas:

Interpretive Listening
27% of the questions

- Short Conversations
- Short Narrations
- Long Conversations and Long Narrations

Structure of the Language
28% of the questions

- Speech Analysis
- Writing Analysis
- Language Analysis
- Grammar Analysis

Interpretive Reading
26% of the questions

- Content and Organization
- Implied Content
- Use of Language

Cultural Perspectives
19% of the questions

- Geography
- Lifestyles and Societies
- Sociolinguistic Elements of German
- History
- Literature and the Arts

Interpretive Listening

The Interpretive Listening section of the test is divided into three different parts: short conversations, short narrations, and long conversations and long narrations. Selections will be read by native speakers of German, followed by questions read orally. Answer choices will appear only in your test book.

Short Conversations

For these questions, you will be asked to listen to a recorded dialogue between two native speakers of German speaking at a normal rate of speech. To complete this task successfully, you must be able to interpret stress and intonation; understand the meaning of key words; understand high-frequency vocabulary, idiomatic expressions, and figures of speech; recognize questions and instructions; understand sentence tenses in different time frames; identify main ideas; and understand conversations on a variety of everyday topics. You also might be asked to make inferences based on the information given.

- Recognize the meaning carried by stress and intonation

  - Rising intonation is used to ask "yes" or "no" questions, whereas unchanging intonation is used to make a statement or give a command. For example, consider the expression *Machen Sie sich Notizen?* The answer would be either *Ja* or *Nein*. However, *Machen Sie sich Notizen!* (spoken forcefully) is a command that requires an action.

  - Intonation can also indicate a particular emotion, including surprise or discontent.

- Understand the meaning of an utterance based on key words

  - Key words allow you to determine where a particular situation may be taking place or what information is being requested. For example, if you hear key words such as *Ihre Pässe, bitte; Wie lange bleiben Sie in der Schweiz?* and finally, *Ihre Flugscheine, bitte,* you will know from the conversation that the speakers are at an airport.

- Understand high-frequency vocabulary, idiomatic expressions, and figures of speech

  - Understand vocabulary used in common, everyday situations, such as at school or at home

  - Understand idiomatic expressions that cannot be translated literally from English to German, such as

    - *Treiben Sie auch viel Sport?* which can be interpreted as "Do you do a lot of sports, too?"

    - *Ich wasche mir die Haare,* which is structurally different from English and translates as "I wash my hair."

    - *Mir gefällt dieses Kostüm,* which translates as "I like this suit."

  - Understand figures of speech that cannot be taken literally, such as

    - *Den Vogel abschießen,* which means "To steal the show."

- Recognize what question has been asked or what instruction has been given

  - When listening to a short conversation, determine what basic problem is being discussed or what instructions are being given

- Understand sentences in different time frames

  - Are the speakers using the perfect tense and therefore speaking about an action that has already taken place?

  - Are the speakers using the present tense and discussing an ongoing activity, an event that they are witnessing, or an event that will happen in the near future?

  - Are the speakers using future tenses in the absence of a descriptive time expression to talk about future plans or an event that will be taking place? For example, *Er reist <u>nächstes Jahr</u> durch Europa,* but *Er wird durch Europa reisen.*

- Identify the main idea of an informal conversation. This may require

  - Identifying a problem

- ▶ Understanding a situation
- ▶ Identifying the conclusion to the situation

- ■ Understand conversations on a variety of everyday topics, such as

  - ▶ Ordering food in a restaurant
  - ▶ Asking for advice
  - ▶ Making a phone call
  - ▶ Talking about entertainment and leisure activities
  - ▶ Discussing health

- ■ Make inferences based on key information in an informal conversation, such as

  - ▶ The place where the conversation occurs
  - ▶ Introduction: formal or informal
  - ▶ The given time frame

Short Narrations

For these questions, you will be asked to listen to one native speaker of German speaking at a normal rate of speech. This person may be telling a brief story, speaking about an event, making an announcement, or providing the type of information you would hear on an answering machine, or during a radio or television broadcast. To answer these questions successfully, you will use many of the same skills involved in answering questions about short conversations.

Long Conversations and Long Narrations

For these questions, you will be asked to listen to one native speaker of German speaking at a normal rate of speech for an extended period of time. You will also listen to two native speakers of German conducting an extended conversation. To answer these questions successfully, you will use many of the same skills involved in answering questions about short conversations and short narrations.

Structure of the Language (Grammatical Accuracy)

This section of the test is divided into four different parts: Speech Analysis, Writing Analysis, Language Analysis, and Grammar Analysis.

Speech Analysis

For these questions, you will be asked to analyze errors in material recorded by nonnative speakers of German. To complete this task successfully, you must be able to detect, describe, and correct errors in grammar, word choice, and pronunciation.

- ■ Demonstrate the ability to detect and describe pronunciation errors in spoken German

  - ▶ Common types of errors may include the incorrect pronunciation of letters or combinations of letters, such as

    - ◆ *ei, ch,* or vowels with or without *Umlaut* or reversed

      - — *ei (Reihe* and not *Riehe)*
      - — *ch (mich* and not *misch* or *mik)*
      - — vowels with or without an *Umlaut (Musik* and not *Müsik, Häuser* and not *Hauser)*

- ■ Demonstrate the ability to detect, describe, and correct grammatical errors in spoken German. This may include errors in phonology or syntax, such as

  - ▶ Incorrect use of gender

    - ◆ Use of masculine articles instead of feminine and vice versa
    - ◆ Use of neuter articles instead of feminine or masculine and vice versa
    - ◆ Incorrect use of masculine, feminine, or neuter possessive adjective

  - ▶ Failure to use the correct noun ending

    - ◆ For example, *der Teil der Maschin (Maschine)*

► Incorrect use of singular or plural

► Failure to use compound words

   ◆ For example, *Der Schlüssel für die Tür vom Haus* combined to become *der Haustürschlüssel*

► Incorrect adjective endings or use of adverbs such as

   ◆ Predicate adjectives: *Sie singt laute (laut)*

   ◆ After indefinite articles: *Ein großes Mann (großer)*

   ◆ Adverbs may directly follow the verb of a sentence or be placed at the beginning or end of the sentence, depending on the intended meaning.

      — *Der Ausflug war* gestern.

      — *Der Ausflug* gestern *war herrlich.*

   ◆ Certain adjectives change in meaning depending on where they are placed in a sentence.

      — *Das Auto fuhr schnell* does not express the same idea as *Das schnelle Auto fuhr . . .* In the first sentence *schnell* describes **how** the car is driving and is therefore an adverb. In the second sentence *schnell* describes the car and is therefore an adjective.

► Incorrect use of adjective endings

   ◆ After *viele, wenige, andere, einige,* and *mehrere; solcher* and *mancher*

      — *Viele alte Freunde* is correct, as opposed to *Viele alten Freunde*

      — *Manche alten Freunde* is correct, as opposed to *Manche alte Freunde*

   ◆ After comparatives or superlatives

      — Basic use of suffixes as in: *billig – billiger – am billigsten*

      — Failure to use *Umlaut* in one-syllable adjectives with the stem vowel *a* and *u: alt – älter – am ältesten; klug – klüger – am klügsten*

► Incorrect use of adverb formulas using positive and comparative forms, such as

   ◆ *Ich gehe öfter wie du ins Theater,* which should be *Ich gehe öfter als du ins Theater* or *Ich gehe so oft wie du ins Theater.*

   ◆ *Karla singt so gut als Else,* which should be *Karla singt so gut wie Else.*

► Incorrect word order of adverbial expressions

   ◆ *Ich fahre morgen nach Ulm* is correct, as opposed to *Ich fahre nach Ulm morgen.*

   ◆ *Wir sind bald da* is correct, as opposed to *Wir bald da sind*

► Incorrect use of negative expressions

   ◆ Expressions using *kein,* as opposed to *nicht*

      — *Er hat kein Geld,* as opposed to the incorrect sentence *Er hat Geld nicht* or *Er nicht Geld hat.*

► Incorrect use of prepositions

   ◆ Certain verbs can be used with different prepositions, depending on the context or meaning.

      • *Ich freue mich auf etwas,* which means "I'm looking forward to something," is different from *Ich freue mich über etwas,* which means "I am happy about something" or "I like something."

   ◆ Cases after two-way prepositions

      — These prepositions require a dative object when the prepositional phrase indicates location, as in *Das Buch liegt auf dem Tisch.*

      — The same preposition, however, requires an accusative object when the phrase describes a motion toward a destination or in a specific direction, as in *Ich lege das Buch auf den Tisch.*

♦ With years, seasons, and definite or indefinite time

— *Er ist 1930 geboren. (The English structure would use "in 1930.")*

— *Wir fahren im Februar nach Hamburg* signifies a specific month.

— *Wir fahren auf einen Monat nach Hamburg* refers to the length of time that something takes, and the accusative case must be used, but *Ich wohne seit einem Monat hier.*

▶ Incorrect use of conjunctions

♦ Confusion between coordinating and subordinating conjunctions and the effect they have on the word order of the clauses they introduce. For example

— *Ich komme nicht, denn ich habe viel zu tun* is correct since *denn* is a coordinating conjunction.

— *Ich komme nicht, weil ich viel zu tun habe* is correct, as opposed to the incorrect sentence *Ich komme nicht, weil ich habe viel zu tun.* (The subordinating conjunction is affecting the word order.)

▶ Incorrect word order in basic sentence structures

♦ Incorrect order of noun and pronoun objects

— *Wir schicken der Frau die Blumen* is correct. Since the direct object *(die Blumen)* is a noun, it must follow the indirect object.

— *Wir schicken sie der Frau* is correct. Since the direct object is now a personal pronoun and must precede the indirect object, it would be incorrect to say, *Wir schicken der Frau sie.*

♦ Words like *nichts, alles,* and *etwas* are called indefinite pronouns and behave like nouns. This means that *Wir schicken der Frau etwas* is

correct, as opposed to *Wir schicken etwas der Frau.*

▶ Incorrect subject-verb agreement in basic sentence structures

♦ Verb does not refer to the subject of the sentence

— *Jeden Morgen steht er (er:* third person singular) *um 7 Uhr auf* is correct, as opposed to *Jeden Morgen stehen er um 7 Uhr auf.* (*Stehen* is the correct form for either first or third person plural.)

— *Schenkt ihr mir einen Hasen?* is correct, as opposed to *Schenken ihr mir einen Hasen?* The verb refers to the second person plural pronoun *ihr* and must therefore have a second person plural ending.

▶ Incorrect use of verbs

♦ Inappropriate auxiliaries with past tenses

— *Ich bin nach Hause gegangen* would be correct, and *haben* would not be used in this case, since *gehen* is an intransitive verb of motion.

— *Er hat Tee getrunken* would be correct since *trinken* uses *haben* as an auxiliary. *Trinken* is transitive.

— *Sie haben den Wagen geschoben* would be correct since *schieben* is not an intransitive verb in this case, even though it involves motion.

♦ Incorrect use of past participles

— Verbs such as *essen, finden, gewinnen, tun* are only a few of the many verbs in German that have irregular past participles.

♦ Incorrect conjugation of irregular verbs in the present and past tenses

— Some common examples are *haben, sein, werden, müssen,* and *sollen.*

- ◆ Incorrect conjugation of verbs with separable and inseparable prefixes
    - — *ab- (ablaufen) auf- (aufhören) mit- (mitmachen) zu- (zugeben)* are only a few examples of verbs with separable prefixes.
    - — Some common examples of verbs with inseparable prefixes are *besuchen, gebrauchen, zerstören, verkaufen.*
- ◆ Incorrect use and conjugation of the "look-alike" verbs that are also related in meaning, such as: *setzen – sitzen, legen – liegen, hängen (transitive) – hängen (intransitive)*
    - — *Sie hängte ihren Mantel auf* as compared to *Der Mantel hing im Schrank.*
- ◆ Failure to use verbs such as *machen, setzen, erinnern* reflexively to complete the meaning of the sentence
    - — In English, one would say "He gets ready"; in German, however, the omission of the reflexive pronoun is not permissible; therefore the sentence must be *Er macht sich fertig.*
- ◆ Incorrect use of verbs that are only used reflexively, such as *sich beeilen, sich erkälten, sich freuen auf/über, sich irren*

- ■ Demonstrate the ability to detect, describe, and correct errors in word choice. This may include errors involving
    - ▶ False cognates
        - ◆ Certain English and German words sound alike but have different meanings.
            - — *Klosett* in German, for example, means "toilet" or "washroom" even though it sounds like the English word "closet," signifying a built-in cupboard or locker.

- ▶ The use of colloquial language in formal situations
    - ◆ Certain expressions in German are very informal and are not acceptable in formal situations, and if used, are considered impolite or rude.
        - — For example, in a department store, one would not say to a salesperson, *Zeigen Sie mir mal Ihre Fähnchen; leichte Sommerkleider* would be the appropriate phrase to use.
        - — Similarly, *meine Karre* is a common expression for an old car in very informal, colloquial situations, but *mein Wagen/Auto* would be the word/s to use when talking with a car dealer.
- ▶ The use of unacceptable anglicisms
    - ◆ Recognize structures that are very different from English
        - — *Wann ist das Konzert zu Ende?* is correct, whereas there may be a tendency to use the conjunction *wenn.*
        - — *Er ist vor einer Woche angekommen* is correct, whereas a sentence such as *Er ist angekommen eine Woche vorher*—a direct translation from English structure—is incorrect.
    - ◆ Occasionally, prepositions used in English are not the same as those used in German.
        - — *Ich warte auf dich* is correct, while *Ich warte für dich* is taken directly from English and is not correct.
        - — In most instances, *nach* is the appropriate preposition to use with reference to cities and countries, as opposed to *zu.*

- ■ Demonstrate the ability to detect, describe, and correct language that is inappropriate to the task and/or the audience addressed
    - ▶ Errors in register

Herr Meier, hast du schon bezahlt? is incorrect; the formal address *Sie* should have been used: *Herr Meier, haben Sie schon bezahlt?*

Writing Analysis

For these questions, you will be asked to analyze errors in writing samples from nonnative speakers of German. Answering these questions requires you to use the same skills you used in answering Speech Analysis questions. In this section, you will have to

■ Demonstrate the ability to detect, describe, and correct basic grammatical errors in written German

▶ Correct use and spelling of adjective endings

♦ Spelling of adjectives that follow definite articles

— *Frisches Brot* becomes *Das frische Brot*

— *Kleiner Vogel* becomes *Dieser kleine Vogel*

♦ Spelling of adjectives that follow indefinite articles

— *alter Freund* becomes *ein alter Freund*

— *gute Dinge* becomes *alle guten Dinge*

▶ Correct combination of preposition and case

♦ Appropriate selection

— *Er warf den Ball über den Zaun* is correct. Other forms, like *über dem,* would be an incorrect combination in this context.

♦ Appropriate usage and spelling of contractions

— *am (an dem), ins (in das)* are correct; *ihr (in ihr)* would be a nonexistent form

— *auf dem* or *hinter das* cannot be contracted

▶ Correct use of conjunction in negation or contrast

♦ *Er ist nicht zu Hause, aber er kommt bald.*

♦ *Ich komme nicht zu dir, sondern du kommst zu uns.*

▶ Correct spelling of diphtongs, as in *rein – Kaiser; neu – Räuber*

▶ Correct word order in main as well as subordinate clauses

— *Er fährt oft mit dem Auto* is correct, as opposed to *Er fährt mit dem Auto oft.*

— *. . . da ich den Film schon gesehen habe* is correct, as opposed to *. . . da ich habe schon gesehen den Film,* which is translated exactly from English

▶ Correct spelling of words with long or short vowels

— *ein bisschen* (short *i* followed by *ss*)

— *eine Prise* (long *i* followed by one *s*)

— *schrieb* (long *i* irregular form of *schreiben*)

— *hoffen* (short *o* followed by *ff*)

— *Hof* (long *o* followed by one *f*)

▶ Appropriate forms and spelling for all verb tenses

♦ Present tense

— Regular verbs (for example, *drehen – drehte – gedreht*)

— Irregular verbs (for example, *sitzen – saß – gesessen*)

♦ Past tenses

— Regular verbs using the ending *-te (spielte)*

— Irregular verbs changing stem vowel *(ging)*

— Verbs of motion or intransitive verbs using *sein* as an auxiliary in perfect and past perfect tense *(bin/war gelaufen)*

— Transitive verbs using *haben* as an auxiliary in perfect and past perfect tense *(habe/hatte gesucht)*

- Word order in perfect or past perfect tense
  - *Er war zu spät zur Feier gekommen.* (The past particle is the last element in a simple sentence.)
- Future tense
  - *werden* followed by infinitives (for example, *Wir werden die Vorlesung besuchen.*)
- Conditional
  - Regular verbs (for example, *Er sagte, er fotografiere gerne.*)
  - Irregular verbs (for example, *Ließe der Regen nach, gingen wir hinaus.*)
- Imperatives
  - All verbs drop the *-en* of the infinitive form in the first person singular and add *-t* in the second person plural form (*geh! – geht!* but *Gehen Sie!*)
- Infinitives and infinitive structures
  - Infinitives with *um – zu, ohne – zu* or *sein + zu +* infinitive (for example, *Das ist nicht zu machen.*)
- Passive voice
  - Agreement with the subject (for example, *Alle Manuskripte wurden gerettet.*)

■ Demonstrate the ability to detect, describe, and correct language that is inappropriate to the task and/or audience addressed. For example, this could call for the recognition of

▶ The misuse of *du* in a formal situation (for example, *Herr Professor, hast du meinen Aufsatz schon gelesen?*)

▶ The misuse of vocabulary, conveying a meaning that is not intended (for example, *Gehen wir heute zum Gewichtheben ins Gymnasium? Gymnasium* is a high school; a gym is a *Turnhalle.*)

■ Demonstrate the ability to detect, describe, and correct errors in capitalization

▶ Correct spelling of all geographical names and compound nouns
  - *Naher Osten, Schweizer Industrie,*
  - *Hochstraße* (compound noun of an undeclined adjective + a noun)
  - *Breite Gasse* (adjective is declined)

▶ Correct spelling of all nouns and proper names
  - *Erde, Wasser, Reichtum*
  - *Anna, Mozart, Berlin, Österreich*

▶ Correct spelling of times of days preceded by adverbs such as *gestern, heute, übermorgen*
  - *gestern Vormittag* or *heute Morgen,* in contrast to *heute früh*

▶ Correct spelling of adjectives, participles, prepositions, and infinitives, when used like nouns; for example, *das Gute, alles Gewollte, das Auf und Nieder, lautes Schreien.*

▶ Correct spelling of all forms of *du* and *Sie*
  - *Ich hoffe, dass es dir/euch gut geht* and *Haben Sie das für Ihre Eltern gemacht?*

▶ Spelling of adjectives that come from a proper name
  - *die platonischen Schriften,* in contrast to *Platos Schriften*

▶ Correct capitalization of all words that start a sentence or are the beginning of a title; for example, *Es ist in Ordnung; Hessisches Hochschulgesetz*

Language Analysis

This section will require you to provide explanations for grammatical and word-use errors. Questions in this section may ask you to

■ Demonstrate knowledge of the structural components of the German language. This may include the identification of the correct use of structures such as

- ▶ Direct and indirect objects
- ▶ Placement of adjectives or adverbs
- ▶ The appropriate use of tenses in *wenn* and *wann* clauses
- ▶ The use of *haben* or *sein* as auxiliaries for perfect and past perfect tenses
- ▶ The singular and plural forms of nouns
- ▶ Idiomatic expressions
- ▶ Cognates
- ▶ Comparative and superlative adjectives
- ▶ Irregular verbs
- ▶ Verb conjugations and tenses

- ■ Demonstrate knowledge of the basic meaningful elements of words. This may include
  - ▶ Verb endings and conjugations of various tenses
    - ♦ Verbs with stem vowel changes
    - ♦ Stems used for conditional and imperfect
  - ▶ Prefixes and suffixes

- ■ Demonstrate knowledge of word order to form phrases, clauses, or sentences. This may include the
  - ▶ Order of subjects and verbs in statements as compared to questions
    - ♦ Using inversion to create questions
    - ♦ Using regular word order and a question mark to indicate a spoken question
  - ▶ Position of verbs
    - ♦ Main clauses
    - ♦ Subordinate clauses
  - ▶ Position of direct and indirect objects
    - ♦ The indirect object is followed by the direct object if both objects are nouns.
      - — *Ich gebe dem Kind* (indirect object) *ein Buch* (direct object).
    - ♦ If the direct object is a personal pronoun, it precedes the indirect object.
      - — *Ich gebe es dem Kind.*

- ♦ If the direct object is an indefinite pronoun, it follows the indirect object.
  - — *Ich gebe dem Kind etwas.*
- ▶ The position of adverbs
  - ♦ Adverbs describing verbs are preceded by the verb.
    - — *Ich spiele gern Tennis.*
    - — *Das Team spielt immer besser.*

- ■ Demonstrate an understanding of the formation of contractions and compound words. This may include
  - ▶ Prepositions and articles
    - — *in* and *dem* become *im.*
    - — *zu* and *der* become *zur,* but *in* and *ihr* cannot be contracted.
  - ▶ Compound words consisting of a base word and one or more modifiers
    - — *Mittagessen* but *Mittagsschlaf*
    - — *reumütig*
    - — *Zollgrenzbezirk*

Grammar Analysis

For these questions, you will read sentences or paragraphs from which words or phrases have been omitted. You will be asked to choose the answer that correctly completes the sentence or paragraph. This part of the test requires knowledge of the following:

- ■ The correct formation and uses of regular and irregular verbs in all moods and tenses. This will include understanding of
  - ▶ Regular verbs in the various tenses
  - ▶ Irregular verbs in the various tenses
  - ▶ Verbs in infinitival clauses
  - ▶ Modal auxiliaries
  - ▶ Stems of verbs for the past and conditional tenses
  - ▶ Applications of tenses in main and subordinate clauses
  - ▶ The use of the subjunctive or the indicative

- The correct formation and uses of nouns, adjectives, adverbs, and articles. This will include understanding of

  ▶ Noun and adjective agreement

  ▶ The derivation of adverbs (refer to "Speech Analysis" above for details)

  ▶ Articles

    ◆ Definite articles

    ◆ Indefinite articles

    ◆ Negatives

    ◆ Gender, case, and number

- The correct formation and use of pronouns. This will include understanding of

  ▶ Direct and indirect object pronouns

  ▶ Placement and use of direct and indirect object pronouns

    ◆ In a statement

    ◆ With imperatives

    ◆ With double object pronouns

- The correct uses of conjunctions and prepositions. This will include understanding of

  ▶ The appropriate use of coordinating and subordinating conjunctions

  ▶ The appropriate use of prepositions

    ◆ Two-way prepositions

    ◆ Time expressions

- The correct formation of sentences based on

  ▶ Rules of subject-verb agreement

  ▶ Rules of the structure of main and subordinate clauses

- The correct formation and use of comparatives and superlatives

  ▶ Adjectives with mandatory *Umlaut* or with no *Umlaut*

  ▶ Irregular adjectives

    ◆ *viel – mehr – am meisten*

- The correct use of flavoring/emphasis words

  ▶ *Nun mach doch schon!* is correct, in contrast to *Nun mach ganz schon!* (wrong choice of emphasis word).

Interpretive Reading

This section is designed to measure how well you understand written German. "Interpretive Reading" refers to the ability to understand, analyze, and evaluate written material. This section of the test covers Content and Organization, Implied Content, and Use of Language. The main topics to consider are presented below, followed by a sample reading.

Content and Organization

For these questions, you will have to read a text and understand the information being presented and the ideas expressed. You will need to do the following:

- Demonstrate understanding of a variety of reading materials

  ▶ Literature

  ▶ Newspapers

  ▶ Periodicals

  ▶ Printed announcements or advertisements

  ▶ Internet articles

- Determine the main idea or purpose from the following types of sources

  ▶ Literary excerpts

  ▶ Internet, newspaper, or magazine articles, reports

  ▶ Announcements and advertisements

- Identify other important ideas from

  ▶ Content and key words

  ▶ Tone of the text

  ▶ Type of language used

    ◆ Past tenses

    ◆ Present tense

    ◆ Future tense

    ◆ Imperative

    ◆ Passive voice

    ◆ Conditional

- Identify supporting details from the content and key words

- Identify paraphrases or summaries of ideas from

  ▶ Content and key words

  ▶ Conclusion of the text

  ▶ Titles

- Identify relationships among ideas directly stated

  ▶ Cause and effect

  ▶ Sequence of ideas

  ▶ Conclusion

- Locate the place in a passage where specific information can be found from key words

Implied Content

For these questions, you will have to determine what is suggested in a text. You will need to do the following:

- Understand the implied content of a variety of reading materials

- Make inferences from directly stated content

- Recognize the attitudes or viewpoints expressed

  ▶ Consider the type of language used

  ▶ Consider the tone

- Distinguish fact from opinion

Use of Language

For these questions, you will be required to demonstrate your understanding and interpretation of the text based on the vocabulary used. You will need to do the following:

- Recognize or infer the meaning of a word or phrase from the context in which it appears

- Understand the function of key transition indicators

  ▶ Specific words, such as *dennoch, sondern, deshalb, indes, weiter*

- Identify the referent of a pronoun

- Determine the meaning of figurative language

The following exercise and annotated sample are intended to give you practice in the kind of interpretive thinking that is expected in this section of the test. Although the format of the annotation exercise is not like that of the multiple-choice questions on the test, the types and levels of understanding and evaluation needed to complete it are comparable. Read the passage and try to annotate key words, phrases, and sentences in the passage. Then, read the annotated version on the following page and compare it with your analysis.

In China wurde seit dem 8. Jahrhundert Porzellan hergestellt. In Europa wurde das weiße chinesische Porzellan durch Reisen Marco Polos bekannt. Doch seine Herstellung blieb ein Geheimnis. Im 17. Jahrhundert lebte in Deutschland ein junger Apotheker-Lehrling namens Johann Friedrich Böttger (1682-1719). Der Mode der Zeit entsprechend experimentierte er mit Alchemie und hatte den Traum, Gold zu erzeugen. Der preußische König versuchte, den kostbaren jungen Apotheker einfangen und an den Hof nach Brandenburg bringen zu lassen. Er sollte hier Gold herstellen! Böttger aber floh nach Sachsen in der Hoffnung, an der Universität Wittenberg untertauchen zu können. Doch auch dort hatte er wenig Glück. Der sächsische Kurfürst, ebenfalls permanent in Geldnöten, erfuhr, wer in seinem Land angekommen war. Er ließ den jungen Apotheker verhaften. Böttger wurde nach Dresden in Sachsen gebracht und musste dort 12 Jahre lang in Gefangenschaft chemische Experimente durchführen. Endlich, im Jahre 1708, gelang ihm ein Durchbruch. Freilich, dies war immer noch nicht das heiß-ersehnte Geheimnis, wie man Gold künstlich machen konnte, doch waren Böttger und seine Helfer auf etwas anderes gestoßen: Sie hatten das Geheimnis zur Porzellanherstellung entdeckt. Mochte August der Starke, der sächsische Kurfürst und König, zunächst enttäuscht gewesen sein, so fand er sich rasch mit der neuen Lage ab, und es erwies sich, dass die Porzellanherstellung beinahe genauso viel wert war wie echtes Gold. 1710 wurde in Meissen in Sachsen die erste europäische Porzellanfabrik gegründet. Die Firma lieferte ihre kostbaren Waren an deutsche und europäische Fürstenhäuser, sodass die Einnahmen bald die leeren Kassen Sachsens füllten. Porzellan aus Meissen ist heute ein Begriff in der ganzen Welt. Der Erfinder des Porzellans, Johann Friedrich Böttger, indes musste sich weiter gedulden. Erst im Jahre 1714 erhielt er seine Freiheit wieder.

Now, compare your annotations with the ones below.

The paragraph opens with a mention of the main topic, *Porzellanherstellung*. The use of the past tense sets the stage and tells us that the story took place many years ago.

This sentence implies that making porcelain was not easy, and that no one in Germany knew how to produce it. *Geheimnis* is the key word.

The reader must be certain who *Er* is. The personal pronoun refers back to the *sächsische Kurfürst*. This correct identification foreshadows the rest of the story.

The author changes into the conditional, indicating that *August der Starke* was not sure in the beginning how porcelain could get his country out of its financial dilemma.

Switching back into the indicative past tense, the author tells us that the king now realizes what *Friedrich Böttger* had developed. Key phrases: *es erwies sich* and *genauso viel wert war wie echtes Gold.*

The introduction of the *Apotheker-Lehrling J.F. Böttger* and his dream "to produce gold" transports the reader into part of Germany's history in the seventeenth and eighteenth centuries (e.g., the financial problems of Brandenburg and Saxony). *Geldnöte* is the key word.

Durchbruch is crucial. It tells the reader that *Friedrich Böttger* found something very important and precious.

The author brings us into the present by using the present tense and proclaiming that *Porzellan aus Meissen* is world renowned.

The author then transitions back into the past using just two key transition indicators: *indes* and *weiter*. The personal pronoun *er* in the last sentence refers back to *Friedrich Böttger*, the founder of porcelain production in the 'Western' world, and not the king.

In China wurde seit dem 8. Jahrhundert Porzellan hergestellt. In Europa wurde das weiße chinesische Porzellan durch Reisen Marco Polos bekannt. Doch seine Herstellung blieb ein Geheimnis. Im 17. Jahrhundert lebte in Deutschland ein junger Apotheker-Lehrling namens Johann Friedrich Böttger (1682-1719). Der Mode der Zeit entsprechend experimentierte er mit Alchemie und hatte den Traum, Gold zu erzeugen. Der preußische König versuchte, den kostbaren jungen Apotheker einfangen und an den Hof nach Brandenburg bringen zu lassen. Er sollte hier Gold herstellen! Böttger aber floh nach Sachsen in der Hoffnung, an der Universität Wittenberg untertauchen zu können. Doch auch dort hatte er wenig Glück. Der sächsische Kurfürst, ebenfalls permanent in Geldnöten, erfuhr, wer in seinem Land angekommen war. Er ließ den jungen Apotheker verhaften. Böttger wurde nach Dresden in Sachsen gebracht und musste dort 12 Jahre lang in Gefangenschaft chemische Experimente durchführen. Endlich, im Jahre 1708, gelang ihm ein Durchbruch. Freilich, dies war immer noch nicht das heißersehnte Geheimnis, wie man Gold künstlich machen konnte, doch waren Böttger und seine Helfer auf etwas anderes gestoßen: Sie hatten das Geheimnis zur Porzellanherstellung entdeckt. Mochte August der Starke, der sächsische Kurfürst und König, zunächst enttäuscht gewesen sein, so fand er sich rasch mit der neuen Lage ab, und es erwies sich, dass die Porzellanherstellung beinahe genauso viel wert war wie echtes Gold. 1710 wurde in Meissen in Sachsen die erste europäische Porzellanfabrik gegründet. Die Firma lieferte ihre kostbaren Waren an deutsche und europäische Fürstenhäuser, sodass die Einnahmen bald die leeren Kassen Sachsens füllten. Porzellan aus Meissen ist heute ein Begriff in der ganzen Welt. Der Erfinder des Porzellans, Johann Friedrich Böttger, indes musste sich weiter gedulden. Erst im Jahre 1714 erhielt er seine Freiheit wieder.

Cultural Perspectives

The Cultural Perspectives section of the test comprises five major topics: geography, lifestyles and societies, sociolinguistic elements of German, history, and literature and the arts. This section is designed to measure your knowledge of the cultures of Germany and German-speaking countries and regions. Below are representative examples of topics that may be covered on the test; this section does not present an exhaustive list of the topics that may appear on the test.

Geography

In this section of the test, your knowledge of geographical facts will be tested. Some of the questions might pertain to

- Identifying and locating Germany, Austria, Switzerland, and Liechtenstein

- Identifying major geographical features of the countries mentioned above
  - Rivers and lakes
  - Mountain ranges
  - Regions
  - Major cities and harbors

- Recognizing major agricultural and industrial regions of the German-speaking world

Lifestyles and Societies

For these questions, your knowledge of the way of life and customs in Germany and in other German-speaking countries and regions will be tested.

- Contemporary lifestyles
  - Food
    - Traditional dishes and specialties
    - Regional specialties
  - Mealtimes
    - Times and names of meals
  - Customs

- Meeting people
- Visiting people
- Greeting people
- Behavior in public places

- Holidays
  - Religious holidays such as
    - *Karfreitag und Ostern*
    - *Pfingsten*
    - *Fronleichnam*
    - *Buß- und Bettag*
    - *Weihnachten*
  - Public holidays
    - *Tag der Arbeit (1. Mai)*
    - *Tag der Deutschen Einheit (3. Oktober)*
    - *Schweizerischer Nationaltag (1. August)*

- Family relationships
  - Families and their homes
  - Relationships with people outside the family
  - Vacations/holidays

- Education
  - School systems
  - Higher education

- Regional variations
  - Specialties

- Foreign influences
  - Relations with other European countries
  - Immigration questions in Germany, Switzerland, and Austria
  - Monetary units (Euro and Swiss Frank)

Sociolinguistic Elements of German

For these questions, your knowledge and understanding of the appropriateness and usage of German will be tested. This includes the following:

- Social interaction patterns

▶ Customary usage of certain expressions in specific situations, particularly in public places

■ Language appropriate to a given task or audience

  ▶ Formal situations

    ◆ Use of *Sie* as opposed to *du*

  ▶ Informal situations

  ▶ Familiar expressions and forms

  ▶ Colloquial language

■ Body language

  ▶ Common gestures and their meanings

■ Identification of cultural aspects that differ from corresponding aspects of United States cultures

History

For these questions, your knowledge of a broad array of historic developments in the four countries (Germany, Austria, Switzerland, and Liechtenstein) will be tested. This may include the following:

■ Origin of present-day political systems in Germany, Austria, Switzerland, and Liechtenstein

■ History of the twentieth century

■ Political organizations of named countries

■ Historic personalities, such as

  ▶ Otto von Bismarck, Kurt Waldheim, Kaiserin Sissi

■ Events with strong historic impact such as

  ▶ *Das Kaiserreich*

  ▶ *Verfassung der Pauls Kirche in Frankfurt*

  ▶ *Weimarer Republik*

  ▶ The First World War

  ▶ The Second World War

  ▶ The first Chancellor (Konrad Adenauer)

▶ Crucial aspects of the history of the German mind

▶ Main lines of intellectual history

▶ Characteristics of different time periods

▶ National icons

▶ Symbols and national identity

▶ Famous buildings and cultural artifacts

■ Contemporary world politics and economics as they affect German-speaking countries and regions

  ▶ Role of the political systems, structures, institutions, parties

    ◆ Elections and voting

    ◆ Court systems

  ▶ Relations with European countries

  ▶ Organization of the government in Germany

  ▶ Recurring topics of public interest

  ▶ German economy, business, and industry

    ◆ Fashion

      — *Trachten*

    ◆ Food

    ◆ Beer and wine

    ◆ Tourism

Literature and the Arts

For these questions, your knowledge of major German authors and their works, as well as events related to the arts, will be tested.

■ Major works and authors of the literature of Germany and other German-speaking countries. For example:

  ▶ Sixteenth- to eighteenth-century German literature

    ◆ Martin Luther

    ◆ Gotthold Ephraim Lessing

    ◆ Heinrich von Kleist

    ◆ Johann Gottfried Herder

    ◆ Johann Wolfgang Goethe

    ◆ Friedrich Schiller

    ◆ Friedrich Hölderlin

- ▶ Nineteenth- to twentieth-century German literature
  - ◆ E.T.A. Hoffmann
  - ◆ Gebrüder Grimm
  - ◆ Günter Grass
  - ◆ Ingeborg Bachmann
  - ◆ Arthur Schnitzler
  - ◆ Max Frisch
  - ◆ Berthold Brecht
  - ◆ Franz Kafka
  - ◆ Thomas Mann
  - ◆ Sarah Kirsch
  - ◆ Ilse Aichinger
  - ◆ Martin Walser
  - ◆ Marie Luise Kaschnitz
  - ◆ Helga Novak
- ■ Significant figures, works, and events in the arts
  - ▶ Traditional theater and opera such as
    - ◆ *Faust* (Johann Wolfgang Goethe)
    - ◆ *Wilhelm Tell* (Friedrich Schiller)
    - ◆ *Der Ring der Nibelungen* (Richard Wagner)
  - ▶ Music
    - ◆ Major composers and conductors, such as
      - • Johann Sebastian Bach
      - • Wolfgang Amadeus Mozart
      - • Ludwig van Beethoven
      - • Johann Strauss
      - • Richard Strauß
      - • Paul Hindemith
      - • Herbert von Karajan
      - • Gustav Mahler

- ■ Art and Architecture
  - ▶ Käthe Kollwitz
  - ▶ Franz Marc
  - ▶ Das Bauhaus
    - ◆ Walter Gropius, Paul Klee, Lyonel Feininger
  - ▶ Adolf Loos
  - ▶ Oskar Kokoschka
- ■ Film
  - ▶ Bernhard Wicki: *Die Brücke*
  - ▶ Rainer Werner-Fassbinder: *Die Ehe der Maria Braun*
  - ▶ Josef von Sternberg: *Der blaue Engel*
- ■ Dance
  - ▶ Regional traditions
  - ▶ The waltz
  - ▶ Reihentanz

Once again, test takers are reminded that this is not an all-inclusive list; nor will these specific examples appear on every test. These are simply areas, topics, events, and figures that represent the major categories that are covered: geography, lifestyles and societies, sociolinguistic elements, history, and literature and the arts.

Chapter 12
Succeeding on Multiple-Choice Questions—*German:*
Content Knowledge

►   ►   ►   ►   ►   ►   ►   ►   ►   ►   ►   ►

Understanding Multiple-Choice Questions

When you read multiple-choice questions on the Praxis *German: Content Knowledge* test, you will probably notice that the syntax (word order) is different from the word order you're used to seeing in ordinary material that you read, such as newspapers or textbooks. One of the reasons for this difference is that many test questions contain the phrase "which of the following."

In order to answer a multiple-choice question successfully, you need to consider carefully the context set up by the question and limit your choice of answers to the list given. The purpose of the phrase "which of the following" is to remind you to do this. For example, look at this question.

Which of the following is a flavor made from beans?

(A)   Strawberry
(B)   Cherry
(C)   Vanilla
(D)   Mint

You may know that chocolate and coffee are also flavors made from beans, but they are not listed, and the question asks you to select from the list that follows ("which of the following"). So the answer has to be the only bean-derived flavor in the list: vanilla.

Notice that the answer can be substituted for the phrase "which of the following." In the question above, you could insert "vanilla" for "which of the following" and have the sentence "Vanilla is a flavor made from beans." Sometimes it helps to cross out "which of the following" and insert the various choices. You may want to give this technique a try as you answer various multiple-choice practice questions.

Looking carefully at the "which of the following" phrase helps you to focus on what the question is asking you to find and on the answer choices. In the simple example above, all of the answer choices are flavors. Your job is to decide which of the flavors is the one made from beans.

The vanilla bean question is pretty straightforward. But the phrase "which of the following" can also be found in more challenging questions. Look at this question:

Which of the following verbs has a past participle that begins with the prefix *"ge-"*?

(A)   *antworten*
(B)   *verstehen*
(C)   *teilnehmen*
(D)   *begleiten*

The placement of "which of the following" tells you that the list of choices consists of several verbs. What are you supposed to find as an answer? You are supposed to remember the past participles of these verbs and identify the one that begins with the prefix *"ge-."*

Educational Testing Service (ETS) question writers and editors work very hard to word each question as clearly as possible. Sometimes, though, it helps to put the question in your own words. Here, you could paraphrase the question as "Which verb, in its past participle form, starts with *'ge-'?*" The correct answer is (A). (The past participle of *"antworten"* is *"geantwortet."*)

You may also find that it helps you to circle or underline each of the critical details of the question in your test book so that you don't miss any of them. It's only by looking at all parts of the question carefully that you will have all of the information you need to answer it. Circle or underline the critical parts of what is being asked in this question.

Unter welcher Bezeichnung ist der deutsche Staat von 1918 bis 1933 in die Geschichte eingegangen?

(A) Die Münchner Räterepublik
(B) Das Wilhelminische Deutschland
(C) Das Alte Reich
(D) Die Weimarer Republik

Here is one possible way you may have annotated the question:

Unter welcher Bezeichnung ist der deutsche Staat von 1918 bis 1933 in die Geschichte eingegangen?

(A) Die Münchner Räterepublik
(B) Das Wilhelminische Deutschland
(C) Das Alte Reich
(D) Die Weimarer Republik

After thinking about the question, you can probably see that you are being asked to look at four titles and to choose the one that is used for the German government between 1918 and 1933. The correct answer is (D). The important thing is understanding what the question is asking. With enough practice, you should be able to determine what any question is asking. Knowing the answer is, of course, a different matter, but you have to understand a question before you can answer it correctly.

Understanding Questions Containing "NOT," "LEAST," or "EXCEPT"

The words "NOT," "LEAST," and "EXCEPT" can make comprehension of test questions more difficult. They ask you to select the choice that *doesn't* fit. You must be very careful with this question type because it's easy to forget that you're selecting the negative. This question type is used in situations in which there are several good solutions, or ways to approach something, but also a clearly wrong way. These words are always capitalized when they appear in The Praxis Series test questions, but they are easily (and frequently) overlooked.

For the following test question, determine what kind of answer you need and what the details of the question are.

Welche der folgenden Städte ist KEIN Seehafen?

(A) Hamburg
(B) Köln
(C) Bremerhaven
(D) Kiel

You're looking for a German city that does NOT have a seaport. (B) is the correct answer. Köln, known in English as Cologne, is landlocked.

> **TIP**
>
> It's easy to get confused while you're processing the information to answer a question that contains a "NOT," "LEAST," or "EXCEPT." If you treat the word "NOT," "LEAST," or "EXCEPT" as one of the details you must satisfy, you have a better chance of understanding what the question is asking.

Be Familiar with Question Types Based on Recorded Excerpts

The first two sections of the *German: Content Knowledge* test will require you to listen to spoken German that is recorded. The recording will be played **only once.** Although some of the recorded material will be printed in the test book, some will not, so it is important that you listen carefully to the spoken material. The questions based on the recorded material will be in several formats.

1. Interpretive Listening—Short Conversations

In this type of question, you listen to a recording of native German speakers conversing at a normal conversational rate of speed. You then are asked one or more questions based on what you have heard. Neither the dialogue nor the questions are printed in your test book. In the following example, first you hear the following dialogue:

(Woman)   *Guten Tag. Ich möchte bitte eine Karte für die Vorstellung heute Abend.*

(Man)   *Möchten Sie eine Karte zu 20, 30 oder 40 Euros?*

(Narrator)   *Wo findet dieses Gespräch statt?*

Then, in your test book you see the following choices:

(A)   Auf der Post.
(B)   Am Flughafen.
(C)   An der Theaterkasse.
(D)   In einem Restaurant.

To answer, you must select the choice that best answers the narrator's question: where is this conversation taking place? The correct answer is (C), because the speakers are discussing the price of a ticket for an evening performance.

2. Interpretive Listening—Short Narrations

This question type is similar to the one discussed in the previous section, except that instead of a conversation you hear a short narration. The narration is not printed in your test book. After each narration, you will hear one or more questions, which are printed in your test book. You may find it useful to take notes in your test book as you listen to the narration.

Here is an example, spoken by one narrator:

(Narrator) *Die Frage bezieht sich auf die folgende Durchsage.*

Auf der Autobahn A7 in der Nähe von Hildesheim wegen Straßenbauarbeiten dichter Verkehr in beiden Richtungen. Es muss mit Stau bis zu 20 Kilometern gerechnet werden.

Then, in your test book you see the following question:

Für wen ist diese Durchsage gemeint?

(A)   Für Bahnbeamte.
(B)   Für Autofahrer.
(C)   Für Radfahrer.
(D)   Für Fußgänger.

The correct answer is (B). The speaker is talking about heavy traffic on the highway due to construction.

3. Interpretive Listening—Long Conversations and Narrations

These formats are the same as those discussed in the previous two sections, except that the narrative passages and conversations are longer. After each narration or conversation, you will hear several questions, which are printed in your test book.

4. Questions about Structure of the Language Based on Recorded Excerpts

Section II of the *German: Content Knowledge* test is called Structure of the Language (Grammatical Accuracy) and includes both listening and reading selections.

In the first part of section II, you hear recorded selections spoken by students who are learning German and who make errors in their speech. Their words are not printed in your test book. The following example begins with the voice of the narrator:

(Narrator)   Question 4 refers to the following selection in which a student explains why she was late for class.

(Female   *Erstens bin ich heute Morgen zu spät aufgeweckt, weil mein Wecker nicht geklingelt*
Student)   *hat. Danach habe ich mich kalt duschen müssen, da es kein heißes Wasser gab.*

(Narrator)   Question Number 4: Identify the grammatical error in the excerpt.

You hear again:

(Female   *Erstens bin ich heute Morgen zu spät aufgeweckt, weil mein Wecker nicht*
Student)   *geklingelt hat.*

In your test book you read the following:

Question 4 refers to the following selection about a student's school and vacation.

4. Identify the grammatical error in the excerpt.

(A) *Erstens*
(B) *Morgen*
(C) *aufgeweckt*
(D) *geklingelt*

The correct answer is (C). The correct past participle of *"aufwachen"* is *"aufgewacht."*

Be Familiar with Question Types Based on Written Excerpts

1. Questions about Structure of the Language Based on Written Excerpts

In the second part of Section II, you read paragraphs written by students who are learning German. The student writing contains errors, and your task is to identify, correct, or describe the type of error made in a particular sentence from the paragraph. Each sentence selected contains only *one* error. When you answer the question, it helps to consider the meaning of the sentence and the type of error in the context of the whole paragraph. You may find it useful to take notes in your test book.

Here is an example:

This question refers to the following selection about a picnic.

(1) Letzten Samstag habe ich mit meinen Freunden Klaus und Heike und ihren zwei Kindern Picknick gemacht. (2) Wir fuhren ungefähr eine Stunde, bis wir in eine schöne waldigen Gegend kamen.

Identify the error in sentence 2.

(A) *Stunde*
(B) *schöne*
(C) *waldigen*
(D) *kamen*

The correct answer is (C) because *"waldigen"* appears in the accusative singular case and as such should not have an *"n"* on the end.

2. Fill-in-the-blank Questions

Some questions in Section II feature German sentences or paragraphs in which words or phrases have been removed and replaced with a blank space. You are presented with four options for filling in the blank. Your task is to choose the option that results in the best sentence or paragraph in written German. Here is an example:

An _____ Geldautomaten der Bank können Sie mit Ihrer Kreditkarte Bargeld bekommen und bis zu 400 Euros pro Tag von Ihrem Konto abheben.

(A)   jeden
(B)   jedem
(C)   jedes
(D)   jeder

The correct answer is (B), because the dative singular is required.

3. Interpretive Reading Questions

In Section III of the *German: Content Knowledge* test, you read several selections in German. Each selection is followed by one or more questions. Your task is to answer each question based only on what is stated or implied in the selection. You may find it helpful to take notes in your test book. Here is an example:

Wir reparieren:
Geschirrspülautomaten
Waschautomaten
Kühlgeräte und
Elektroherde

Kundendienst
Meisterbetrieb

Helmut Wolske
Castrop-Rauxel
Lange Straße 98

Tel. 7 57 25

Was wird repariert?

(A)   Telephonanlagen
(B)   Waschmaschinen
(C)   Mikrowellenherde
(D)   Dienstwagen

You are being asked to look at the advertisement and choose what the advertiser is offering to repair. The correct answer is (B) because the advertisement states that large washing machines will be repaired.

Other Formats

New formats are developed from time to time in order to find new ways of assessing knowledge with multiple-choice questions. If you see a format you are not familiar with, read the directions carefully. Then read and approach the question the way you would any other question, asking yourself what you are supposed to be looking for and what details are given in the question that help you find the answer.

Other Useful Facts about the Test

1. You can answer the questions that do not require listening in any order. You can go through the questions with written prompts from beginning to end, as many test takers do, or you can create your own path. Perhaps you will want to answer questions in your strongest area of knowledge first and then move from your strengths to your weaker areas. There is no right or wrong way. Use the approach that works best for you.

You do not have this liberty with the questions that require you to listen to a recording. You must answer those questions in the order in which you hear them and in the time that the recording permits. You are not allowed to pause the recording for extra time.

2. There are no trick questions on the test. You don't have to find any hidden meanings or worry about trick wording. All of the questions on the test ask about subject matter knowledge in a straightforward manner.

3. Don't worry about answer patterns. There is one myth that says that answers on multiple-choice tests follow patterns. There is another myth that there will never be more than two questions with the same lettered answer following each other. There is no truth to either of these myths. Select the answer you think is correct based on your knowledge of the subject.

4. There is no penalty for guessing. Your test score for multiple-choice questions is based on the number of correct answers you have. When you don't know the answer to a question, try to eliminate any obviously wrong answers and then guess at the correct one.

5. It's OK to write in your test booklet. You can work out problems right on the pages of the booklet, make notes to yourself, mark questions you want to review later, or write anything at all. Your test booklet will be destroyed after you are finished with it, so use it in any way that is helpful to you. But make sure to mark your answers on the answer sheet.

Smart Tips for Taking the Test

1. Put your answers in the right "bubbles." It seems obvious, but be sure that you are filling in the answer "bubble" that corresponds to the question you are answering. A significant number of test takers fill in a bubble without checking to see that the number matches the question they are answering.

2. Skip the nonlistening questions you find extremely difficult. In the section of the test that does not require listening to a recording, there are sure to be some questions that you think are hard. Rather than trying to answer these on your first pass through this part of the test, leave them blank and mark them in your test booklet so that you can come back to them later. Pay attention to the time as you answer the rest of the questions on the test, and try to finish with 10 or 15 minutes remaining so that you can go back over the questions you left blank. Even if you don't know the answer the second time you read the questions, see if you can narrow down the possible answers, and then guess.

3. Keep track of the time. In the part of the test that requires you to listen to a recording, you must answer within a specific period of time. For the rest of the test, however, you will need to budget your time for yourself. Bring a watch to the test, just in case the clock in the test room is difficult for you to see. You will probably have plenty of time to answer all of the questions, but if you find yourself becoming bogged down in one section, you might decide to move on and come back to that section later.

4. Read all of the possible answers before selecting one—and then reread the question to be sure the answer you have selected really answers the question being asked. Remember that a question that contains a phrase such as "Which of the following does NOT…" is asking for the one answer that is NOT a correct statement or conclusion.

5. Check your answers. If you have extra time left over at the end of the test, look over each question and make sure that you have filled in the "bubble" on the answer sheet as you intended. Many test takers make careless mistakes that they could have corrected if they had checked their answers.

6. Don't worry about your score when you are taking the test. No one is expected to answer all of the questions correctly. Your score on this test is *not* analogous to your score on the SAT, the GRE, or other similar-looking (but in fact very different!) tests. It doesn't matter on this test whether you score very high or barely pass. If you meet the minimum passing scores for your state and you meet the state's other requirements for obtaining a teaching license, you will receive a license. In other words, your actual score doesn't matter, as long as it is above the minimum required score. With your score report you will receive a booklet entitled *Understanding Your Praxis Scores,* which lists the passing scores for your state.

Chapter 13

Practice Questions—*German: Content Knowledge*

▶   ▶   ▶   ▶   ▶   ▶   ▶   ▶   ▶   ▶   ▶   ▶

Now that you have studied the content topics and have worked through strategies relating to multiple-choice questions, you should answer the following practice questions. You may find it helpful to simulate actual testing conditions, giving yourself 90 minutes to work on the test. You can cut out and use the answer sheet provided if you wish.

When you have finished the practice questions, you can score your answers and read the explanations for the best answer choices in chapter 14.

The listening section for this practice test is found on the German CD included with this study guide. Tracks 1-5 refer to the *German: Content Knowledge* test. (Note that tracks 6-13 refer to the *German: Productive Language Skills* test; you will not need to listen to this section of the CD unless you are planning to take that test as well.) As you listen to the CD, you will notice that pauses have been included in the narration. During the pauses, you may bubble in your answers on the answer sheet.

To simulate actual testing conditions, do not stop your CD player during the practice test.

Keep in mind that the test you take at an actual administration will have different questions, although the proportion of questions in each area and major subarea will be approximately the same. You should not expect the percentage of questions you answer correctly on this practice test to be exactly the same as when you take the test at an actual administration, since numerous factors affect a person's performance in any given testing situation.

THE **PRAXIS**
S E R I E S
Professional Assessments for Beginning Teachers ®

TEST NAME:

German: Content Knowledge (0181)

90 Practice Questions

Time—90 minutes

(**Note:** At the official test administration, there will be 120 questions,
and you will be allowed 120 minutes to complete the test.)

DO NOT USE INK

PAGE 1

Use only a pencil with soft black lead (No. 2 or HB) to complete this answer sheet.
Be sure to fill in completely the oval that corresponds to the proper letter or number.
Completely erase any errors or stray marks.

ETS

THE PRAXIS SERIES
Professional Assessments for Beginning Teachers®

Answer Sheet L

1. NAME
Enter your last name and first initial.
Omit spaces, hyphens, apostrophes, etc.

Last Name (first 6 letters) | F I

2.

YOUR NAME: (Print)
Last Name (Family or Surname) | First Name (Given) | M. I.

MAILING ADDRESS: (Print)
P.O. Box or Street Address | Apt. # (if any)
City | State or Province
Country | Zip or Postal Code

TELEPHONE NUMBER: ( ) Home ( ) Business

SIGNATURE:

TEST DATE:

3. DATE OF BIRTH
Month | Day
Jan. Feb. Mar. April May June July Aug. Sept. Oct. Nov. Dec.

4. SOCIAL SECURITY NUMBER

5. CANDIDATE ID NUMBER

6. TEST CENTER / REPORTING LOCATION
Center Number | Room Number
Center Name
City | State or Province
Country

7. TEST CODE / FORM CODE

8. TEST BOOK SERIAL NUMBER

9. TEST FORM

10. TEST NAME

51055 • 14725 • TF24E50 • printed in U.S.A.

MH04023   I.N. 202984   Q3032-06,07

1   2   3   4

PAGE 2

BE SURE EACH MARK IS DARK AND COMPLETELY FILLS THE INTENDED SPACE AS ILLUSTRATED HERE: ● .

1 Ⓐ Ⓑ Ⓒ Ⓓ	31 Ⓐ Ⓑ Ⓒ Ⓓ	61 Ⓐ Ⓑ Ⓒ Ⓓ	91 Ⓐ Ⓑ Ⓒ Ⓓ
2 Ⓐ Ⓑ Ⓒ Ⓓ	32 Ⓐ Ⓑ Ⓒ Ⓓ	62 Ⓐ Ⓑ Ⓒ Ⓓ	92 Ⓐ Ⓑ Ⓒ Ⓓ
3 Ⓐ Ⓑ Ⓒ Ⓓ	33 Ⓐ Ⓑ Ⓒ Ⓓ	63 Ⓐ Ⓑ Ⓒ Ⓓ	93 Ⓐ Ⓑ Ⓒ Ⓓ
4 Ⓐ Ⓑ Ⓒ Ⓓ	34 Ⓐ Ⓑ Ⓒ Ⓓ	64 Ⓐ Ⓑ Ⓒ Ⓓ	94 Ⓐ Ⓑ Ⓒ Ⓓ
5 Ⓐ Ⓑ Ⓒ Ⓓ	35 Ⓐ Ⓑ Ⓒ Ⓓ	65 Ⓐ Ⓑ Ⓒ Ⓓ	95 Ⓐ Ⓑ Ⓒ Ⓓ
6 Ⓐ Ⓑ Ⓒ Ⓓ	36 Ⓐ Ⓑ Ⓒ Ⓓ	66 Ⓐ Ⓑ Ⓒ Ⓓ	96 Ⓐ Ⓑ Ⓒ Ⓓ
7 Ⓐ Ⓑ Ⓒ Ⓓ	37 Ⓐ Ⓑ Ⓒ Ⓓ	67 Ⓐ Ⓑ Ⓒ Ⓓ	97 Ⓐ Ⓑ Ⓒ Ⓓ
8 Ⓐ Ⓑ Ⓒ Ⓓ	38 Ⓐ Ⓑ Ⓒ Ⓓ	68 Ⓐ Ⓑ Ⓒ Ⓓ	98 Ⓐ Ⓑ Ⓒ Ⓓ
9 Ⓐ Ⓑ Ⓒ Ⓓ	39 Ⓐ Ⓑ Ⓒ Ⓓ	69 Ⓐ Ⓑ Ⓒ Ⓓ	99 Ⓐ Ⓑ Ⓒ Ⓓ
10 Ⓐ Ⓑ Ⓒ Ⓓ	40 Ⓐ Ⓑ Ⓒ Ⓓ	70 Ⓐ Ⓑ Ⓒ Ⓓ	100 Ⓐ Ⓑ Ⓒ Ⓓ
11 Ⓐ Ⓑ Ⓒ Ⓓ	41 Ⓐ Ⓑ Ⓒ Ⓓ	71 Ⓐ Ⓑ Ⓒ Ⓓ	101 Ⓐ Ⓑ Ⓒ Ⓓ
12 Ⓐ Ⓑ Ⓒ Ⓓ	42 Ⓐ Ⓑ Ⓒ Ⓓ	72 Ⓐ Ⓑ Ⓒ Ⓓ	102 Ⓐ Ⓑ Ⓒ Ⓓ
13 Ⓐ Ⓑ Ⓒ Ⓓ	43 Ⓐ Ⓑ Ⓒ Ⓓ	73 Ⓐ Ⓑ Ⓒ Ⓓ	103 Ⓐ Ⓑ Ⓒ Ⓓ
14 Ⓐ Ⓑ Ⓒ Ⓓ	44 Ⓐ Ⓑ Ⓒ Ⓓ	74 Ⓐ Ⓑ Ⓒ Ⓓ	104 Ⓐ Ⓑ Ⓒ Ⓓ
15 Ⓐ Ⓑ Ⓒ Ⓓ	45 Ⓐ Ⓑ Ⓒ Ⓓ	75 Ⓐ Ⓑ Ⓒ Ⓓ	105 Ⓐ Ⓑ Ⓒ Ⓓ
16 Ⓐ Ⓑ Ⓒ Ⓓ	46 Ⓐ Ⓑ Ⓒ Ⓓ	76 Ⓐ Ⓑ Ⓒ Ⓓ	106 Ⓐ Ⓑ Ⓒ Ⓓ
17 Ⓐ Ⓑ Ⓒ Ⓓ	47 Ⓐ Ⓑ Ⓒ Ⓓ	77 Ⓐ Ⓑ Ⓒ Ⓓ	107 Ⓐ Ⓑ Ⓒ Ⓓ
18 Ⓐ Ⓑ Ⓒ Ⓓ	48 Ⓐ Ⓑ Ⓒ Ⓓ	78 Ⓐ Ⓑ Ⓒ Ⓓ	108 Ⓐ Ⓑ Ⓒ Ⓓ
19 Ⓐ Ⓑ Ⓒ Ⓓ	49 Ⓐ Ⓑ Ⓒ Ⓓ	79 Ⓐ Ⓑ Ⓒ Ⓓ	109 Ⓐ Ⓑ Ⓒ Ⓓ
20 Ⓐ Ⓑ Ⓒ Ⓓ	50 Ⓐ Ⓑ Ⓒ Ⓓ	80 Ⓐ Ⓑ Ⓒ Ⓓ	110 Ⓐ Ⓑ Ⓒ Ⓓ
21 Ⓐ Ⓑ Ⓒ Ⓓ	51 Ⓐ Ⓑ Ⓒ Ⓓ	81 Ⓐ Ⓑ Ⓒ Ⓓ	111 Ⓐ Ⓑ Ⓒ Ⓓ
22 Ⓐ Ⓑ Ⓒ Ⓓ	52 Ⓐ Ⓑ Ⓒ Ⓓ	82 Ⓐ Ⓑ Ⓒ Ⓓ	112 Ⓐ Ⓑ Ⓒ Ⓓ
23 Ⓐ Ⓑ Ⓒ Ⓓ	53 Ⓐ Ⓑ Ⓒ Ⓓ	83 Ⓐ Ⓑ Ⓒ Ⓓ	113 Ⓐ Ⓑ Ⓒ Ⓓ
24 Ⓐ Ⓑ Ⓒ Ⓓ	54 Ⓐ Ⓑ Ⓒ Ⓓ	84 Ⓐ Ⓑ Ⓒ Ⓓ	114 Ⓐ Ⓑ Ⓒ Ⓓ
25 Ⓐ Ⓑ Ⓒ Ⓓ	55 Ⓐ Ⓑ Ⓒ Ⓓ	85 Ⓐ Ⓑ Ⓒ Ⓓ	115 Ⓐ Ⓑ Ⓒ Ⓓ
26 Ⓐ Ⓑ Ⓒ Ⓓ	56 Ⓐ Ⓑ Ⓒ Ⓓ	86 Ⓐ Ⓑ Ⓒ Ⓓ	116 Ⓐ Ⓑ Ⓒ Ⓓ
27 Ⓐ Ⓑ Ⓒ Ⓓ	57 Ⓐ Ⓑ Ⓒ Ⓓ	87 Ⓐ Ⓑ Ⓒ Ⓓ	117 Ⓐ Ⓑ Ⓒ Ⓓ
28 Ⓐ Ⓑ Ⓒ Ⓓ	58 Ⓐ Ⓑ Ⓒ Ⓓ	88 Ⓐ Ⓑ Ⓒ Ⓓ	118 Ⓐ Ⓑ Ⓒ Ⓓ
29 Ⓐ Ⓑ Ⓒ Ⓓ	59 Ⓐ Ⓑ Ⓒ Ⓓ	89 Ⓐ Ⓑ Ⓒ Ⓓ	119 Ⓐ Ⓑ Ⓒ Ⓓ
30 Ⓐ Ⓑ Ⓒ Ⓓ	60 Ⓐ Ⓑ Ⓒ Ⓓ	90 Ⓐ Ⓑ Ⓒ Ⓓ	120 Ⓐ Ⓑ Ⓒ Ⓓ

PRAXIS GERMAN: CONTENT KNOWLEDGE

90 Multiple-Choice Questions
(Time—90 minutes)

RECORDED PORTION OF THE TEST

Section I	Interpretive Listening	Parts A, B, C
Section II	Structure of the Language (Grammatical Accuracy)	Part A

[The following directions will be heard on the CD.]

This is the recorded portion of the study guide for the Praxis *German: Content Knowledge* test. All the directions you will hear for this portion of the test are also printed in your test book.

In a moment, you will hear an introductory statement by two of the people who recorded this test. The purpose of this introduction is to familiarize you with the speakers' voices. Listen to the following passage.

Die Schüler haben von Montag bis Freitag Unterricht, Feiertage ausgenommen. Am 20. und 27. Januar dieses Jahres fallen die Nachmittagsstunden aus, damit die Lehrer an einer Lehrerkonferenz teilnehmen können.

[Heard Twice]

GO ON TO THE NEXT PAGE

SECTION I

INTERPRETIVE LISTENING

Approximate time—23 minutes

Section I is designed to measure how well you understand spoken German.

Part A: Questions 1–9

Directions: In Part A, you will hear short conversations between two people. After each conversation, you will hear one or more questions. The conversations and questions are not printed in the test book.

During the pause after each question, read the four answer choices printed in your test book and choose the <u>one</u> most appropriate answer. Indicate your choice on your answer sheet.

For example, you will hear:

[Recorded conversation and question]

In your test book you will read:

SAMPLE ANSWER

(A) Auf der Post.
(B) Am Flughafen.
(C) An der Theaterkasse.
(D) In einem Restaurant.

Ⓐ Ⓑ ● Ⓓ

Of the four answer choices, (C) is the most appropriate answer. Therefore, you would fill in space (C) on your answer sheet.

You may take notes, but <u>only</u> in your test book.

Now we will begin Part A with the conversation for questions 1 and 2.

Frage 1 und Frage 2 beziehen sich auf eine Reservierung.

1. (A) An der Rezeption.
   (B) Im Café.
   (C) An der Bar.
   (D) Im Hotelzimmer.

2. (A) Ein Begrüßungsgetränk.
   (B) Komputeranschluss.
   (C) Eine Straßenkarte.
   (D) Zimmerschlüssel.

---

3. (A) Im Kino.
   (B) Im Theater.
   (C) Im Hörsaal.
   (D) Im Stadion.

Frage 4 und Frage 5 beziehen sich auf das folgende kurze Gespräch.

4. (A) In Deutschland.
   (B) In Frankreich.
   (C) In Österreich.
   (D) In der Schweiz.

5. (A) Sie hat dort Urlaub gemacht.
   (B) Sie hat früher dort gearbeitet.
   (C) Sie hat dort mit ihrer Familie gewohnt.
   (D) Sie hat dort eine Universität besucht.

Frage 6 und Frage 7 beziehen sich auf ein Gespräch zwischen Gertrud und Dirk.

6. (A) In der Autowerkstatt.
   (B) Im Parkhaus.
   (C) Im Auto.
   (D) Auf dem Bahnsteig.

7. (A) Ein Warndreieck aufstellen.
   (B) Einen Parkplatz suchen.
   (C) Andere Autofahrer um Hilfe bitten.
   (D) Die Straßenwacht anrufen.

Frage 8 und 9 Frage beziehen sich auf das folgende Gespräch.

8. (A) Sie müssen sich auf ein Seminar
       vorbereiten.
   (B) Sie müssen in eine Vorlesung gehen.
   (C) Sie wollen eine Party geben.
   (D) Sie wollen zusammen einkaufen gehen.

9. (A) Anglistik.
   (B) Geschichte.
   (C) Mathematik.
   (D) Kunst.

GO ON TO THE NEXT PAGE

Part B: Questions 10–15

Directions: In Part B, you will hear short narrations. The narrations are not printed in your test book. After each narration, you will hear two or more questions, which are printed in your test book.

During the pause after each question, read the four answer choices printed in your test book and choose the <u>one</u> most appropriate answer. Indicate your choice on your answer sheet.

For example, you will hear:

[Recorded narration and question]

In your test book you will read:

Die Frage bezieht sich auf die folgende Durchsage.

Für wen ist diese Durchsage gemeint?

(A) Für Bahnbeamte.
(B) Für Autofahrer.
(C) Für Bauarbeiter.
(D) Für Mechaniker.

SAMPLE ANSWER
Ⓐ ● Ⓒ Ⓓ

Of the four answer choices, (B) is the most appropriate answer. Therefore, you would fill in space (B) on your answer sheet.

You may take notes, but <u>only</u> in your test book.

Now we will begin Part B with the narration for questions 10 and 11.

Frage 10 und Frage 11 beziehen sich auf den folgenden Bericht.

10. Worum geht es in dem Bericht?

   (A)   Um eine Gartenausstellung.
   (B)   Um ein Ferienlager.
   (C)   Um einen Feiertag.
   (D)   Um einen Sommertag.

11. Warum machten die Gastwirte ein gutes Geschäft?

   (A)   Sie stellten mehr Tische auf.
   (B)   Die Zoos waren geschlossen.
   (C)   Die Ausflugslokale organisierten Ostereiersuchen.
   (D)   Das Wetter war herrlich warm.

Frage 12 und Frage 13 beziehen sich auf einen Ausflug auf Inline-Skates.

12. Wie wird die Gegend südöstlich von München beschrieben?

   (A)   Sie ist ländlich.
   (B)   Sie ist gebirgig.
   (C)   Sie zieht viele Touristen an.
   (D)   Sie ist mehrere Autostunden von München entfernt.

13. Wie kann man sich vom Inlineskating erholen?

   (A)   Man kann auf Feldwegen joggen.
   (B)   Man kann auf Pferden reiten.
   (C)   Man kann bayrische Spezialitäten essen.
   (D)   Man kann die sommerliche Hitze genießen.

Frage 14 und Frage 15 beziehen sich auf die folgende Nachricht auf einem Anrufbeantworter.

14. Worum geht es bei der Nachricht?

   (A)   Um einen Kinobesuch.
   (B)   Um eine Einladung.
   (C)   Um eine Bestellung.
   (D)   Um einen Umzug.

15. Was soll Thomas tun?

   (A)   Zu Hause bleiben.
   (B)   Mit Karin ausgehen.
   (C)   David einladen.
   (D)   Karin anrufen.

GO ON TO THE NEXT PAGE

Part C: Questions 16–24

Directions: In Part C, you will hear narrations and conversations that are longer than those in Parts A and B. The narrations and conversations are not printed in your test book. After each narration or conversation you will hear several questions, which are printed in your test book.

During the pause after each question, read the four answer choices printed in your test book and choose the one most appropriate answer. Indicate your choice on your answer sheet.

There is no sample question for this part.

You may take notes, but only in your test book.

Now we will begin Part C with the conversation for questions 16–18.

Fragen 16 bis 18 beziehen sich auf eine Unterhaltung zwischen zwei Freunden.

16. Warum schlägt Uwe vor, nach Berlin zu fahren?

   (A)   Er plant, dort Architektur zu studieren.
   (B)   Er hat darüber Interessantes gelesen.
   (C)   Seine Tante will ihn sehen.
   (D)   Günter kennt sich dort aus.

17. Warum will Günter nicht in die Staatsoper gehen?

   (A)   Er interessiert sich nur für italiensiche Opern.
   (B)   Er will lieber in die Neue Nationalgalerie gehen.
   (C)   Er hatte schon Konzertkarten bestellt.
   (D)   Er will lieber ein berühmtes Orchester spielen hören.

18. Wo werden Günter und Uwe übernachten?

   (A)   In einem Hotel.
   (B)   In einer Jugendherberge.
   (C)   Bei einer Verwandten von Uwe.
   (D)   In einer Ferienwohnung in Kreuzberg.

Fragen 19 bis 21 beziehen sich auf die folgende Reportage.

19. Woher kommt die Reportage?

   (A)   Aus einer Fahrschule.
   (B)   Aus einer Automobilfabrik.
   (C)   Von einer Automobilmesse.
   (D)   Von einem Autorennen.

20. Welcher Autohersteller ist dieses Jahr eine Sensation?

   (A)   Eine kleine deutsche Firma.
   (B)   Eine ausländische Firma.
   (C)   Eine bekannte deutsche Firma.
   (D)   Eine ganz neue Firma.

21. Welche interessante Nachricht erfährt man?

   (A)   Geländewagen werden immer billiger.
   (B)   Elektroautos werden immer beliebter.
   (C)   Auslandsexporte sind wenig gestiegen.
   (D)   Elektroautos werden meistens in Frankfurt verkauft.

Fragen 22 bis 24 beziehen sich auf das folgende Gespräch.

22. Wo findet das Gespräch statt?

    (A)   Im Kaufhaus.
    (B)   Auf dem Markt.
    (C)   In der Gärtnerei.
    (D)   Auf dem Flugplatz.

23. Was hat die Frau vor?

    (A)   Ihren Stand zu verkaufen.
    (B)   Drei Wochen zu arbeiten.
    (C)   Urlaub zu machen.
    (D)   Italien zu sehen.

24. Was findet Herr Schwingenstein teuer?

    (A)   Die Kartoffeln.
    (B)   Die Karotten.
    (C)   Die Tomaten.
    (D)   Die Trauben.

GO ON TO THE NEXT PAGE

SECTION II

STRUCTURE OF THE LANGUAGE (Grammatical Accuracy)

Approximate time—26 minutes

Part A (recorded portion)—3 minutes
Parts B, C, and D—23 minutes

Section II is designed to measure your knowledge of the structure of the German language.

Part A: Questions 25–29

Directions: In Part A, you will hear selections spoken by students who are learning German and who make errors in their speech. The selections are not printed in your test book. After hearing a selection, you will hear one or more excerpts from the selection. Each excerpt contains only <u>one</u> error. You will be asked to identify, correct, or describe the type of error in the excerpt. When answering each question, consider the error in the context of the entire selection. The questions are printed in your test book.

During the pause after each question, read the four answer choices printed in your test book and choose the <u>one</u> most appropriate answer. Indicate your choice on your answer sheet.

For example, you will hear:

[Recorded selection and question]

Then you will hear again:

[Recorded excerpt]

In your test book you will read:

The question refers to the following selection in which a student explains why she was late for class.

Identify the grammatical error in the following excerpt.

(A) *Erstens*
(B) *Morgen*
(C) *aufgeweckt*
(D) *geklingelt*

SAMPLE ANSWER

Ⓐ Ⓑ ● Ⓓ

Of the four answer choices, (C) is the most appropriate answer. Therefore, you would fill in space (C) on your answer sheet.

You may take notes, but <u>only</u> in your test book.

Now we will begin Part A with the selection for questions 25 and 26.

Questions 25–26 refer to the following talk by a student who just returned from a trip to Germany.

25. Identify the grammatical error in the following excerpt.

(A) *liegt*
(B) *im*
(C) *dann*
(D) *weiter*

26. Identify the grammatical error in the following excerpt.

(A) *ist*
(B) *große*
(C) *Bundesland*
(D) *kleinste*

Questions 27–29 refer to the following talk in which a student tells her classmates about her travel experience.

27. Identify the grammatical error in the following excerpt.

(A) *Die*
(B) *zu*
(C) *war*
(D) *wirklich*

28. Identify the grammatical error in the following excerpt.

(A) *wollten*
(B) *nehmen*
(C) *haben*
(D) *geflogen*

29. Identify the grammatical error in the following excerpt.

(A) Incorrect word order
(B) Incorrect conjunction
(C) Incorrect verb tense
(D) Incorrect adjective ending

STOP.

THIS IS THE END OF THE RECORDED PORTION OF THE TEST.

AT THE ACTUAL TEST ADMINISTRATION, YOU MUST NOT TURN THE PAGE UNTIL YOU ARE TOLD TO DO SO.

Part B: Questions 30–35

Directions: In Part B, you will read paragraphs written by students who are learning German. Each paragraph contains errors. You will be asked to identify, correct, or describe the type of error in some of the sentences from each paragraph; each of these sentences contains only one error. When answering each question, consider the error in the context of the entire paragraph.

For each question, choose the <u>one</u> most appropriate answer from the four answer choices printed in your test book. Indicate your choice on your answer sheet.

For example:

The question refers to the following selection about a picnic.

(1) Letzten Samstag habe ich mit meinen Freunden Klaus und Heike und ihren zwei Kinder Picknick gemacht. (2) Wir fuhren ungefähr eine Stunde, bis wir in eine schöne waldigen Gegend kamen.

Identify the error in sentence 1.

(A) *Letzten*
(B) *Freunden*
(C) *Kinder*
(D) *gemacht*

SAMPLE ANSWER
Ⓐ Ⓑ ● Ⓓ

Of the four answer choices, (C) is the most appropriate answer. Therefore, you would fill in space (C) on your answer sheet.

You may take notes, but <u>only</u> in your test book.

Questions 30–32 refer to the following passage written by a student.

(1) Viele Menschen treiben Sport in ihrer Freizeit, um einen Ausgleich zu haben, besonders wann sie den ganzen Tag am Komputer sitzen. (2) Viele interessieren für Sport nur als Zuschauer. (3) Wie auch immer, als aktiver Sportler oder passiver Sportfan, die meisten begeistern sich von uns für die eine oder andere Sportart.

30. In sentence 1, *"wann"* is used incorrectly. Which of the following is correct in the context of the sentence?

    (A) *denn*
    (B) *wie*
    (C) *wenn*
    (D) *als*

31. In sentence 2, the verb is used incorrectly. Which of the following forms is the correct one?

    (A) *interessiert*
    (B) *interessiert sich*
    (C) *interessieren sich*
    (D) *sich interessieren*

32. In sentence 3, the word order of the last part of the sentence is incorrect. Identify the correct word order.

    (A) *die meisten sich begeistern von uns für die eine oder andere Sportart.*
    (B) *die meisten von uns sich begeistern für die eine oder andere Sportart.*
    (C) *die meisten von uns begeistern für sich die eine oder andere Sportart.*
    (D) *die meisten von uns begeistern sich für die eine oder andere Sportart.*

Questions 33–35 refer to the following passage about Albert Einstein written by a student.

(1) Albert Einstein wurde 14. März 1879 in Ulm geboren. (2) 1880 zog die Familie nach München. (3) Später studierte er an die Technischen Hochschule in Zürich und belegte die Fächer Mathematik und Physik. (4) Nach seinem Studium ist Einstein technischer Beamter in Bern und später Privatdozent an der Universität Zürich.

33. In sentence 1, a preposition is missing. Identify the missing preposition.

    (A) *vor*
    (B) *im*
    (C) *auf*
    (D) *am*

34. In sentence 3, *"an die"* is used incorrectly. How would you correct the error?

    (A) *an dem*
    (B) *an der*
    (C) *an den*
    (D) *an das*

35. In sentence 4, *"ist"* is incorrect. Identify the correct verb.

    (A) *wurde*
    (B) *arbeitete*
    (C) *bewarb*
    (D) *sollte*

Part C: Questions 36–41

Directions: In Part C, you will read questions about the structure of the German language. For each question, choose the <u>one</u> most appropriate answer from the four answer choices printed in your test book. Indicate your choice on your answer sheet.

For example:

Which of the following verbs has a past participle that begins with the prefix *"ge-"*?

(A) *antworten*
(B) *verstehen*
(C) *teilnehmen*
(D) *begleiten*

SAMPLE ANSWER

● Ⓑ Ⓒ Ⓓ

Of the four answer choices, (A) is the most appropriate answer. Therefore, you would fill in space (A) on your answer sheet.

You may take notes, but <u>only</u> in your test book.

36. Which of the following verbs takes an umlaut in the second and third person singular present tense?

    (A) *achten*
    (B) *fragen*
    (C) *tragen*
    (D) *lachen*

37. Which of the following prepositions is used with the verb *"sich ärgern"* when the meaning is "to be upset about something"?

    (A) *auf*
    (B) *mit*
    (C) *an*
    (D) *über*

38. Choose the adjective that correctly completes the sentence *"Uschi lebt jetzt in der Schweiz und arbeitet dort bei einer...Firma."*

    (A) *deutscher*
    (B) *deutsche*
    (C) *deutschen*
    (D) *deutsch*

39. The vowel in the word *"Stadt"* is most similar to the vowel in

    (A) *Staat*
    (B) *mag*
    (C) *hatte*
    (D) *sage*

40. Which of the following German words is the correct translation of the English word "gift" in the sentence "He bought his mother a gift for her birthday"?

    (A) *Gift*
    (B) *Geschenk*
    (C) *Gipfel*
    (D) *Geschäft*

41. Which of the following verb forms correctly completes the sentence *"Ich sollte vielleicht ein Glas Wasser..."*?

    (A) *trinke*
    (B) *getrunken*
    (C) *trinken*
    (D) *trank*

Part D: Questions 42–50

Directions: In Part D, you will read sentences or paragraphs from which words or phrases have been omitted. Each sentence is followed by four possibilities for completing the sentence. For each blank, choose the <u>one</u> answer that results in the best sentence or paragraph in written German. When choosing your answer, consider it in the context of the entire sentence or paragraph. Indicate your choice on your answer sheet.

For example:

An _____ Geldautomaten der Bank können Sie

mit Ihrer Kreditkarte Bargeld bekommen und bis

zu 400 Euros pro Tag von Ihrem Konto abheben.

SAMPLE ANSWER

Ⓐ ● Ⓒ Ⓓ

(A) jeden
(B) jedem
(C) jedes
(D) jeder

Of the four answer choices, (B) is the most appropriate answer. Therefore, you would fill in space (B) on your answer sheet.

You may take notes, but <u>only</u> in your test book.

Gestern haben wir den ganzen Nachmittag im
Zoo __(42)__ . Überall gab es viel __(43)__ sehen.
Die Affen flitzten über Äste und kletterten an Seilen
hoch. Ein Affe klaute __(44)__ meine Banane. Er
sah so nett __(45)__ , dass ich ihm nicht böse sein
konnte. Der Löwe riss __(46)__ Maul weit auf und
gähnte. Dann legte er sich auf die Seite und __(47)__ .
Ich glaube, er langweilte __(48)__ sehr. Die
Elefanten waren __(49)__ toll. Am Abend gingen
wir müde __(50)__ .

42. (A) verbracht
    (B) gebracht
    (C) angebracht
    (D) eingebracht

43. (A) mehr
    (B) nach
    (C) für
    (D) zu

44. (A) mich
    (B) mir
    (C) ihm
    (D) ihr

45. (A) vor
    (B) aus
    (C) über
    (D) um

46. (A) sein
    (B) mein
    (C) euer
    (D) dein

47. (A) einschlief
    (B) schläft ein
    (C) schlief ein
    (D) eingeschlafen

48. (A) ihn
    (B) unsere
    (C) dich
    (D) sich

49. (A) eigens
    (B) besonders
    (C) rar
    (D) kaum

50. (A) nach Hause
    (B) zu Hause
    (C) im Haus
    (D) von Hause aus

SECTION III

INTERPRETIVE READING

Suggested time—26 minutes

Section III is designed to measure how well you can understand written German.

Section III: Questions 51–73

Directions: In Section III, you will read several selections or passages in German. Each selection or passage is followed by questions. For each question, choose the <u>one</u> most appropriate answer from the four answer choices printed in your test book. Indicate your choice on your answer sheet.

When answering the questions, consider them in the context of the entire selection or passage. Base each answer <u>only</u> on what is stated or implied in the selection or passage.

There is no sample question for this part.

You may take notes, but <u>only</u> in your test book.

Fragen 51 und 52 beziehen sich auf die folgende Anzeige.

> **Frische Luft ist gut für die Menschen. Nur nicht 24 Stunden lang!**
>
> **Horizont e.V. Initiative für Obdachlose.**
>
> **Spendenkonto: Stadtsparkasse München**

51. Worauf macht die Anzeige aufmerksam?

   (A) Menschen sollen mehr Sport treiben.
   (B) Weniger frische Luft ist besser für die Menschen.
   (C) Heimatlose Menschen sollen nicht auf der Straße leben.
   (D) 24 Stunden Freizeit ist einfach zu viel.

52. Was möchte die Anzeige bewirken?

   (A) Man soll einen Verein gründen.
   (B) Man soll mit Geldspenden helfen.
   (C) Man soll ein Bankkonto eröffnen.
   (D) Man soll seinen Horizont erweitern.

Fragen 53–55 beziehen sich auf den folgenden Artikel über eine Ausstellung in der Schweiz.

Zeile

Die Schweiz ist Mitglied der Vereinten Nationen geworden und hat es gewagt, in der Expo 2002 für sich selbst ein optimistisches Bild ihrer Identität, ihrer Einheit zu entwerfen. Es

5 dauerte lange, bis man sich auf den richtigen Standort der Expo, das Drei-Seen-Gebiet an der deutsch-französischen Sprachgrenze, geeinigt hatte. Als die Expo jedoch zu Ende ging, hatte sie 10 Millionen Besucher in diese Region der

10 Schweiz gelockt.

Zweifellos entschied über den Erfolg dieser Schau zum einen die Distanzierung von Folklore und Kitsch und zum anderen die überraschend futuristische Architektur. Alles, was nach

15 staatsbürgerlichem Unterricht aussehen könnte, wurde vermieden.

Es hätte drei Tage gebraucht, um alle Gebäude, Galerien und Ausstellungsräume zu besuchen. Wer dafür die Bahn oder das

20 Tragflügelschnellboot nicht abenteuerlich genug fand, konnte sich ein Fahrrad oder Inline-Skates für die Zickzacktour leihen. Die Expo feierte sich selbst als immerwährendes Fest in theatralischen oder musikalischen „Events".

25 Die Schweiz blieb in diesem Sommer von großen Naturkatastrophen verschont. Kein ernsthaftes Unglück trübte die Stimmung. So wird man verschmerzen können, dass die Expo mit einem Defizit schloss.

53. Was wollte die Schweiz mit der Expo erreichen?

(A) Sie wollte sich von einer neuen Seite zeigen.
(B) Sie wollte die Geschichte des Landes erzählen.
(C) Sie wollte ländliche Atmosphäre vermitteln.
(D) Sie wollte staatliche Gebäude zur Schau stellen.

54. Welches Transportmittel konnte man auf dem Ausstellungsgelände benutzen?

(A) Das Dampfschiff
(B) Den Zug
(C) Das Motorrad
(D) Den Bus

55. Womit hatten die Schweizer bei der Expo großes Glück?

(A) Die Expo brachte viel Geld ein.
(B) Man einigte sich schnell auf einen Standort.
(C) Die Expo fand nicht im Sommer statt.
(D) Es gab keine Probleme mit dem Wetter.

Fragen 56–60 beziehen sich auf eine Sage aus dem Riesengebirge.

Zeile

Im Riesengebirge hauste ein riesiger Berggeist. Eines Tages beobachtete er die schöne Königstochter Emma, die mit ihren Freundinnen im Wald spielte. Sie gefiel ihm so gut, dass er sie
5 zu heiraten beschloss. Der Berggeist entführte Emma und brachte sie in sein herrliches Schloss. Er selbst erschien ihr als schöner junger Mann. So hoffte er, Emma würde nun seine Frau werden und immer bei ihm bleiben.
10 Nach einigen Tagen merkte er aber, dass die Königstocher traurig and gelangweilt war. Deshalb wollte er ihr Gesellschaft herbeizaubern. Er zog ein paar Rüben aus einem Feld und brachte sie ihr. Sobald Emma die Rüben mit
15 einem Zauberstab berührte, bekamen sie die menschliche Gestalt, die sie wünschte. Emma gab den Rüben die Gestalten ihrer Freundinnen, Dienerinnen, einer kleinen Katze und eines Hundes. Aber nach einigen Wochen wurden sie
20 alt und faltig, weil die Rüben verwelkt waren. Der Berggeist wollte neue Rüben holen, aber er fand keine; inzwischen war nämlich die Ernte vorbei und die Felder waren leer. Nun säte er ein ganzes Feld voll Rüben and
25 ließ sie besonders schnell wachsen. Emma wurde jedoch nicht fröhlich, denn sie hatte einen Verlobten, und an ihn musste sie nun immer denken. Als die Rüben reif wurden, hatte Emma
30 schon einen Plan gefasst, wie sie den Berggeist überlisten könnte. Sie verwandelte eine Rübe in einen Vogel, den sie als Boten zu ihrem Verlobten schickte. Sie bat ihn, in drei Tagen am Fuß des Gebirges auf sie zu warten.
35 Als der Berggeist sie wieder bat, seine Frau zu werden, versprach sie es ihm—unter einer Bedingung; er solle die Rüben auf dem Feld zählen, damit sie wissen könne, wie viele Hochzeitsgäste sie haben werde.
40 Sofort machte sich der Geist an die Arbeit und zählte. Er zählte noch einmal und ein drittes Mal. Immer wieder verzählte er sich und musste von neuem beginnen. Emma verwandelte in der Zwischenzeit eine
45 schöne große Rübe in ein Pferd und ritt eilig fort, über das Gebirge bis ins Tal, wo ihr Verlobter schon auf sie wartete.

Zeile

Als der Berggeist nach dem Zählen Emmas Fehlen bemerkte, war es zu spät, sie
50 zurückzuholen, denn sie hatte das Gebirge und damit die Grenzen seines Reiches schon verlassen. Während die schöne Emma im Tal Hochzeit hielt, tobte und stürmte der zornige Geist im
55 Riesengebirge.

56. Was geschah der Königstochter Emma?

    (A)   Der Berggeist raubte sie.
    (B)   Sie verirrte sich im Wald.
    (C)   Ihr Verlobter entführte sie.
    (D)   Sie wurde in eine Rübe verzaubert.

57. Warum wurde Emma nicht froh?

    (A)   Sie hatte ihren Zauberstab verloren.
    (B)   Sie vermisste besonders ihre Eltern.
    (C)   Sie konnte ihren Verlobten nicht vergessen.
    (D)   Die Rüben wuchsen nicht schnell genug.

58. Wie versuchte der Berggeist, Emma aufzuheitern?

    (A)   Er baute ihr ein Schloss.
    (B)   Er schenkte ihr ein Pferd.
    (C)   Er lud ihre Freundinnen ein.
    (D)   Er zauberte Unterhaltung herbei.

59. Welche List benutzte die Königstochter, um dem Berggeist zu entkommen?

    (A)   Sie bat ihn, mehr Rüben zu säen.
    (B)   Sie beschäftigte ihn mit Rübenzählen.
    (C)   Sie verwandelte sich in einen Vogel.
    (D)   Sie versteckte sich im Gebirge.

60. Warum konnte der Berggeist Emma nicht zurückholen?

    (A)   Er hatte viel Arbeit mit dem Rübenfeld.
    (B)   Er konnte sein Pferd nirgends finden.
    (C)   Sie war nicht mehr in seinem Reich.
    (D)   Sie hatte den Zauberstab mitgenommen.

Fragen 61–62 beziehen sich auf das Gedicht „die sonne scheint" von Ernst Jandl.

Jandl benützt keine Satzzeichen und er schreibt die Substantive auch nicht groß. Er spielt in seinem Gedicht mit dem Wort „scheinen".

Zeile   *die sonne scheint*
       die sonne scheint unterzugehen
       die sonne scheint untergegangen
       die sonne scheint aufzugehen
  5   *die sonne scheint aufgegangen*
       die sonne scheint

61. Was deutet die Wiederholung des s-Lautes an?

(A) Glühende Hitze
(B) Das Sinken
(C) Angenehme Ruhe
(D) Vielzahl der Sterne

62. Scheinen heißt „leuchten". Welche Bedeutung hat das Verb „scheinen" in den Zeilen 2 und 5 ?

(A) sinken
(B) leuchten
(C) anscheinend
(D) glänzen

Fragen 63–67 beziehen sich auf die Jugenderinnerungen des österreichischen Skifahrers Karl Schranz.

Zeile Meine Mutter und mein Vater waren die unsportlichsten Menschen, die man sich vorstellen kann. Sie haben in ihrem ganzen Leben nicht auf Skiern gestanden, denn alles,
5 was sie kannten, war Arbeit. Für meinen Vater war der Ski-Sport überhaupt nur etwas für Nichtstuer. „Schau dir doch deine drei Onkel an", sagte er verächtlich, „die sind Skilehrer".

Ich wäre stolz gewesen, ihm zu beweisen,
10 was man mit diesem Sport erreichen kann. Doch mein Vater starb, kurz nachdem ich in die Nationalmannschaft aufgenommen worden war. Meine Erfolge hat er nicht mehr miterlebt und leider auch nicht die Lebensqualität, die ich
15 später durch das Skifahren erkämpfte.

Das tut mir sehr leid, umso mehr, als wir zu den armen Familien in unserem Heimatort Sankt Anton zählten. Mein Vater arbeitete bei der Eisenbahn. Seine Aufgabe war es, täglich durch
20 den Arlbergtunnel zu gehen, um die Gleise zu inspizieren. Einmal konnte er ein Unglück verhindern, als er entdeckte, dass auf der Strecke ein Stück Schiene fehlte. Man hat meinem Vater dafür eine Prämie ausbezahlt, und das war
25 sicherlich eine Sternstunde seines sonst an Höhepunkten nicht reichen Lebens.

Meine Mutter war gelernte Köchin aus Wien. Ihre böhmische Küche und Mehlspeisen waren berühmt! Die Eltern hatten fünf Kinder und
30 betrieben eine kleine Bauernwirtschaft. Als ich sieben Jahre alt war, traf unsere Familie jedoch ein Schicksalsschlag. Unser Haus fing Feuer und brannte bis auf die Grundmauern ab. Über Nacht standen wir vor dem Nichts. In meiner
35 kindlichen Naivität wäre mir der Verlust des Hauses egal gewesen, aber dass meine Skier auch der Katastrophe zum Opfer gefallen waren, traf mich schwer. Lange Jahre mussten wir zu siebt in Notunterkünften leben, eine harte Zeit.
40 Mein Vater baute das Haus später mit eigenen Händen wieder auf, und als ich schließlich mit siebzehn Jahren in die österreichische Ski-Nationalmannschaft aufgenommen wurde, erfüllte dies meine Eltern mit Stolz. Für sie blieb
45 es immer unglaublich, dass es Touristen und Wintergäste gab, die ihren Sohn von Kinowochenschauen und aus dem T.V. kannten. Als erfolgreicher Sportler konnte ich endlich für die ganze Familie sorgen. Schade, dass es mein
50 Vater nicht mehr erlebte.

63. Karl Schranz beschreibt seine Eltern als

   (A)   sportlich
   (B)   arbeitsam
   (C)   sorgenfrei
   (D)   unbescheiden

64. Welche Einstellung hatte der Vater am Anfang zum Ski-Sport?

   (A)   Er nahm den Ski-Sport nicht ernst und verachtete ihn.
   (B)   Er glaubte, dass sich mit Ski-Sport viel Geld verdienen ließe.
   (C)   Er bewunderte alle, die Skilehrer wurden.
   (D)   Er hatte weder eine gute noch eine schlechte Meinung.

65. Wofür erhielt der Vater einmal eine Auszeichnung?

   (A)   Er hatte verunglückte Skifahrer gerettet.
   (B)   Er hatte jahrelang seine Onkel unterstützt.
   (C)   Er hatte allein ein neues Haus gebaut.
   (D)   Er hatte einen Zug vor Entgleisung bewahrt.

66. Was erfahren wir über die Mutter?

   (A)   Sie hat den Erfolg ihres Sohnes nicht mehr erlebt.
   (B)   Sie war eine ausgezeichnete Köchin.
   (C)   Sie zählte zu den schönsten Frauen Sankt Antons.
   (D)   Sie hatte ein großes Vermögen in Wien.

67. Was war das einschneidende Ereignis in Karl Schranz' Jugend?

   (A)   Der Vater hatte einen schweren Unfall.
   (B)   Viele Touristen kamen nach Sankt Anton.
   (C)   Das Haus der Familie wurde in einem Feuer zerstört.
   (D)   Karl wurde in die Nationalmannschaft aufgenommen.

Fragen 68 und 69 beziehen sich auf eine internationale Vergleichsstudie.

Zeile   Bildung ist in der föderalen Bundesrepublik Ländersache. Das Prinzip der Bundestreue verpflichtet die einzelnen Länder zwar dazu, im gesamten Bundesgebiet anerkannte
5 Schulabschlüsse zu erarbeiten, eine Aufgabe, die von der Kultusministerkonferenz erfüllt wird. Dennoch sichert das Grundgesetz die Kultur- und Bildungshoheit den Ländern zu.
    Mit der Ankündigung, die Bildungspolitik in
10 Zukunft zur „nationalen Aufgabe" zu machen, reagierte die Regierung auf die Ergebnisse der internationalen Vergleichsstudie PISA, die untersuchte, über welche Kompetenzen 15-jährige Schüler im Leseverständnis und
15 in der mathematisch-naturwissenschaftlichen Grundbildung verfügen. Die PISA Studie wurde im Dezember 2001 im internationalen Bereich durchgeführt.

68. Wer ist für die Bildung in Deutschland verantwortlich?

(A) Die Europäische Union
(B) Die einzelnen deutschen Städte
(C) Die Länder Deutschlands
(D) Die deutsche Bundesregierung

69. Was wollte die internationale Studie unter anderem herausfinden?

(A) Wie gut 15-jährige Schüler rechnen und lesen können
(B) Wie die Lehrerausbildung verbessert werden kann
(C) Wie viele Schüler vor dem Schulabschluss ausscheiden
(D) Wie die Bildungspolitik aussehen soll

Fragen 70–73 beziehen sich auf diesen Artikel aus der Zeit der Einführung des Euros.

Zeile
Der Euro kommt, Europas neue Währung. Jahre und Monate hatten sie gewarnt, der Euro starte viel zu früh und gefährde die Stabilität. Briten und Schweden wollten gar nicht beitreten.

5 Doch bald gerät das Euro-Volk von Helsinki bis Athen, von Berlin bis Lissabon völlig aus dem Häuschen. Die Pessimisten verkrümeln sich beschämt in ihre Ecken, und alle Welt schaut selig in eine rosige Zukunft der

10 Gemeinschaftswährung.
Hundertausende feiern in der Silvesternacht 2001 am Brandenburger Tor und begeistern sich an einem Feuerwerk. Mit der Beethoven-Hymne „Freude, schöner Götterfunken" begrüßen die

15 Frankfurter den Euro. Als dann—ausnahmsweise am Neujahrstag—einige Banken öffnen, wartet die Kundschaft geduldig in langen Schlangen vor den Schaltern.
Auf den Geldrausch folgt die Ernüchterung.

20 Erste alarmierende Meldungen von Preiserhöhungen, vor allem für Obst und Gemüse, tragen Mitte Januar Unruhe unter deutsche Dächer. Verbraucherschützer rechnen sofort nach, denn plötzlich kostet das Steak nicht

25 mehr 25 Mark, sondern 15 Euro, entdecken aber vorerst keine böse Absicht. Verblüffend ist doch, dass auch viele Nahrungsmittel und vor allem die Preise in der Gastronomie steigen. Es steigen auch die Park- und Müllgebühren, ein halbes

30 Pfund Butter kostet stellenweise zwei Euro, im Restaurant explodiert der Preis für das Jägerschnitzel. Überall lauern Betrüger. Missmutige Eurologen sehen sich in ihren düsteren Vorahnungen bestätigt.

35 Die Deutschen hadern so mit dem Euro, weil sie sich innerlich noch nicht von ihrer geliebten Mark verabschiedet haben, vor allem die Ostdeutschen, die nur wenige Jahre in den Genuss des jahrzehntelang ersehnten Westgeldes

40 gekommen waren.

70. Fast alle Länder Europas begrüßten den Euro zur Zeit seiner Einführung mit

   (A) Begeisterung
   (B) Stabilität
   (C) Missmut
   (D) Alarm

71. Was wurde zur Feier des Tages erlaubt?

   (A) Müll durfte abgeholt werden.
   (B) Banken durften ihre Schalter öffnen.
   (C) Feuerwerk wurde ausnahmsweise in der Stadt gestattet.
   (D) Ostmark durften für Euros eingetauscht werden.

72. Welche Auswirkung hatte der Euro auf die deutsche Wirtschaft?

   (A) Mehr Restaurants wurden eröffnet.
   (B) Mehr Nahrungsmittel wurden verkauft.
   (C) Feuerwerke wurden populärer.
   (D) Preise wurden höher.

73. Worüber waren die Deutschen traurig?

   (A) Sie konnten keine Schillinge mehr bekommen.
   (B) Die Ostmark war wieder im Handel.
   (C) Die D-Mark war nicht mehr gültig.
   (D) Das Englische Pfund wurde zu teuer.

SECTION IV

CULTURAL PERSPECTIVES

Suggested time—15 minutes

Section IV is designed to measure your knowledge of the cultures of German-speaking countries and regions.

Section IV: Questions 74–90

Directions: For each question in Section IV, choose the <u>one</u> most appropriate answer from the four answer choices printed in your test book. Indicate your choice on your answer sheet.

For example:

Welches der folgenden Länder grenzt an Österreich?

(A) Polen
(B) Rumänien
(C) Ungarn
(D) Frankreich

SAMPLE ANSWER

Ⓐ Ⓑ ● Ⓓ

Of the four answer choices, (C) is the most appropriate answer. Therefore, you would fill in space (C) on your answer sheet.

You may take notes, but <u>only</u> in your test book.

74. Wie viele Länder hat die Bundesrepublik Deutschland?

   (A)   Zehn
   (B)   Zwölf
   (C)   Fünfzehn
   (D)   Sechzehn

75. Mit der Redewendung „wo sich die Füchse gute Nacht sagen" kann man ausdrücken, dass eine Person

   (A)   in einer einsamen Gegend wohnt
   (B)   bis spät in die Nacht arbeitet
   (C)   Tiere gern hat
   (D)   schlafen geht

76. Mit Hilfe der historischen Berliner „Luftbrücke" wurde von 1948 bis 1949

   (A)   West Berlin 462 Tage lang versorgt
   (B)   Berlin ständig von alliierten Flugzeugen bombadiert
   (C)   das zerstörte Berlin wieder aufgebaut
   (D)   Ost Berlin von sowjetischen Flugzeugen geschützt

77. In welcher Stadt ist die älteste Universität Deutschlands?

   (A)   Heidelberg
   (B)   Freiburg
   (C)   Leipzig
   (D)   Berlin

78. Wie würde man einen Professor ansprechen, wenn man Hilfe braucht?

   (A)   He, komm mal her!
   (B)   Darf ich Sie um Hilfe bitten?
   (C)   Was darf's sein?
   (D)   Kann ich euch helfen?

79. Das 18. Jahrhundert brachte eine neue geistige Strömung. Wie wurde sie genannt?

   (A)   Das Barock
   (B)   Die Aufklärung
   (C)   Das Biedermeier
   (D)   Der Realismus

80. Welche Farben hat die deutsche Nationalflagge?

   (A)   Rot, weiß, gelb
   (B)   Schwarz, rot, gold
   (C)   Blau, weiß, grün
   (D)   Grün, weiß, rot

81. Welche der folgenden Städte liegt in der Schweiz?

   (A)   Graz
   (B)   Vaduz
   (C)   Würzburg
   (D)   Luzern

82. Wie wird in Deutschland ein 16-jähriger Lehrling genannt?

   (A)   Student
   (B)   Vorarbeiter
   (C)   Azubi
   (D)   Meister

83. Was versteht man unter den „Neuen Bundesländern"?

   (A)   Das sind Länder, die seit dem Jahr 2000 zur EU gehören.
   (B)   Das sind die Teile Deutschlands, die vor 1990 zur DDR gehörten.
   (C)   Das sind die Gebiete Europas, in denen Deutsch gesprochen wird.
   (D)   Das ist eine andere Bezeichnung für das Land Österreich.

84. Welches der folgenden literarischen Werke handelt von der Entstehung der Schweiz?

   (A) *Doktor Faustus*
   (B) *Wilhelm Tell*
   (C) *Die Räuber*
   (D) *Der zerbrochene Krug*

85. Welche der folgenden Städte ist KEIN Seehafen?

   (A) Hamburg
   (B) Köln
   (C) Bremerhaven
   (D) Kiel

86. Wer schrieb die Geschichte *Emil und die Detektive?*

   (A) Erich Kästner
   (B) Kurt Tucholsky
   (C) Günter Grass
   (D) Bernard Schlink

87. Im Jahre 1919 gründete Walter Gropius die internationale Hochschule Bauhaus in Weimar. Diese Hochschule war für

   (A) Bildende Künste und Architektur
   (B) Wirtschaft und politische Wissenschaft
   (C) Oper, Operette und Konzert
   (D) Literatur und Literaturwissenschaft

88. Unter welcher Bezeichnung ist der deutsche Staat von 1918 bis 1933 in die Geschichte eingegangen?

   (A) Die Münchner Räterepublik
   (B) Das Wilhelminische Deutschland
   (C) Das Alte Reich
   (D) Die Weimarer Republik

89. Wann wird der Tag der Deutschen Einheit heute gefeiert?

   (A) Am 1. Mai
   (B) Am 17. Juni
   (C) Am 3. Oktober
   (D) Am 26. Dezember

90. Was wird mit dem gelben Verkehrsschild „Umleitung" angedeutet?

   (A) Einbahnstraße
   (B) Fußgängerzone
   (C) Baustelle
   (D) Autobahn

Chapter 14
Right Answers and Explanations for the Practice Questions—*German: Content Knowledge*

▶   ▶   ▶   ▶   ▶   ▶   ▶   ▶   ▶   ▶   ▶   ▶

Now that you have answered all of the practice questions, you can check your work. Compare your answers to the multiple-choice questions with the correct answers in the table below.

Question Number	Correct Answer	Content Category	Question Number	Correct Answer	Content Category
1	A	Interpretive Listening—Short Conversation	35	A	Structure of the Language—Writing
2	D	Interpretive Listening—Short Conversation	36	C	Structure of the Language—Language Analysis
3	A	Interpretive Listening—Short Conversation	37	D	Structure of the Language—Language Analysis
4	A	Interpretive Listening—Short Conversation	38	C	Structure of the Language—Language Analysis
5	D	Interpretive Listening—Short Conversation	39	C	Structure of the Language—Language Analysis
6	C	Interpretive Listening—Short Conversation	40	B	Structure of the Language—Language Analysis
7	D	Interpretive Listening—Short Conversation	41	C	Structure of the Language—Language Analysis
8	C	Interpretive Listening—Short Conversation	42	A	Structure of the Language—Grammar
9	B	Interpretive Listening—Short Conversation	43	D	Structure of the Language—Grammar
10	C	Interpretive Listening—Short Narration	44	B	Structure of the Language—Grammar
11	D	Interpretive Listening—Short Narration	45	B	Structure of the Language—Grammar
12	A	Interpretive Listening—Short Narration	46	A	Structure of the Language—Grammar
13	C	Interpretive Listening—Short Narration	47	C	Structure of the Language—Grammar
14	B	Interpretive Listening—Short Narration	48	D	Structure of the Language—Grammar
15	D	Interpretive Listening—Short Narration	49	B	Structure of the Language—Grammar
16	B	Interpretive Listening—Long Conversation	50	A	Structure of the Language—Grammar
17	D	Interpretive Listening—Long Conversation	51	C	Interpretive Reading—Content and Organization
18	C	Interpretive Listening—Long Conversation	52	B	Interpretive Reading—Content and Organization
19	C	Interpretive Listening—Long Narration	53	A	Interpretive Reading—Content and Organization
20	A	Interpretive Listening—Long Narration	54	B	Interpretive Reading—Implied Content
21	B	Interpretive Listening—Long Narration	55	D	Interpretive Reading—Content and Organization
22	B	Interpretive Listening—Long Conversation	56	A	Interpretive Reading—Content and Organization
23	C	Interpretive Listening—Long Conversation	57	C	Interpretive Reading—Content and Organization
24	D	Interpretive Listening—Long Conversation	58	D	Interpretive Reading—Content and Organization
25	C	Structure of the Language—Speech	59	B	Interpretive Reading—Content and Organization
26	B	Structure of the Language—Speech	60	C	Interpretive Reading—Content and Organization
27	B	Structure of the Language—Speech			
28	C	Structure of the Language—Speech			
29	B	Structure of the Language—Speech			
30	C	Structure of the Language—Writing			
31	C	Structure of the Language—Writing			
32	D	Structure of the Language—Writing			
33	D	Structure of the Language—Writing			
34	B	Structure of the Language—Writing			

Question Number	Correct Answer	Content Category
61	A	Interpretive Reading—Implied Content
62	C	Interpretive Reading—Use of Language
63	B	Interpretive Reading—Content and Organization
64	A	Interpretive Reading—Content and Organization
65	D	Interpretive Reading—Content and Organization
66	B	Interpretive Reading—Content and Organization
67	C	Interpretive Reading—Content and Organization
68	C	Interpretive Reading—Content and Organization
69	A	Interpretive Reading—Content and Organization
70	A	Interpretive Reading—Content and Organization
71	B	Interpretive Reading—Content and Organization
72	D	Interpretive Reading—Content and Organization

Question Number	Correct Answer	Content Category
73	C	Interpretive Reading—Content and Organization
74	D	Cultural Perspectives—Geography
75	A	Cultural Perspectives—Sociolinguistic Elements
76	A	Cultural Perspectives—History
77	A	Cultural Perspectives—History
78	B	Cultural Perspectives—Sociolinguistic Elements
79	B	Cultural Perspectives—Literature and the Arts
80	B	Cultural Perspectives—Lifestyles and Societies
81	D	Cultural Perspectives—Geography
82	C	Cultural Perspectives—Lifestyles and Societies
83	B	Cultural Perspectives—History
84	B	Cultural Perspectives—Literature and the Arts
85	B	Cultural Perspectives—Geography
86	A	Cultural Perspectives—Literature and the Arts
87	A	Cultural Perspectives—Literature and the Arts
88	D	Cultural Perspectives—History
89	C	Cultural Perspectives—History
90	C	Cultural Perspectives—Lifestyles and Societies

Explanations of Right Answers

1. This conversation is about room reservations and also deals with an inquiry about a coffee shop location. The question asks where Mrs. Meier and Mr. Fisch are at the moment of the dialogue. (A) is the correct answer, since Mrs. Meier and Mr. Fisch just arrived and inquired about their room reservations at the reception desk. (B) is incorrect for this question because the gentleman asks for directions to a coffee shop. (C) is incorrect because they are not ordering something to drink. (D) is incorrect because they are inquiring about their reservations and are not in their rooms yet.

2. Question 2 asks what the two people received at the reception desk. (A) is incorrect because nothing is said about a welcome drink. (B) is incorrect because nobody mentions anything about a computer connection. (C) is incorrect because they do not ask for a road map. At the reception desk, Mrs. Meier's and Mr. Fisch's reservations are confirmed and both receive keys to their rooms. Therefore, the correct answer is (D).

3. Question 3 tests your understanding of a short dialogue in a movie theater. The question asks you where this dialogue takes place. (A) is the correct answer, since movies are shown most of the time in *Kinos,* the German word for movie house. (B) is incorrect because the man talks about a movie and not a play. (C) is incorrect because a *Hörsaal* is normally used for lectures and/or presentations. (D) is incorrect because sporting events take place in a *Stadion;* no sporting event is mentioned in this short dialogue.

4. This is a conversation between a man and a woman who apparently do not know one another well. They talk about many different places where they have lived throughout the years. The question asks where the man is presently living. The man hails from Austria and has lived in Switzerland and in France. He tells the woman that he is presently living with his family in Stuttgart, Germany. Therefore, the correct answer is (A).

5. This question asks why the woman once had lived in Switzerland. The woman explains that she was a student at a university in Zürich. Therefore, the correct answer is (D).

6. This conversation is between two people whose car has a flat tire. Moreover, they are stuck in heavy traffic. This question asks the listener to identify where the conversation takes place. According to the context, (C) is the best answer, since Gertrud, the female speaker, asks the male speaker to pull over and stop. (A) and (B) assume that the car is already parked. (D) is also not an option, since cars are not allowed on a train platform.

7. This question asks you to identify the solution Gertrud proposes. (A), (B), and (C) suggest possibilities for solving the problem but do not mention the use of a cell phone; only (D) suggests with the verb *anrufen* that the woman will use her cell phone to call the road service right away; therefore, (D) is the correct answer.

8. This conversation is between Gerlinde and Erich, who are discussing preparations for a party. The question asks the listener what Erich and Gerlinde are planning. (A) is incorrect, since nothing is said about preparing for a seminar or class. (B) is incorrect because they both are at home, and Erich asks Gerlinde if she bought chips. (C) is the correct answer, since Erich mentions the starting time of the party in the first sentence. (D) is incorrect because Gerlinde offers to go to the shop alone, while Erich takes care of setting up the chairs.

9. This question asks what course of study Erich and Gerlinde are taking. (A), (C), and (D) mention course subjects, but only (B), "history," can be applied to the course Professor Weichert is teaching. Both Erich and Gerlinde talk about how much Professor Weichert loves to talk about the Romans and the Middle Ages; (B) is therefore the correct answer.

10. This question refers to a short report about a beautiful Easter day. The question asks what the report is describing. Easter is a holiday. Therefore, the correct answer is (C).

11. This question focuses on one detail of the report. The weather was beautiful, almost like a summer day. Sidewalk cafes, ice-cream stores, and restaurants were full of people, thus making the proprietors quite happy about business. Therefore, the correct answer is (D).

12, This question refers to a narration about a leisure time activity, namely, in-line skating. The question asks how the region southeast of Munich is described. (A) is the correct answer, because the narrator talks about paths through lovely landscapes passing cows and horses. There is hardly any traffic. (B) is incorrect, because the person talks about a fairly flat landscape and does not mention mountains. (C) is incorrect, since the person tells us that it is a very quiet region with hardly any traffic or people *(. . . ist verhältnismäßig wenig los),* just cows and horses. (D) is incorrect, because the person mentions that Munich is only one hour away from this remote location *(. . . nur eine Autostunde von München entfernt).*

13. This question asks about the possibility of recovering from the in-line skating exercise. (A) is incorrect because it describes how one can jog on gravel paths. (B) is incorrect because it talks about the possibility of horseback riding, another activity, but not rest. (C) is correct, since the narrator talks about the possibility of sitting outside of a restaurant and enjoying regional food and drinks. (D) is incorrect because it is not desirable or restful to sit in the summer heat after strenuous in-line skating.

14. This question refers to a message left on a telephone answering machine. This becomes obvious with the introductory greeting *Hallo* and the request to call back *(Ruf doch bitte kurz zurück . . .).* The question asks about the topic of the telephone message. The caller is inviting somebody to a birthday party for her brother. The correct answer is therefore (B).

15. This question asks what the person who received the call should do. The female caller requests a call back to confirm the invitation. The correct answer is therefore (D).

16. This question refers to a conversation between two friends who plan a weekend trip to Berlin. It asks why Uwe makes the suggestion to go to Berlin. (A) is incorrect, since there is no mention of whether the two men are students or of what they are doing professionally. (B) is the correct answer. Uwe discovered in the latest travel digest *(Baedecker)* many interesting things one could do or see in Berlin.

17. This question asks why Günter does <u>not</u> want to go to the opera. (A) is incorrect because this answer would imply that he loves the opera, especially Italian operas. (B) is incorrect because he does not say that he prefers to go to the museum instead of the opera. (C) is incorrect because it is not mentioned that Günter had bought tickets to a concert already. (D) is the correct answer. Günter mentions that he would rather listen to a concert by the Berlin Philharmonic orchestra than go to an opera.

18. This question asks where the two friends, Günter and Uwe, will be staying while they are in Berlin. (A) is incorrect; the possibility of a hotel is never mentioned. (B) is incorrect because they are not staying at a youth hostel. (C) is the correct answer. Günter and Uwe are staying with Uwe's aunt because she has a spacious apartment in Berlin. (D) is incorrect because they will go to Kreuzberg only to visit the Jewish Museum.

19. This narration refers to a radio program. This becomes clear since the announcer addresses his audience as *Liebe Zuhörer* (esteemed listeners). The reporter calls in from an international car show in Frankfurt. The question asks where the broadcast is taking place. It is at a car show *(Automobilmesse).* (A), (B), and (D) describe different places where cars play a major role, such as in a driving school, a car manufacturing plant, and a race track. The correct answer is (C); cars are presented and exhibited at a car show.

20. This question asks about the car manufacturer who attracts most of the attention at the car show. The reporter describes a small German company, Hauser, as being sensational and the star of the show. The correct answer is therefore (A).

21. This question asks about the most surprising news from the car show. We learn that the company that produces electric cars is selling an increasing number of electric cars in Germany. Electric cars are becoming more and more popular. The correct answer, therefore, is (B).

22. This question refers to a dialogue between a salesperson and a customer at a fruit and vegetable stand. It is a friendly chat about vacation plans and the quality and prices of goods. The question asks where the dialogue takes place. (A) and (D) are not correct answers to the question asked, since one cannot find the described type of fruit and vegetable stand in a department store or in a German airport. (C) is also incorrect, since one does not buy vegetables or fruit in a *Gärtnerei*. Cut flowers, flower arrangements, plants, or flower pots are normally bought in a *Gärtnerei*. Thus, (B) is the correct answer.

23. This question asks about the plans of the woman who sells her goods to Mr. Schwingenstein. (A) is incorrect, since there is no mention of her selling her stand. (B) is incorrect. The three weeks are not referring to her work schedule but to the length of her vacation. (C) is the best answer according to the context. The woman says that she wants to take a vacation (*Urlaub machen*) and wants to fly to Spain. (D) is incorrect. The woman does not want to go to Italy. Instead, the grapes she is selling come from Italy.

24. This question asks you which goods the customer finds very expensive. The dialogue states that a kilogram of Italian grapes costs 9 euros and 80 cents. The customer finds that too expensive. Therefore, (D) is the correct answer. All other goods mentioned in options (A), (B), and (C) are goods Mr. Schwingenstein purchased; he never questioned the prices for those.

25. This question refers to a short talk by a student who just returned from a trip to Germany. It tests your ability to identify the speaker's use of an incorrect comparative conjunction. (A), (B), and (D) are used correctly in this sentence; however, (C) *(dann)* is used incorrectly. The

correct comparative conjunction for this sentence should be *als*. In this sentence, the geographical location of two German states is compared. The correct sentence, therefore, is *Niedersachsen liegt weiter im Norden als Hessen,* which makes (C) the correct answer.

26. This question tests your ability to identify the incorrect form of an adjective. (A), (C), and (D) are all correct in the context of the spoken sentence. The speaker uses the positive form in a sentence where the superlative is asked for. The correct superlative form of *das große* is *das größte;* therefore, (B) is the correct answer.

27. This question refers to a talk by a student about her travel experience going from Basel to Berlin. It asks you to identify a grammatical error in the excerpt. (A) is not a mistake because the feminine definite article of *Reise* is *die*. (C) is not a mistake because to describe a situation in the past, one needs to use *war*. (D) is not a mistake because the adverb *wirklich* is used correctly to modify the participle *anstrengend*. The correct preposition used to express "from . . . to" is *nach*. The correct answer, therefore, is (B).

28. This question asks you to identify the grammatical error in the excerpt. (A) is not a mistake, because the sentence is written in past tense. (B) is not a mistake, because *nehmen* is the correct infinitive form used with the modal auxiliary *wollen*. The auxiliary verb used in the construction of the present perfect tense is a form of "to be." Here, *sind* must be used with the verb *fliegen;* therefore, (C) is the correct answer. (D) is not a mistake, because it is the correct past participle form of the verb *fliegen*.

29. This question asks you to identify the grammatical error in the excerpt describing what happened at the arrival at the airport. (A), (C), and (D) are not mistakes. The conjunction *wenn* is used to express a hypothetical situation. In order to repeat something in the past tense, one needs to use the conjunction *als*. Therefore, (B) is the correct answer.

30. This question refers to a composition about sports. The subordinate clause in sentence (1) uses the wrong conjunction. *Wann* is a

temporal conjunction; however, a causal conjunction is required here. (A), (B), and (D) are either coordinating or temporal conjunctions. (C) *Wenn* is therefore the correct answer in the context of the sentence.

31. The context of the sentence requires a reflexive of the verb *interessieren*. The subject is plural; therefore, the verb must also have a plural ending. (A), (B), and (D) do not correct the error in the sentence. Only in (C) *interessieren sich* is the correct plural ending used and the reflexive in the correct place. (C) is therefore the correct answer.

32. The word order in a German main clause always follows this pattern: entire subject, predicate (verb), object. The subject in this sentence is *die meisten von uns* and must therefore not be separated. The object *sich* follows the verb *begeistern* and should also not be separated from the verb. (A), (B), and (C) do not follow the grammatically correct word order. (D) is written in the correct order and is therefore the correct answer.

33. This question refers to a short passage about Albert Einstein. He was born in Ulm, studied mathematics and physics in Zürich, and later became a lecturer at the University of Zürich. In sentence (1), a preposition is missing. (A) is incorrect because it means "before," and Einstein could not have been born before his actual date of birth. (B) is incorrect because it is a preposition of place, as in "in the house." (C) is incorrect because it is a preposition of place, as in "on the table." (D) *Am* is a contraction of the preposition *an* and the dative of the definite masculine article *der*, which is *dem. Am (an dem)* is a preposition of time and is therefore the correct answer.

34. This question asks you to identify and correct the error in sentence 3. How would you correct *an die*? The preposition an can be followed by a dative or an accusative. *An* with the dative answers the question "where" (*wo*). In this scenario, the question actually is "Where did Einstein study?" A dative form of a noun with or without an article is required. (B) The noun *Hochschule* ("university") is a feminine noun.

The dative form of the definite feminine article is *der*; therefore, the correct answer is (B).

35. This question asks you to apply your knowledge of vocabulary and correct use of tenses. "To become" is correctly translated as *werden*. The third-person singular past tense of *werden* is *wurde*. (A) is therefore the correct answer. (B), (C), and (D) are all verbs in the correct tense and person, but they do not fit the context.

36. This question asks you to apply your knowledge of basic verb forms in the present tense. In most cases the second- or third-person singular present tense is formed by adding -*st* or -*t* to the stem of the verb as in (B) *fragen (du fragst, er fragt)* and (D) *lachen (du lachst, er lacht)*. In both verbs, the stem vowel does not change. If the verb stem ends in -*d* or -*t*, the second- and third-person singular endings begin with an -*e* as in (A) *achten (du achtest, er achtet)*. The stem vowel again does not change. On the other hand, strong or irregular verbs like (C) *tragen* add not only -*st* or -*t* to the stem, but their stem vowels also change in most cases to an umlaut. The correct second- and third-person singular present tense therefore has to be *du trägst, er trägt*. (C) is therefore the correct answer.

37. This question focuses on the correct use of prepositions with a particular verb. In German, "To be upset about something" needs a reflexive verb with the preposition *über*. Therefore, (D) is correct.

38. This question asks you to determine the correct adjective ending according to the gender and case of the noun and the adjective following an indefinite article. (A) is incorrect, because the adjective ending -*er* is the ending used for the singular masculine nominative following an indefinite article. (B) is incorrect, because it is the singular feminine nominative adjective ending following an indefinite article. (D) is incorrect because it is an adverb, which takes no endings. (C) is correct because the adjective ending -*en* is used in the feminine dative form following an indefinite article.

39. This question tests your knowledge of correct pronunciation. *Stadt* ("city") is pronounced with the short vowel "*a*." However, (A) *Staat* ("state"), (B) *mag* ("to like"), and (D) *sage* ("to say") are pronounced with the long vowel "*a*." Only (C) *hatte* is also pronounced with a short vowel. Therefore, the correct answer is (C).

40. This question tests your knowledge of vocabulary and the recognition of "false friends." (A) is incorrect, because *Gift* (the false friend) means "poison." The correct answer is (B), because the literal translation of the English word "gift" (or "present") is *Geschenk*. The translation for (C) is "mountain top," and (D) means "store." Both are incorrect.

41. This question tests your knowledge of structure, especially when using modals as auxiliaries. A modal auxiliary is always combined with an infinitive. (A), (B), and (D) are not infinitive verb forms and are therefore incorrect. (C) *trinken* is thus the correct answer.

42. This question tests your knowledge of the appropriate past participle form of the verb *verbringen*. The past participle is used to indicate that an action is completed. *Verbringen,* which means here "to spend time," is a strong or irregular verb with an inseparable prefix that changes its stem vowel in the past tense. (A) is the only answer that completes the sentence correctly. (B), (C), and (D) are also past participles, but of other verbs with *bringen* in the stem. (B) *gebracht* means "did bring." (C) *angebracht* means "did attach" or "attached." (D) *eingebracht* means "did bring in" or "earned."

43. This question tests your knowledge of infinitive constructions. (A) *mehr* is the comparative of the adjective *viel.* (B) *nach* and (C) *für* are prepositions. (D) is not a preposition here but a conjunction followed by an infinitive. Therefore, (D) completes the sentence correctly.

44. This question tests your knowledge of the personal pronouns as indirect objects. The indirect object here is the person for whom the action was intended. The indirect object is in the dative case. (A) *mich* is the accusative case

of the personal pronoun *ich* and is therefore incorrect, since the dative singular is required. (B) is the correct answer, because *mir* is the dative case of the personal pronoun *ich.* (C) *ihm* is the dative case of the personal pronoun *er* but is incorrect in the context of the sentence, because what is said is "the monkey stole my banana." (D) *ihr* is the dative case of the personal pronoun *sie* and is also incorrect, because the monkey did not steal her banana.

45. This question tests your knowledge of separable prefixes with the verb *sehen.* (A) *vorsehen (sah-vor)* is normally used reflexively *(sich vorsehen)* and means "to be cautious." (B) *aussehen (sah aus)* means "to look" and is very often combined with an adverb. (B) is the correct answer because *aus* completes the sentence correctly. (C) *übersehen* means "to overlook," and (D) *umsehen* means "to look back." Neither (C) nor (D) completes the sentence correctly.

46. This question tests your knowledge of possessive adjectives. (A) *sein* here is a possessive adjective describing the lion's *(der Löwe)* mouth and is therefore the correct answer. (B), (C), and (D) are pronouns that could be used as possessive adjectives; however, they do not fit into the sentence contextually.

47. This question tests your mastery of the conjugation of verbs with separable prefixes. (A), (B), and (D) are correct forms of the verb *einschlafen;* however, the context of the sentence requires the third-person singular in the past tense. Therefore, (C) is the correct answer.

48. This question tests your knowledge of the correct use of reflexive verbs. A verb becomes a reflexive when the object is identical with the subject. (A), (B), and (C) are all reflexive pronouns but do not refer back to the lion. (D) is the correct answer because *sich* completes the sentence correctly; the subject pronoun *(er)* and the object pronoun *(sich)* both refer to the lion.

49. This question tests your knowledge of adverbs. (A), (C), and (D) are adverbs but do not modify the descriptive adverb *toll* correctly according to the context of the sentence. (B) *besonders* acts as an attribute for the adverb *toll* and is therefore the correct answer.

50. This question tests your knowledge of German idioms. (A) completes the idiom *nach Hause gehen* ("to go home") correctly. (B), (C), and (D) are prepositional phrases that all refer to "home" as well, but they do not fit the context of the sentence.

51. This question refers to an advertisement concerned with raising money for homeless children. The text is very short. A brief, general statement is combined with another short sentence; this makes it very clear that the text is not about "fresh air" in general, but about homeless people. The question asks about the problem to which this advertisement wants to draw attention. Although fresh air is mentioned, it is not mentioned in a positive way. Fresh air, the text concedes, is beneficial for people, but not for 24 hours a day. People should not have to live without shelter and on the streets. The correct answer is therefore (C).

52. This question asks about the purpose of the ad. Readers are not just being made aware that homeless people do exist. The name of one charity is given, including its bank account. Readers are encouraged to donate money. The correct answer is therefore (B).

53. This question refers to a description of a World's Fair expo hosted by Switzerland. The expo gave Switzerland an opportunity to project a new image of itself, defying old clichés. The question asks about the goals for the expo that Switzerland had set for itself. Switzerland did not want to show old, commonplace ideas of the alps, countryside, and indigenous rural culture, but instead wanted to present modern aspects of its culture like architecture, music, and theater productions. The correct answer, therefore, is (A).

54. This question refers to the big area of the expo site and asks about the means of transportation that were made available to visitors. The expo featured trains, hydrofoils, bicycles, and in-line skates. The choices (A) "steamboat," (C) "motorcycle," and (D) "balloon" are not even mentioned in the text; therefore, the only possible answer is (B) "train" *(Bahn = Zug),* as mentioned in line 19.

55. This question asks about a favorable circumstance of this expo. Good weather and an absence of major accidents are implied in lines 25–27. Therefore, the correct answer is (D).

56. This question refers to a fable about a giant and a princess. The question is about the first paragraph of the story, and it asks what had happened to the princess. The answer can be found in lines 5–6. The correct answer is (A), because *Der Berggeist raubte sie* means the same as *Der Berggeist entführte Emma.*

57. This question asks why the princess is not happy. (C) is the correct answer, because we read in lines 25–28 that *Emma wurde jedoch nicht fröhlich, denn sie hatte einen Verlobten, und an ihn musste sie nun immer denken.*

58. This question asks the reader how the giant is trying to cheer Emma up. (A), (B), and (C) are not mentioned in the text at all; only (D) states what the giant was trying to do. *Er zauberte Unterhaltung herbei* is basically a summary of lines 12–19. Therefore, (D) is the correct answer.

59. This question asks the reader how Emma was planning to trick *(List)* the giant in order to be set free. All options could potentially be correct, but (B) is the only correct answer, because Emma tells the giant to count the beets, as stated in lines 37–39.

60. This question asks the reader why the giant was helpless and could not get Emma back. The answer can be found in lines 48 and 49. (C) is correct, because *Sie war nicht mehr in seinem Reich* is a rephrasing of lines 50–52.

61. This question tests your understanding of a poem by Ernst Jandl. The author uses neither punctuation nor the German convention of capitalizing the first letter of all nouns. The poem is a play with and on the word *scheinen,* which can mean "to shine" or "to seem." The question asks what the repetition of the "s" sound suggests. The repetition of the "s" sound

suggests sizzling, searing heat, or glaring sun and (A), therefore, is the correct answer. (B) is incorrect because the thought of a sunset does not give one the sensation of a sizzling hot sun. (C) is incorrect because comfort and calm are not connected with sizzling heat. (D) is also incorrect because the view of a number of stars does not portray the feeling of burning.

62. This question asks about the meaning of the word *scheinen*. *Scheinen* can mean "to shine," "to gleam," "to sizzle," or "to glow," but it can also mean, as in lines 2 and 5, "apparently" or "it seems." (A) *sinken* means "to go down"; however, in line 2, *scheinen* is used to say that the sun seems to go down, so (A) is incorrect. (B) *leuchten* means "to shine" or "to glow," but lines 2 and 5 indicate that the sun appears to go up or down, so (B) is also incorrect. (D) *glänzen* means "to glitter" or "to be shining" and is incorrect for the same reasons as (A) and (B). (C) *anscheinend* means "apparently" or "it seems to be," and in the context of the poem, this is the correct meaning. Therefore, (C) is the correct answer.

63. This question refers to an autobiographic account by Karl Schranz, a famous Austrian skier and athlete of the 1960s and 1970s. The question asks about Karl Schranz's parents. How does the author describe them? Karl Schranz's parents were humble and hardworking. They did not have much money and apparently did not show any interest in sporting activities. The correct answer, therefore, is (B).

64. This question asks about how Karl Schranz's father viewed the sport of skiing. In lines 7–8, the words *Nichtstuer* and *verächtlich* describe perfectly what Karl's father thought of skiing or teaching others how to ski. Therefore, (A) is the correct answer, because it says that he did not take the sport seriously and actually despised it.

65. This question asks about an award that Karl Schranz's father once received. The father was a railroad man whose daily task was to inspect the railroad tracks leading through the famous *Arlberg* (Arl Mountain). One day he discovered a missing piece of track in time to save trains

from derailing (lines 21–23). The correct answer is therefore (D).

66. This question asks about Karl Schranz's mother. She was a cook by profession (lines 27–29). The correct answer is therefore (B).

67. This question asks about a significant event in Karl Schranz's youth. According to lines 30–39, his home burned down and the family had to live in tight quarters. He was sad particularly about the loss of his skis. (C) is therefore the correct answer.

68. This question refers to a passage about the internationally conducted PISA study. This study compares the knowledge of 15-year-old students in reading, mathematics, and the sciences. The text informs the reader that according to article 7 of the German Basic Law (*Grundgesetz*), all schools are under the supervision of the individual states. The standing conference of the Minister of Education and Cultural Affairs of the *Länder* in the Federal Republic of Germany is responsible for coordinating the recognition of certificates awarded by elementary schools, high schools, and vocational schools in all the states. The question asks who is responsible for education in the Federal Republic of Germany. (A) is incorrect because the European Union is not responsible. (B) is incorrect because German cities are not responsible. (D) is incorrect because the government of the Federal Republic of Germany is also not responsible. The German states are responsible for schools and education, as stated in lines 1 and 2. Therefore, the correct answer is (C).

69. This question asks what the international study wanted to find out. Lines 13–16 state that the study aimed to find out how well 15-year-old students perform in math and reading. Therefore, (A) is the correct answer. (B) is about how the teacher training could be improved and is therefore incorrect. (C) is about how many students drop out of school before graduation. (D) is about how educational politics of the Federal Republic of Germany should look.

70. This question refers to an article published at the time the euro was introduced as the common European currency. The question asks the reader to describe how the euro was greeted when it was finally introduced. (A) *Begeisterung* describes what we can read in lines 11–15 and is therefore the correct answer. (B) "Stability" is not mentioned in the article and is therefore incorrect. (C) "Discontent" and (D) "alarm" are also not mentioned or described in lines 11–15 and are therefore incorrect.

71. This question asks what exceptions were made on the day the euro was officially introduced. (A) is incorrect because it talks about garbage collection. (B) is the correct answer because in line 15, the word *ausnahmsweise* tells the reader that an exception was made. (C) is incorrect because fireworks are an annual tradition in Germany to welcome the new year. (D) is also incorrect because at the time of the euro, the *Ostmark* did not exist anymore.

72. This question is about what influence the euro had on the German economy. (A), (B), and (C) talk about greater consumption and popularity of items, but only (D) reveals that prices were rising, which the reader can find in lines 26–32. (D) is therefore the correct answer.

73. This question asks what caused sadness among Germans. (A), (B), and (D) talk about other currencies and are therefore incorrect. (C) is the correct answer because it tells us that the D-Mark was not accepted any more. Many Germans are still not accustomed to the euro and find it difficult to say good-bye to a currency they had used for many years (lines 35–40).

74. This question tests your knowledge of German geography and contemporary issues. In 1947, after the Second World War, the allied forces established a federal structure of states *(Länder)*. Five of those states—Sachsen, Sachsen-Anhalt, Brandenburg, Mecklenburg-Vorpommern, and Thüringen in the Soviet-occupied zone—were abolished by the German Democratic Republic in 1952. After the reunification in 1990, those former GDR states were reestablished in the Federal Republic of Germany. (A), (B), and (C) are incorrect, because the FRD consisted of 11 states *(Länder)* until 1990. (D) is the correct answer because Germany has included 16 states *(Länder)* since the reunification on October 3, 1990.

75. This question asks you to apply your understanding of sociolinguistic elements as well as culturally idiomatic usage of German. The idiom itself puts the reader in a fairy tale situation that happens in a remote area. (B), (C), and (D) take only some words from the idiom but do not capture its true meaning and are therefore incorrect. The correct answer is (A) "to live in a very remote area".

76. This question tests your knowledge of German history. After the Second World War, Germany was divided by the four allied forces (The United States, Great Britain, France, and Russia) into four administrative zones. Berlin had a special status as a city; it was also divided into four allied zones. The city of Berlin was situated in the middle of the Russian sector. From 1948 to 1949 the Soviet Union blocked all ways to enter Berlin by land or sea, thus cutting off Berlin from all necessary daily supplies. As a result of this blockade, the United States created the famous airlift *(Luftbrücke)* in order to ensure the continued delivery of essential supplies. (A) is correct because it states that Berlin was supplied by air for 462 days. (B) is incorrect because the war was over. (C) is incorrect because the reconstruction was not sustained by air. (D) is also incorrect because the airlift *(Luftbrücke)* was a relief effort solely conducted by the United States.

77. This question also tests your knowledge of German history. All four cities have universities founded at different times. (A) is the correct answer, since Heidelberg has the oldest university. It was founded in 1386. (B) The University of Freiburg was founded in 1457; (C) the University of Leipzig was founded in 1409; and (D) the University of Berlin was founded in 1810.

78. This question tests your knowledge of sociolinguistic elements of German. Professors are highly respected and are therefore addressed in a formal way. If you ask a professor for help, you use the formal singular form of address in your request. (A) is incorrect because it is very informal and almost impolite. (B) is the correct answer because the question is stated in the proper polite, formal way. (C) is incorrect because it does not ask for help but asks what you want to order. (D) is incorrect because it is a question in the second-person plural form.

79. This question tests your knowledge of historical time periods and their intellectual movements. The major figures of enlightenment were the philosophers, who popularized new ideas for the general reading public. The supreme importance of the individual formed the basis of the ethics of Immanuel Kant, who had supreme faith in rationality. (A) is incorrect because *Das Barock* (baroque) is an art and architecture style developed in Europe during the seventeenth century. (B) *Die Aufklärung* was an intellectual movement during the eighteenth century that attacked spiritual and scientific authority, dogmatism, intolerance, censorship, and economic and social restraint and is thus the correct answer. (C) is incorrect because *Das Biedermeier* is applied to a period of culture and a style of furniture and decoration originating in Germany early in the nineteenth century. (D) is incorrect because *Der Realismus* (realism) was a movement in art and literature in the mid-nineteenth century that attempted to describe life without idealization or romantic subjectivity.

80. This question asks about general cultural perspectives and tests your familiarity with everyday culture. The colors of the German flag are black, red, and gold. This flag was adopted as the official German flag in 1948. The correct answer is therefore (B).

81. This question tests your knowledge of the geography of German-speaking regions. (A) Graz is the second largest city in Austria. (B) Vaduz is the capital of the principality of Liechtenstein, and (C) Würzburg is a city in Germany. (D) is the correct answer because Luzern is not only a province of Switzerland but also the capital of this Swiss province.

82. This question asks you to apply your knowledge of German idiomatic expressions. When young Germans decide not to go to university but rather to vocational school, they work during their education in the field in which they want to become proficient. These apprentices are called (C) *Auszubildende* (in short, *Azubi*). (A) is incorrect because a student is a person studying at the university. (B) is incorrect because a *Vorarbeiter* is someone who is already through basic training and who works with the boss. (D) is incorrect because a *Meister* is a very experienced and educated person (a master of a trade).

83. This question asks you to apply your knowledge of recent German history. Germany was, until the reunification in 1990, divided into two German countries: East Germany, or Deutsche Demokratische Republik (DDR), and West Germany, or Bundesrepublik Deutschland (BRD). In 1990 all former East German states became part of the Federal Republic of Germany, or Bundesrepublik Deutschland (BRD). Therefore, the correct answer is (B).

84. This question tests your knowledge of literature. Wilhelm Tell is the name of a legendary Swiss patriot who played a crucial role in the formation of Switzerland in 1291. Historic research, however, has revealed that he might never have existed. (A) *Doktor Faustus* (1847), a novel by Thomas Mann, is the portrait of a brilliant but increasingly insane musician. (B) is the correct answer because the German dramatist Friedrich von Schiller (1759-1809) wrote his play *Wilhelm Tell,* a story about the Swiss patriot, in 1804, masterfully intertwining legend, fiction, and historic events. (C) is incorrect because *Die Räuber* is a drama by Friedrich von Schiller written in his revolutionary phase in 1781 that does not mention Switzerland at all. (D) is incorrect because *Der zerbrochene Krug* (1806) is a comedy by Heinrich von Kleist mocking hypocrisy in a small German village.

85. This question tests your knowledge of German geography. (A) is incorrect because Hamburg is located at the mouth of the river Elbe at the Atlantic Ocean and is known as one of the most important ports of Germany. (B) is the correct answer because Köln is the only landlocked city. (C) is incorrect because Bremerhaven lies directly at the Atlantic coast. (D) is also incorrect because Kiel is a well-known port on the Baltic Sea.

86. This question tests your knowledge of popular German literature. (B), (C), and (D) are writers known for their adult literature; only (A) Erich Kästner wrote predominantly children's literature. *Emil and the Detectives* is definitely written for younger audiences. (A) is therefore the correct answer.

87. This question tests your knowledge of the arts in the twentieth century. The Bauhaus, founded by Walter Gropius (1883-1969) in 1919, became world famous. It started as a school for design, and its philosophy spread to the far corners of the world. Today, masterpieces of its synthesis of architecture, technology, and functionality can be found all over the world. (A) is the correct answer because it talks about fine arts and architecture. (B) talks about economics and does not fall into the category of arts at all. (C) and (D) talk about different forms of the arts, namely music and literature, but not architecture and design, and are therefore incorrect.

88. This question tests your knowledge of German history. During the nineteenth and twentieth centuries, Germany experienced several political upheavals and changes before it became the democratic and unified state of today. After Germany was defeated in the First World War in 1918, the Weimarer Republik (Weimar Republic) was founded as a first attempt to establish a democratic society. But the Weimarer Republik was toppled by the rise of National Socialism in 1933. (A) is incorrect because the Münchner Räterepublik was a short-lived communist experiment after the First World War. (B) is also incorrect because the Wilhelminische Deutschland ended with the reign of Emperor Wilhelm II in 1918. (C) is also not correct because the Alte Reich (Holy Roman Empire) was brought to its demise by the French Revolution and Napoleon in 1806. The correct answer is (D), because the Weimarer Republik lasted from 1918 to 1933.

89. This question tests your knowledge of history and contemporary issues in Germany. On October 3, 1990, the German Democratic Republic officially acceded to the Federal Republic of Germany in accordance with Article 23 of the German Basic Law. (A) is incorrect because May 1 is Labor Day in Germany. (B) is incorrect because until 1990, the German national holiday was June 17, in memory of the June uprising of 1953. (D) is incorrect because December 26 is celebrated in Austria as *Stephanitag,* in Britain as Boxing Day, and in Germany as the official second day of Christmas. Therefore, (C) is the correct answer.

90. This question tests your knowledge of contemporary issues focusing on everyday life. (A) is incorrect because *Einbahnstraße* denotes a one-way street. (B) is also incorrect because *Fußgängerzone* is a section reserved for pedestrians. (C) is the correct answer because *Umleitung* is a detour. This traffic sign is used when roads are closed due to construction. (D) is incorrect because *Autobahn* is a highway.

Chapter 15
Preparing for *German: Productive Language Skills*

► ► ► ► ► ► ► ► ► ► ► ►

The purpose of this chapter is to provide you with strategies for listening to, reading carefully, and understanding the questions on the Praxis *German: Productive Language Skills* (*PLS*) test, in order for you to be able to provide proficient oral and written responses in German.

Introduction to the Test

The test is designed for candidates applying for licenses/credentials to teach German in grades K-12. The *PLS* test in German measures the speaking and writing proficiency of prospective/beginning teachers of German. The test questions elicit samples of speaking and writing skills that a teacher of German needs in order to clearly and accurately demonstrate the language in the classroom and to develop and improve students' performance in all four language skills: listening, speaking, reading, and writing. This test is designed to gather evidence about your knowledge of the German language and your ability to use it.

The test contains a total of 9 questions.

- Six questions consist of stimuli or situations to which you must provide spoken responses in German.

- Three questions consist of stimuli or situations to which you must provide written responses in German.

In all nine questions, you will have to demonstrate that you can speak or write in a way that is comprehensible to educated native speakers of German, express and organize ideas effectively, and describe situations accurately and fluently. You must use a level of language appropriate to the task and/or audience and be able to communicate without major errors in vocabulary, syntax, structure, and grammar.

What to Study

Success on this test is not simply a matter of learning more about how to respond to the question types of this *PLS* test; it also takes real knowledge of the German language and culture. You must show the ability to produce comprehensible and proficient oral or written responses to each question. It must be obvious that your ability in all four language skills (reading, listening, speaking, and writing) in German is strong enough to serve as a solid, desirable model in guiding your students in the classroom to develop and improve their own capabilities in the German language.

Therefore, it would serve you well to consider the following areas for review prior to taking the test.

1. Familiarize yourself with the test content and format by reviewing this chapter and answering the practice questions included in this study guide.

2. Review the chapter containing sample responses to the practice questions and explanations for how the responses were scored. Compare your responses to the high-scoring responses in this chapter to develop a sense of the areas in which you need further review and practice. Then, refer to additional resources to help you brush up on those areas.

Based on your German-language skills, you may find the following materials helpful.

Hoecherl-Alden, Gisela and Barbara Beckman Sharon. *Übungsbuch Kaleidoskop: Kultur, Literatur und Grammatik.* (Workbook edition) 1999.

Moeller, Jack. *Kaleidoskop: Kultur, Literatur, und Grammatik.* Houghton Mifflin Textbooks, 2001.

Rankin, Jammie, and Larry D. Wells. *Handbuch zur Deutschen Grammatik: Wiederholen und Anwenden.* Houghton Mifflin Company, 2000.

Turneaure, Brigitte M. *Der treffende Ausdruck.* W.W. Norton & Company, 1998.

Wells, Larry D., and Rosmarie T. Morewedge. *Mitlesen Mitteilen: Literarische Texte zum Lesen, Sprechen, Schreiben und Hören (with Audio CD).*

Zorach, Cecile, and Charlotte Melin. *English Grammar for Students of German.* Olivia & Hill Pr., 2001.

You may also wish to consult available tape/CD/CD-ROM/video materials that complement German-language texts, as well as separate computer software and online Internet resources that focus on learning and improving all four language skills in German. A good place to start would be www.goethe.de or www.dw-world.de or your modern language department's own (German) Web pages.

The above-mentioned materials are particularly relevant to the types of knowledge, topics, and skills covered on the test. Note, however, that the test is not based on these resources. Instead, the list of works is intended to help you revisit topics you have already covered in your German courses.

Understanding What the Questions Are Asking

It is impossible to produce orally, or in written form, a successful response to a question unless you thoroughly understand the question. Test takers often jump into their responses without taking enough time to understand exactly what the question is asking, how different parts of the question need to be addressed, and how the information in the written prompts and picture stimuli need to be approached and used. The appropriate time and attention you invest in making sure you understand what the question is asking will definitely pay off in a better performance.

Examine the overall question closely; then identify what specific information and details your responses must contain. In the preparation time allotted for each question, mentally organize your response and take notes in the space provided in your test book. Write down key words and outline your answer. Leave yourself plenty of time to speak or write your answer.

Question Types Used In the Speaking Section

To illustrate the importance of understanding the question before you begin answering, let's look at the question types for the Presentational Speaking section.

1. Role playing/phone message

This question type describes a situation that requires you to request a favor from someone in order to solve a problem. Listen to and carefully read in your test book the description of the situation. You should outline your answer by writing down key words and brief notes to guide your spoken response. Make sure that you clearly and accurately address each of the information items you are required to include in your response.

2. Picture description

This question type presents a picture of an everyday scene, which usually shows an incident in progress. For a good response, you should demonstrate the ability to use different verb tenses such as present, past, future, and conditional. Make sure that, once again, you clearly address each of the prompts/tasks that accompany the picture. Someone who cannot see the picture must be able to visualize it from the detailed description of your response.

Prior to taking the test, you might want to practice key verbs in major tenses by describing an interesting picture from a magazine or book. Within a two-minute period, explain in German what has just happened, what is currently happening, what people would probably say, what will most likely happen next, and how the incident could have been avoided.

3. Giving instructions or giving a narration of a series of pictures

In this question, you are required to give instructions (using the imperative) or tell a story (using past tenses) describing a progression of activities. A sequence of six to nine pictures is provided to assist you in formulating your response. The necessary vocabulary can be fairly specific. It is imperative that you say something about each picture in the logical sequence. Do not try to lump two or more pictures together in your description. Don't forget that you are speaking to someone who cannot see the pictures you are describing. There is always a lead-in prompt that clearly suggests how to start out your response and points out which register (formal or informal) you should use. Scorers advise that candidates use appropriate verb forms (correct address: informal or formal, as well as tenses) and do not elaborate into areas that are not illustrated in the pictures. Stay on task.

4. Stating and defending an opinion

In this question type, you must carefully use the allotted preparation time to take notes and outline the presentation of your opinion. Jot down key vocabulary words that you will use to support as many specific examples as possible in the defense of your opinion. Clarity in stating your point of view is critical and should be immediately apparent in the introduction of your response. You then should give, in an orderly fashion, detailed examples that clearly address and support the objectives of your answer.

5. Oral paraphrase

First, it is assumed by scorers that you fully understand what "paraphrase" means. If you are uncertain, the *New Oxford American Dictionary* definition is "Rewording or restating the meaning of a spoken or written passage using different words [if possible] to achieve greater clarity." In this question, you will hear a passage read twice. While listening to the readings, you will have the opportunity to take notes. You will be required to retell the story in German in your own words. You must demonstrate your listening comprehension skills in order to produce an accurate recreation of the passage with appropriate vocabulary. You do not translate, analyze, or critique the passage; you simply restate the contents of the passage. It need not be word for word; it can be in your own words, but your paraphrase must contain all the essential points of the story, including the ending, which at times may reveal a surprise conclusion. The keys to a good response are accuracy and completion.

6. Brief talk

This question type requires that you prepare and deliver a short, formal talk to a particular gathering of people. The directions establish the premise of a determined situation. The prompts for this question usually have two parts: (1) Greetings, thanks, and acknowledgement of the situation and (2) substantial, detailed information about the purpose or intended results of the situation. This second part should make up the greater portion of your response. Listen to and read very carefully what specific information is expected in the content of your speech. Outline your talk with key words and details so that your delivery will flow smoothly, with a minimum of hesitation, and will have the proper degree of formality.

Question Types Used in the Writing Section

It is obvious and quite natural that errors will show up much more clearly in a written response than in a spoken one. Inappropriate or limited vocabulary and idiomatic expressions, wrong word order, spelling, and, most of all, poor grammatical control are all quickly exposed in written responses. Common errors in standard written German include the following:

- Missing or wrong definite or indefinite article

- Missing or wrong adjective ending

- Subject-verb agreement errors

- Misuse of tenses, particularly the past tense and present perfect tense

- Incorrect auxiliary words

- Incorrect use of the *du* form or the *Sie* form

- Misuse and confusion of direct and indirect object pronouns

- Poor use of, or missing connectors and prepositions

- Wrong genders

- Wrong word order

- Wrong or incorrect style (e.g., the date and greeting in a letter)

- "Anglicisms": American syntax, vocabulary, and idiomatic expressions transcribed into German words

To illustrate the importance of understanding the question before you begin answering, let's look at the question types for the Presentational Writing section.

7. Picture narration

This question type presents a series of pictures (usually six) for which you must write a continuous narrative. There is always a lead-in prompt that clearly suggests the use of past tenses. *Letzte Woche* or *Letzten Sommer* are common examples. Scorers will expect at least the appropriate, simultaneous use of the past tenses (imperfect and present or past perfect). Do not deviate from what you see in the pictures. Make sure you write something about each picture and keep the narrative flowing. You must assume that the reader cannot see the pictures.

8. Writing a letter or e-mail

You may wish to practice writing a formal letter or e-mail at home before taking the actual test. Check out samples of formal or business letters in a university-level advanced grammar/composition textbook. Possibilities are a business letter to a store or company concerning purchase of merchandise, or a cover letter for a job application. Be aware of the specific types of opening and closing salutations in German. The directions and prompts for this type of question are very specific. Include information requested in each of the prompt items in the order provided. These prompts will very likely suggest the use of various verb tenses (e.g., past, future, conditional, subjunctive) and specialized vocabulary. Communicating formally in writing requires that you do not use the *du* form in addressing people. Use the *Sie* form.

9. Writing questions

Here, in response to a particular situation described in the test book, you are required to write four questions addressed to one or more people. The situation could relate to one person you are expected to interview, for example. The four questions should be very clear and deal only with the subject presented in the prompt. One can be a short-answer question; the other three questions should call for longer answers such as an opinion, a description, or a narration. You may ask a two-part question but do not bunch several questions into one question. Do not ask silly, personal, or insensitive questions such as "What is your name?" or "Are you divorced/married?" Maintain a proper degree of politeness and formality. Never use the *du* form; always use the *Sie* form. Your complete written response will involve a relatively small amount of text, so individual errors may be costly; your grammar, sentence construction, and spelling will count a great deal in determining your score. Check your questions carefully after you have finished. You may wish to practice at home prior to taking the *PLS* test. For example, assume that you are writing four questions that you will ask an exchange German teacher who has just arrived at your school.

How the Test Scorers Evaluate Your Responses

Even if you feel confident about your language skills and knowledge of the content to be tested, you still may want to know how the scorers evaluate your answers. The fact is that you can find out what the test scorers want by carefully looking at the questions themselves. The *German: PLS* questions are worded as clearly as possible regarding what specific tasks you are expected to do. The German educators who evaluate your responses base your score on two considerations:

1. Whether you do all the tasks that the question requests

2. How well you do them using the German language skills you possess

The *German: PLS* tests are scored by expert teachers of German from high schools, community colleges, and universities—educators who have many years of experience scoring Praxis German tests. The team of scorers/readers is made up of both native and nonnative speakers of German, representative of diverse personal backgrounds. Scorers follow strict procedures to ensure that scoring is fair and consistent. Scores are based on carefully established criteria in the scoring guide. They do not reflect the scorers' personal opinions or preferences. At the readings, or scoring sessions, the process involves critical steps to confirm the quality of the scoring process.

- All scorers, whether they are long-experienced readers or not, undergo rigorous training before and during the scoring session.

- The scoring guide is completely reviewed and studied so that everyone clearly understands the criteria for each score (ranging from 0 to 4).

- Old benchmark responses are used prior to the actual scoring to illustrate how the criteria determine every score of 0 to 4 for each question.

- During the actual scoring of your test, each question is scored twice, once each by two different scorers working independently. Both scores for the same question must never be more than one point apart. When scores are more than one point apart, it is considered a discrepancy that is immediately resolved by the scoring leader, who scores the response a third time. This step reinforces strict adherence to the criteria set forth in the scoring guide.

■ The scorers' performances are continuously monitored by the scoring leader in order to keep everyone focused on the consistent and accurate application of the scoring criteria.

■ The PLS exams are scored holistically. Scorers assess the quality and overall comprehensibility of the response. The four key factors in the criteria that make a difference between one score and another (e.g., between 2 and 3) are as follows:

1. *Comprehensibility.* How much of an effort does the scorer have to make to understand what is being said or written?

2. *Accuracy of content.* Is each task of every question addressed appropriately and accurately? Is the content relevant?

3. *Grammatical control.* Strong grammatical control of basic structures that are used with high frequency by speakers and writers in ordinary situations, or by teachers of German in a classroom, is essential for scores of 3 and 4. Many errors or error patterns in basic structures would pull the score down to a 2.

4. *Fluency.* Spoken and written fluency should demonstrate control of complex sentences, connectors, and transition words, and there should be some elaboration to give substance to a response. A response made up of single words or short, memorized phrases, poorly formulated sentences, limited vocabulary with little or no idiomatic constructions, and no elaboration will very likely receive a score of 2.

Sample Questions

To answer more specifically the question "How do the scorers evaluate your responses?" we should look at sample questions much like the ones you will encounter on the test.

Sample Question 1: Picture Description—Speaking

Directions: In this question, you are asked to describe in German the picture in your test book. Do <u>not</u> assume that the person listening to your response can see the picture. In your description, include all of the following details:

- Where this incident is taking place
- What is happening
- What is probably going to happen next
- How this situation could have been avoided

Before you are asked to speak, you will have <u>2 minutes</u> to study the picture, go over each bulleted point silently, and think about your response. Then you will have <u>2 minutes</u> to give your response.

NOTES

Reading the Question—Key Components of the Question

Just focus on understanding the question: what are the parts of the question and what does each part ask. Here you are to give a description of the picture and to provide *details for each of the four tasks*, which tell you in general terms what your response should address.

Organizing Your Response

Successful responses start with successful planning, either with an outline or with at least some notes. By planning your response, you greatly decrease the chances that you will forget to answer any part of the question. You increase your chances of creating a well-organized response, which is something the scorers look for.

To illustrate a possible strategy for planning a response, let us focus again on this sample picture-description question. By analyzing the question, we find that it asks for four tasks to be addressed. You might begin by numbering those parts on your notes page, leaving space under each. This will ensure that you address each part when you begin speaking.

First, look at the picture carefully and remember that you are to describe what is happening, not what the people were doing before, or your opinion of their personal relationship. Then, jot down key vocabulary words for everything you see and have to incorporate into your answer. Decide which verb tenses you have to use for each of the four tasks required.

Sample Notes

Start by identifying each part of the question and quickly writing down the main vocabulary and verb tenses you want to address in each part. Your notes could include some of the following:

1. Herr und Frau Neubeck, zu Hause im Wohnzimmer (present tense)
2. Herr Neubeck sucht ein Buch, Bücherregal, Blumentöpfe, Schachtel, Bilderrahmen, Frau Neubeck, Sessel, erstarrt, schrecklich, erschreckt, zuschauen, Bücher umfallen, das oberste Brett rutschen, Buchlawine aufhalten (present and future tense)
3. Frau Neubeck hilft nicht, alle Bücher fallen, Krach (future tense)
4. Bücherbrett ausbalancieren oder befestigen (conditional, past subjunctive II)

You have now created the skeleton of your oral response and have enough vocabulary to choose from to provide information for each task.

Speaking Your Response

Now the important step of *speaking* your response begins. The scorers will **not** consider your notes when they score your response, so it is crucial that you integrate all the important ideas from your notes into your actual oral response.

Sample Response (Transcribed with Mistakes) That Earned a Score of 4

Keep in mind that a score of 4 need not be perfect. There may be some small mistakes, but your oral response must be completely comprehensible, even to a native speaker of German who is not accustomed to dealing with nonnative learners of the language. It must be completely accurate with appropriate elaboration, strong grammatical control, and broad, precise vocabulary. Your overall fluency should rarely be hesitant and your pronunciation may be slightly nonnative, but always easily comprehensible. *Speak clearly and loudly into your microphone.*

> Herr und Frau Neubeck sitzen an einem Sonntagnachmittag zu Hause in Wohnzimmer. Frau Neubeck sitzt in einem Sessel und liest ein interessant Buch.
>
> Ihr Mann ist noch immer dabei, sich ein Buch auszusuchen. Auf dem Bücherregal sind viele Bücher und zwischendrin stehen auch einige Blumentopfe, ein Bild und eine Schachtel. In dem Moment, in dem Herr Neubeck sein gewähltes Buch vom Regal nehmen will, fallen alle Bücher um, und das oberste Brett beginnt zu rutschen. Herr Neubeck versucht krampfhaft die Buchlawine aufhalten, während seine Frau völlig erstarrt im Sessel sitzenbleibt und ihrem Mann schrecklich zuschaut.
>
> Es sieht so aus, als ob Frau Neubeck ihrem Mann nicht helfen wirst, und so kann er trotz größter Anstrengung die Buchlawine nicht aufhalten. Alle Bucher landen krachend auf dem Boden.
>
> Herr Neubeck hätte sich schon längst vergewissern sollen, dass entweder alle Bücherbretter gut ausbalanciert oder befestigt sind.

Commentary on Sample Response that Earned a Score of 4

The response is complete and very comprehensible. All four parts of the prompt have been addressed with some elaboration. One could easily recreate this picture from the description given. The verb tenses are correctly used and show very good grammatical control. Very impressive are the sentence structures the candidate uses (e.g., *Ihr Mann ist noch immer dabei sich ein Buch auszusuchen* or *In dem Moment, in dem Herr Neubeck sein gewähltes Buch vom Regal nehmen will, fallen alle Bücher um, und das oberste Brett beginnt zu rutschen*). Minor mistakes include, for example, a missing pronoun (*in Wohnzimmer* should be *in ihrem Wohnzimmer*), an incorrect adjective ending (*ein interessant Buch* should be *ein interessantes Buch*), or the wrong choice of an adverb (*schrecklich* should be *erschreckt*). The fact that the candidate sometimes does not use the umlaut (e.g., *Blumentopfe* or *Bucher*) definitely does not distract from the overall comprehensibility. There are also NO error patterns. Overall, the candidate clearly demonstrates proficiency in her response by having an excellent knowledge of the German language and a full understanding of all four parts of the question.

Sample Question 2: Picture Narration—Writing

Directions: In this question, you are asked to write a <u>continuous</u> story in German based only on the six pictures below. In your story, tell what is happening in each of the six pictures, but do not assume that the reader of the story can see the pictures.

Start the story with the words *"Letzte Woche . . ."*

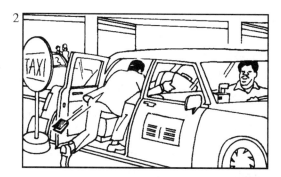

Reading the Question—Key Components of the Question

Focus on the content of the six pictures for which you will have to write a continuous story (based only on the six pictures). Your story should be written in the past tenses because the prompt tells you to start with *"Letzte Woche . . ."* ("Last week . . .").

Organizing Your Response

First, look at the pictures carefully. Remember that you are to tell something about each picture in order to describe an event that happened "last week." In your notes, jot down key vocabulary that you would like to use in your story. The German verb tenses you are likely to use are imperfect, present, and/or past perfect.

Sample Notes

Your notes for each of the six pictures might include some of the following words and verbs, depending on your knowledge of the German language:

1. U-bahn, aussteigen, Geldbeutel, herausfallen
2. Taxi einsteigen, es eilig haben
3. Frau mit Handtasche, Geldbeutel aufheben
4. Fundbüro, Geldbeutel abgeben, eine andere Dame
5. Telefonanruf vom Fundbüro
6. Freude, Geldbeutel zurückbekommen

Writing Your Response

Now the important step of writing your response begins. The scorers will not consider your notes in determining your score, so it is crucial that you integrate all the details of the pictures from your notes into your actual written response.

Sample Response that Earned a Score of 4

Keep in mind that a score of 4 need not be perfect. There may be some small mistakes (such as spelling, wrong or missing endings, and/or prefixes), but your written response must be completely comprehensible, even to a native speaker of German who is not accustomed to dealing with nonnative learners of the language. It must be completely accurate with appropriate elaboration, strong grammatical control, and broad, precise vocabulary. Your word choice should be generally idiomatic, rarely awkward, and easily comprehensible. Address all six pictures!

Letzte Woche war ich in Berlin. Ich bin aus der U-Bahn ausstiegen, und musste sehr schnell in ein Taxi eingesteigen. Weil ich es so eilig hatte, habe ich beim Einstiegen des Taxis meinen Geldbeutel verloren. Er ist wahrscheinlich einfach von meiner Tasche ausgefallen. Eine Frau, die gerade vorbeiging, hob den Gelbeutel auf und brachte ihn im Fundbüro. Sie gab ihn an der Information ab. Später bekam ich vom Fundbüro einen Anruf. Mir wurde gesagt, dass eine nette Dame meinen Geldbeutel auf der Straße gefunden habe und ihn zum Fundbüro abgegeben. Der Anruf hat mir nämlich große Freude bereitet und ich bin so schnell wie möglich zum Fundbüro gefahren, um meinen Geldbeutel zurückzubekommen.

Commentary on Sample Response that Earned a Score of 4

The response is concise and very comprehensible. All six picture frames have been described with some elaboration. It would be quite easy to recreate these pictures from the description given. The verb tenses are correctly used and show very good grammatical control. The mistakes do not interfere with the overall communication. In the second sentence, however, the writer should have elaborated a little more (for example, *Weil ich es so eilig hatte, bemerkte ich es nicht, dass ich beim Einsteigen in das Taxi meinen Geldbeutel verlor*). In the next sentence, the preposition *von meiner Tasche* should have been *aus*, thus making the sentence more accurate: *Er ist wahrscheinlich einfach aus meiner Tasche gefallen.* The syntax in the sentence *Mir wurde gesagt, dass eine nette Dame meinen Geldbeutel auf der Straße gefunden habe und ihn im Fundbüro abgegeben* is excellent; however, the writer forgot to add *habe* after *abgegeben* to make this sentence a perfect example of indirect speech. The word *nämlich* in the sentence *Der Anruf hat mir nämlich große Freude bereitet* is superfluous but does not distract from what the writer intended to convey. Overall, the response demonstrates an excellent knowledge of the language and a full understanding of the sequence of events in the six pictures.

Sample Response that Earned a Score of 1

A score of 1 definitely demonstrates lack of proficiency. Even a sympathetic reader must make a constant effort to understand and interpret the intended meaning of the response. There is hardly any grammatical control, and the vocabulary is very limited. The response, which is missing most of the tasks, is poorly organized and mostly incoherent.

> Letze Woch Mann stiegt aus, fallen in Taxi. Frau sehen purse and Frau pick up und einkaufen Information und telephoning Mann im Kreis. Man zeigen Frau mit purse.

Commentary on Sample Response that Earned a Score of 1

It is obvious that this response is too short, very poorly written, and generally incomprehensible. There is no apparent control of syntax. Grammatical and spelling mistakes appear in every sentence. The writer only uses isolated words and in the case of *Geldbeutel, aufheben,* or *anrufen,* the candidate just writes English words. The pictures are hardly described, and it is very difficult to recreate them from this very poorly written effort. This candidate clearly demonstrates lack of proficiency in writing or composing a German description.

In Conclusion

The important thing is that your answers be clearly comprehensible, complete, and detailed. You need to be certain that you do the following:

- Answer all parts of the question.

- Select appropriate vocabulary and grammatical constructions.

- Demonstrate language-specific knowledge and proficiency in your answers.

- Refer to the data in the stimulus: pictures, written prompts, and directions.

Even though you may be teaching first-year German now, your daily experiences in teaching beginning students are not enough to prepare you adequately to take this test. You need to practice and be exposed to a more advanced level than first-year German. Facility with basic verb tenses, correct endings, and basic syntax is critical not only in teaching students to speak and write German, but in successfully demonstrating in this test that you have a thorough knowledge of basic and advanced German. Develop your vocabulary by reading different types of materials, fiction and nonfiction. Access the Internet and read German newspapers online. Talk to German-speaking friends whenever you can; listen to the language in films and on cable television, if possible.

It is highly recommended that you use the practice questions provided in chapter 17 to help you develop a plan for taking the Praxis *German: PLS* test on the actual testing day.

Chapter 16

Succeeding on Constructed-Response Questions—
German: Productive Language Skills

► ► ► ► ► ► ► ► ► ► ► ►

This chapter provides advice for maximizing your success on the *German: Productive Language Skills* test, with special focus on the scoring guides and procedures used by the scorers. Chapter 15 offers step-by-step strategies for working through questions, lists of the topics covered, and lists of sources you can use to prepare.

TIP **Advice from the Experts**

Scorers who have scored hundreds of real tests were asked to give advice to teacher candidates planning to take the *German: Productive Language Skills* test. The scorers' advice boiled down to the practical pieces of advice described below.

1. *Read and answer the question accurately.*

   Be sure to dissect the parts of the question and analyze what each part is asking you to do. If the question asks you to *describe* or *discuss*, keep those requirements in mind when composing your response—do not just give a list.

2. *Answer everything that is asked in the question.*

   This seems simple, but many test takers fail to provide a complete response. If a question asks you to do three distinct things in your response, don't give a response to just two of those things. No matter how well you speak or write about those two things, the scorers will not award you full credit.

3. *Give a thorough and detailed response.*

   Your response must indicate to the scorers that you have a thorough command of the German language. The scorers will not read into your response any information that is not specifically stated. If something is not spoken or written, they do not know that you know it and will not give you credit for it.

   A word of caution: Superfluous speaking or writing will obscure your points and will make it difficult for the scorers to be confident of your full understanding of the material. Be straightforward in your response. Do not try to impress the scorers. If you do not know the answer, you cannot receive full credit, but if you do know the answer, provide enough information to convince the scorers that you have a full understanding of what is being asked.

4. *Do not change the question or challenge the basis of the question.*

   Stay focused on the question that is asked. You will receive no credit or, at best, a low score if you choose to answer another question or if you state, for example, that there is no possible answer. Answer the question by addressing the fundamental topic at hand. Do not venture off-topic, for example, to demonstrate your command of vocabulary that is not specifically related to the question. This undermines the impression that you understand the topic adequately.

5. *Reread your written response, both to improve your writing and to check that you have written what you thought you wrote.*

   Frequently, sentences are left unfinished or clarifying information is omitted.

General Scoring Guides for the *German: Productive Language Skills* Test

The scorers' advice above corresponds with the official scoring criteria used at scoring sessions. It is a good idea to be familiar with the scoring rubrics so that you can maximize your success and spend your time on things that matter (e.g., demonstrating understanding of the prompt and providing good examples) rather than spending time on things that don't matter (e.g., writing a very long narration or letter).

The following scoring rubrics provide the overarching framework for scoring the questions in the *German: Productive Language Skills* test.

Each question on the test is scored on a scale from 0 to 4. The response is considered in its entirety when the scorer assigns the score. The following general scoring guides are used.

Presentational Speaking Section

This scoring guide is used to evaluate responses in the Presentational Speaking section. The score range is 0 to 4.

4
- Is completely and easily comprehensible, even to an unsympathetic listener[1]
- Gives a complete and entirely accurate, relevant response, with appropriate elaboration, to all (or almost all) parts of the question
- May make sporadic errors, but they rarely or never interfere with communication
  - has strong grammatical control (no errors in basic, high-frequency structures; few errors in complex, low-frequency structures; no marked error patterns)
  - employs a broad, precise vocabulary adequate for almost all topics, with word choice that is generally idiomatic and varied and rarely awkward
  - has overall fluency: speech is occasionally or rarely hesitant, with frequent use of complex sentences and "connectors" when appropriate or required
  - may have a slightly nonnative pronunciation, with few or no phonological errors and no error patterns, but is always comprehensible

3
- Is generally comprehensible, even to an unsympathetic listener, but occasionally requires the listener's effort and interpretation of the intended meaning
- Gives a mostly accurate, relevant response to most parts of the question
- Is likely to make errors and/or produce error patterns, but they only occasionally interfere with communication
  - has moderate grammatical control (few errors in basic, high-frequency structures; some errors and/or error patterns in complex, low-frequency structures)

[1] "Unsympathetic listener" refers to a native speaker of the language who is NOT accustomed to dealing with nonnative learners of the language. An unsympathetic listener does not make any special effort to understand the examinee.

— employs vocabulary adequate for most general topics, with word choice that is often idiomatic but occasionally awkward

— has considerable fluency: speech is sometimes hesitant, with some use of complex sentences and "connectors" when appropriate or required

— may have a markedly nonnative pronunciation with some phonological errors and/or error patterns, but is nearly or always comprehensible

2 ■ Is somewhat comprehensible to a sympathetic listener,[2] but often requires the listener's effort and interpretation of the intended meaning

■ Gives a somewhat accurate, relevant response to some parts of the question

■ Produces errors and/or error patterns that may often interfere with communication

— has limited grammatical control (many errors and/or error patterns in basic, high-frequency structures; no control of complex, low-frequency structures)

— employs a limited vocabulary, with word choice that is often unidiomatic and awkward

— has limited fluency, with halting speech and mostly short, simple sentences; suggests inability to use complex sentences and "connectors" when appropriate or required

— has a markedly nonnative pronunciation, with many phonological errors and/or error patterns, and is sometimes incomprehensible

1 ■ Is generally incomprehensible, even to a sympathetic listener, despite the listener's constant effort to interpret the intended meaning

■ Gives an incomplete and/or mostly inaccurate and/or irrelevant response

■ Produces errors and/or error patterns that very often interfere with communication

— has very little grammatical control (many serious errors and/or error patterns in virtually all structures)

— employs very little vocabulary, with some "formulaic speech" (memorized phrases, fixed expressions) used inappropriately

— has virtually no fluency: speech is fragmentary and halting, interrupted often by long pauses and repetitions, and consists only of isolated words, memorized phrases, and fixed expressions

— has a markedly nonnative pronunciation, with many serious phonological errors and/or error patterns, and is very often incomprehensible

0 ■ Is completely incomprehensible, even to a sympathetic listener, despite the listener's constant effort to interpret the intended meaning

■ Gives an entirely inaccurate, irrelevant response or fails to respond at all

■ Produces errors and/or error patterns that always interfere with communication

— has no grammatical control (many serious errors and/or error patterns in all structures)

---

[2] "Sympathetic listener" refers to a native speaker of the language who is accustomed to dealing with nonnative learners of the language. A sympathetic listener tends to make a conscious effort to understand the examinee, interpreting his or her speech for its intended meaning.

— employs no vocabulary, not even "formulaic speech" (memorized phrases and fixed expressions)

— has no fluency

— has a markedly nonnative pronunciation and is always incomprehensible

Presentational Writing Section

This scoring guide is used to evaluate responses in the Presentational Writing section. The score range is 0 to 4.

4
- Is completely and easily comprehensible, even to an unsympathetic reader[3]

- Gives a complete and entirely accurate, relevant response, with appropriate elaboration, to all (or almost all) parts of the question

- May make sporadic errors, but they rarely or never interfere with communication

    — has strong grammatical control (no errors in basic, high-frequency structures; few errors in complex, low-frequency structures; no marked error patterns)

    — employs a broad, precise vocabulary adequate for almost all topics, with word choice that is generally idiomatic and varied and rarely awkward

    — has very few or no errors in mechanics, which rarely or never interfere with meaning

    — is completely coherent and well organized, with frequent use of complex sentences and "connectors" when appropriate or required

    — uses language that is appropriate for the intended task and/or audience

3
- Is generally comprehensible, even to an unsympathetic reader, but occasionally requires the reader's effort and interpretation of the intended meaning

- Gives a mostly accurate, relevant response to most parts of the question

- Is likely to produce errors and/or error patterns, but they only occasionally interfere with communication

    — has moderate grammatical control (few errors in basic, high-frequency structures; some errors and/or error patterns in complex, low-frequency structures)

    — employs a vocabulary adequate for most general topics, with word choice that is often idiomatic but occasionally awkward

    — makes some errors in mechanics (spelling, punctuation, etc.), but they only occasionally interfere with meaning

    — is generally coherent and organized, with some complex sentences and "connectors" when appropriate or required

    — is likely to use language that is appropriate for the intended task and/or audience

---

[3] "Unsympathetic reader" refers to a native speaker of the language who is NOT accustomed to dealing with nonnative learners of the language. An unsympathetic reader does not make any special effort to understand the examinee.

2 ■ Is somewhat comprehensible to a sympathetic reader,[4] but often requires the reader's effort and interpretation of the intended meaning

■ Gives a somewhat accurate, relevant response to some parts of the question

■ Produces errors and/or error patterns that may often interfere with communication

— has limited grammatical control (many errors and, or error patterns in basic, high-frequency structures; no control of complex, low-frequency structures)

— employs a limited vocabulary, with word choice that is often unidiomatic and awkward

— makes several errors in mechanics (spelling, punctuation, etc.), which may often interfere with meaning

— is partly or often incoherent, with little evidence of organization; suggests inability to use complex sentences and "connectors" when appropriate or required

— is likely to use language that is inappropriate for the intended task and/or audience

1 ■ Is generally incomprehensible, even to a sympathetic reader, despite the reader's constant effort to interpret the intended meaning

■ Gives an incomplete, mostly inaccurate and/or irrelevant response

■ Produces errors and/or error patterns that very often interfere with communication

— has very little grammatical control (many serious errors and/or error patterns in virtually all structures)

— employs very little vocabulary, with some "formulaic language" (memorized phrases, fixed expressions) used inappropriately

— makes many serious errors in mechanics (spelling, punctuation, etc.) in virtually all structures, which very often interfere with meaning

— is mostly incoherent, with very little or no evidence of organization

— uses language that is inappropriate for the intended task and/or audience

0 ■ Is completely incomprehensible, even to a sympathetic reader, despite the reader's constant effort to interpret the intended meaning

■ Gives an entirely inaccurate, irrelevant response or fails to respond at all

■ Produces errors and/or error patterns that always interfere with communication

— has no grammatical control (many serious errors and/or error patterns in all structures)

— employs no vocabulary, not even "formulaic language" (memorized phrases and fixed expressions)

— makes many serious errors in mechanics (spelling, punctuation, etc.) in all structures, which always interfere with meaning

— is completely incoherent

---

[4] "Sympathetic reader" refers to a native speaker of the language who is accustomed to dealing with nonnative learners of the language. A sympathetic reader tends to make a conscious effort to understand the examinee, interpreting his or her writing for its intended meaning.

A Sample Question From the
German: Productive Language Skills Test

In this question from the Presentational Speaking Section, you are asked to tell a <u>continuous</u> story in German based on the six pictures below. In your narration, describe in German what is happening in all six picture frames, but do not assume that the people listening can see the pictures.

Before you are asked to speak, you have up to two minutes to study the pictures and think about your instructions. You have up to two minutes to speak. Start the story with the words *"Letzte Woche . . . "*

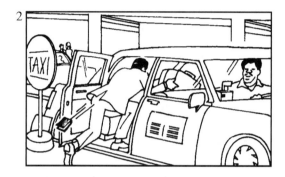

What You Should Know About How the *German: Productive Language Skills* Test is Scored

As you build your skills in writing and speaking answers to constructed-response questions, it is important to have in mind the process used to score the test. If you understand the process by which experts determine your scores, you may have a better context in which to think about your strategies for success.

How the Test is Scored

After each test administration, test books and recorded responses are returned to ETS. The test booklets in which constructed-response answers are written and the recordings of the spoken responses are sent to the location of the scoring session.

The scoring sessions usually take place over two days. The sessions are led by scoring leaders, highly qualified German teachers who have many years of experience scoring test questions. All of the remaining scorers are experienced German teachers and German teacher-educators. An effort is made to balance experienced scorers with newer scorers at each session; the experienced scorers provide continuity with past sessions, and the new scorers ensure that new ideas and perspectives are considered and that the pool of scorers remains large enough to cover the test's needs throughout the year.

Preparing to Train the Scorers

The scoring leaders meet several days before the scoring session to assemble the materials for the training portions of the main session. Training scorers is a rigorous process, and it is designed to ensure that each response gets a score that is consistent both with the scores given to other responses and with the overall scoring philosophy and criteria established for the test when it was designed.

The scoring leaders first review the "General Scoring Guides," which contain the overall criteria, stated in general terms, for awarding the appropriate score.

To begin identifying appropriate training materials for an individual question, the scoring leaders first listen to and read through many responses to get a sense of the range of answers. They then choose a set of benchmarks, one response at each score level. These benchmarks serve as solid representative examples of the kind of response that meets the scoring criteria at each score level and are considered the foundation for score standards throughout the session.

The scoring leaders then choose a larger set of test-takers' responses to serve as sample responses. These samples represent the wide variety of possible responses that the scorers might see. The sample responses serve as the basis for practice scoring at the scoring session, so that the scorers can rehearse how they will apply the scoring criteria before they begin.

The process of choosing a set of benchmark responses and a set of sample responses is followed systematically for each question to be scored at the session.

Training at the Main Scoring Session

At the scoring session, the scorers are placed into groups according to the question they are assigned to score. New scorers are distributed equally across all groups. One of the scoring leaders is placed with each group. The chief scorer is the person who has overall authority over the scoring session and plays a variety of key roles in training and in ensuring consistent and fair scores.

For each question, the training session proceeds in the same way:

1. All scorers carefully listen to or read through the question they will be scoring.

2. All scorers review the "General Scoring Guides."

3. For each question, the leader guides the scorers through the set of benchmark responses, explaining in detail why each response received the score it did. Scorers are encouraged to ask questions and share their perspectives.

4. Scorers then practice on the set of sample responses chosen by the leader. The leader polls the scorers on what scores they would award and then leads a discussion to ensure that there is consensus about the scoring criteria and how they are to be applied.

5. When the leader is confident that the scorers will apply the criteria consistently and accurately, the actual scoring begins.

Quality-Control Processes

A number of procedures are followed to ensure that accuracy of scoring is maintained during the scoring session. Most importantly, each response is scored twice, with the first scorer's decision hidden from the second scorer. If the two scores for a response are the same or differ by only one point, the scoring for that response is considered complete, and the test taker will be awarded the sum of the two scores. If the two scores differ by more than one point, the response is scored by a scoring leader, who has not seen the decisions made by the other two scorers. If this third score is midway between the first two scores, the test taker's score for the question is the sum of the first two scores; otherwise, it is the sum of the third score and whichever of the first two scores is closer to it.

Another way of maintaining scoring accuracy is through back-reading. Throughout the session, the leader for each question checks random samples of scores awarded by all the scorers. If the leader finds that a scorer is not applying the scoring criteria appropriately, that scorer is given more training.

At the beginning of the second day of scoring, additional sets of responses are scored using the consensus method described above. This helps ensure that the scorers are refreshed on the scoring criteria and are applying them consistently.

Finally, the scoring session is designed so that several different scorers (usually four) contribute to any single test taker's total score. This minimizes the effects of a scorer who might score slightly more stringently or generously than other scorers.

The entire scoring process—general scoring guides, standardized benchmarks and samples, consensus scoring, adjudication procedures, back-reading, and rotation of test questions to a variety of scorers—is applied consistently and systematically at every scoring session to ensure comparable scores for each administration and across all administrations of the test.

Given the information above about how constructed responses are scored and what the scorers are looking for in successful responses, you are now ready to look at specific questions, suggestions of how to approach the questions, and sample responses and scores given to those responses.

Chapter 17
Practice Questions—*German: Productive Language Skills*

▶ ▶ ▶ ▶ ▶ ▶ ▶ ▶ ▶ ▶ ▶ ▶

Now that you have worked through preparation and strategies for taking for the *German: Productive Language Skills* test, you should respond to the following practice questions. The practice questions are from actual Praxis tests, now retired. You will probably find it helpful to simulate actual testing conditions, giving yourself 60 minutes to work on the questions. You can use the lined answer pages provided if you wish.

When you have finished the practice questions, you can read through the sample responses with scorer annotations in chapter 18.

The speaking and listening sections for these practice questions are found on the *German* CD included with this study guide. Tracks 6–13 refer to the *German: Productive Language Skills* test. (Note that tracks 1–5 refer to the *German: Content Knowledge* test; you will not need to listen to that section of the CD unless you are planning to take that test as well.)

To simulate actual testing conditions, you might find it helpful to use your own tape recorder to record your responses to the questions presented on this CD. As you listen to the CD, you will notice that pauses have been included in the narration. During the pauses, you may prepare your responses and record your responses on your tape recorder.

Keep in mind that the test you take at an actual administration will have different questions. You should not expect your level of performance to be exactly the same as when you take the test at an actual administration, since numerous factors affect a person's performance in any given testing situation.

THE **PRAXIS**
S E R I E S
Professional Assessments for Beginning Teachers ®

TEST NAME:

German: Productive Language Skills (0182)

9 Practice Questions

Time—60 minutes

Note that for questions 1 through 6, you must answer the question in the time allotted on the CD. For questions 7–9, you will be allotted 35 minutes to answer the questions. If you finish before time is called, you may go back and review your responses to questions 7–9 only.

PRESENTATIONAL SPEAKING SECTION

Questions 1–6
Time—25 Minutes

General Directions

These questions are designed to elicit responses that demonstrate how well you speak German. There are six different questions, and special directions will be given for each one. You will be told how long you have for answering the questions. Although you need not speak for the entire time period, you should give as complete an answer as possible within the time allotted.

As you speak, your voice will be recorded. Your score for these questions will be based only on what is on the recording. Be sure to speak loudly enough for the recording device to clearly record what you say. You are not expected to know all the words you may feel you need. If you do not know specific vocabulary, try to express yourself as well as you can, using circumlocution if necessary. You may take notes in your test book.

Your speaking will be evaluated on the following:

- Overall comprehensibility to a native speaker of German who is not accustomed to dealing with nonnative speakers

- Accuracy and appropriateness of the content

- Presentation of ideas in a related and logical manner, supported by relevant reasons, examples, and details

- Appropriateness of vocabulary

- Accuracy of grammar and pronunciation

- Fluency of delivery and cohesiveness (including use of varied sentence structure and transitional expressions where appropriate)

- Appropriateness for a given task and/or listener

- The extent to which all of the assigned tasks are completed

If you make a mistake and correct it soon afterward, it will not be considered a mistake.

Speaking Section Directions

[The following directions will be heard on the recording.]

This is the Presentational Speaking section of the *German: Productive Language Skills* practice test.

The practice test questions contained on this CD are similar to the kinds of questions you will encounter during an actual test. The test questions you will hear are also printed in the Practice Questions chapter of the study guide.

To simulate actual testing conditions, you might find it helpful to use your own tape recorder to record your responses to the questions presented on this CD. As you listen to the CD, you will notice that pauses have been included in the narration. During the pauses, you may prepare your responses and record your responses on your tape recorder.

To simulate actual testing conditions, do not stop your CD player or your tape recorder during the practice test.

In a moment, you will hear an introductory statement by the person who recorded the German portions of questions one through six. The purpose of this introduction is to familiarize you with the speaker's voice. Listen to the following passage.

> *Die Schüler haben von Montag bis Freitag Unterricht, Feiertage ausgenommen. Am 20. und 27. Januar dieses Jahres fallen die Nachmittagsstunden aus, damit die Lehrer an einer Lehrerkonferenz teilnehmen können.*

For each speaking question in the test, you will be given time to prepare your response and time to record your response.

Listen for the voice on the CD to direct you to answer the question; begin speaking *only* after you have been told to start your response. You will <u>not</u> be given credit for anything recorded during the preparation time.

GO ON TO THE NEXT PAGE

Practice Questions

In this part of the test, you are asked to answer in German two warm-up questions that will not be scored. Listen to the directions for each question.

Practice Question A

Directions: Answer the following question in German. You will have 20 seconds to prepare your response. Then you will have <u>20 seconds</u> to record your response. Remember, do not begin speaking until you hear the words "Answer Practice Question A now."

> *Erzählen Sie, was Sie am Wochenende gerne machen.*

Practice Question B

Directions: Read aloud the following passage in German. Before you are asked to speak, you will have <u>1 minute</u> to read the passage silently. Then you will have <u>1 minute</u> to record your reading of the passage.

> *Sagen Sie nicht, Pflanzen haben im Büro nichts zu suchen. Im Gegenteil: Wo Pflanzen sind, lässt es sich besser arbeiten. Verschiedene Versuchsreihen bestätigen, dass Pflanzen schädliche Stoffe abbauen, die in jedem Gebäude auftreten können. Das Raumklima verbessert sich spürbar. Sie fühlen sich wohler und leben gesünder. Die natürlichen Klimaanlagen bekommen Sie im Garten- und Blumenfachhandel in Ihrer Nähe. Grün arbeiten, besser arbeiten.*

NOTES

GO ON TO THE NEXT PAGE

Question 1

Directions: In this question, you are asked to persuade someone to help you out of a difficult situation. You are required to leave a message in German on a telephone answering machine.

In your message

- include as many details as possible, and

- be as persuasive as possible.

You will have 2 minutes to review the description of the situation and to prepare your message. Then you will have 1 minute to record your message.

> Pretend that you are taking a class at a university in Germany. On the morning of an important exam, you wake up feeling very sick. You call the department office to request to take the exam on another day. However, when you call, the office staff is not in, so you must leave a recorded message in German on the answering machine.

NOTES

GO ON TO THE NEXT PAGE

Question 2

Directions: In this question, you are asked to describe in German the picture in your test book. Do <u>not</u> assume that the person listening can see the picture. In your description, include <u>all</u> of the following details:

- Where this incident is taking place
- What has just occurred
- What is probably going to happen next
- How this situation could have been avoided
- What the woman would probably say (or think) to herself in this situation

Before you are asked to speak, you will have <u>2 minutes</u> to study the picture, go over each bulleted point silently, and think about your response. Then you will have <u>2 minutes</u> to give your response.

NOTES

GO ON TO THE NEXT PAGE

Question 3

Directions: In this question, you are asked to give instructions to a German-speaking friend who wishes to transfer a plant from a pot to the garden. Based <u>only</u> on what you see in the pictures in your test book, give clear, step-by-step instructions in German. In your instructions, include the information presented in <u>all</u> the pictures, but do <u>not</u> assume that the people listening can see the pictures.

Before you are asked to speak, you will have <u>1 minute</u> to study the pictures and think about your instructions. Then you will have <u>2 minutes</u> to speak. Start your instructions with the words "*Mach zuerst die Schublade auf . . .*"

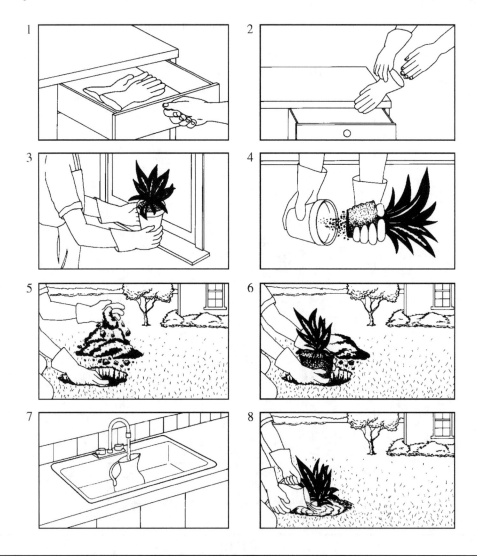

NOTES

GO ON TO THE NEXT PAGE

Question 4

Directions: In this question, you are asked to give your opinion in German. You will have <u>1 minute</u> to prepare your response before you are asked to speak. Then you will have <u>2 minutes</u> to give your response.

Should companies provide day-care facilities for their employees' children?

- State and defend your opinion.
- Use specific examples to support your ideas.

NOTES

GO ON TO THE NEXT PAGE

Question 5

Directions: In this question, you are asked to paraphrase in German a passage after you have heard it read twice in German. You may take notes in your test book during the readings. Before you are asked to speak, you will have <u>1 minute</u> to review any notes you may have taken and to prepare your response. Then you will have <u>1½ minutes</u> to paraphrase the passage.

NOTES

GO ON TO THE NEXT PAGE

Question 6

Directions: In this question, you are asked to give a brief talk in German based on the following situation.

You have been selected to represent your city on a trip to its sister city in Germany. When you arrive in Germany, you are asked to give a brief talk in German to the local chamber of commerce, in which you

- thank the people of the sister city for their hospitality, and
- explain how your trip will help foster good relations between the two cities.

Be sure to observe the appropriate degree of formality for such a talk.

You will have <u>2 minutes</u> to prepare your talk. Then you will have <u>1½ minutes</u> to give your talk.

NOTES

THIS IS THE END OF THE PRESENTATIONAL SPEAKING SECTION.

AT THE ACTUAL TEST ADMINISTRATION, YOU MUST NOT TURN THE PAGE UNTIL YOU ARE TOLD TO DO SO.

END OF RECORDING.

PRESENTATIONAL WRITING SECTION

Questions 7–9
Time—35 minutes

General Directions

There are three questions in this section. Be sure to answer each question completely. For each question, there is a suggested time limit so that you can pace yourself as you work.

Write your answers in German as clearly and neatly as possible on the lined pages provided. Your written German should be acceptable to a wide range of educated native speakers.

You may use the area marked "NOTES" to plan and take notes on each question. These notes will not be used in evaluating your response.

Your writing will be evaluated on the following:

- Overall comprehensibility to a native speaker of German who is not accustomed to dealing with the writing of nonnative learners

- Accuracy and appropriateness of content

- Presentation of ideas in a related and logical manner, supported by relevant reasons, examples, and details

- Appropriateness of vocabulary

- Accuracy of grammar and mechanics (including spelling)

- Cohesiveness (including use of varied sentence structure and transitional expressions where appropriate)

- Appropriateness for a given task and/or reader

- The extent to which all the assigned tasks are completed

Use only the lined pages provided for your response. Although you need not use all of the space on the lined pages provided, you should give as complete a response as possible.

Question 7
(Suggested time—10 minutes)

Directions: In this question, you are asked to write a <u>continuous</u> story in German, based on the six pictures below. In your story, tell what is happening in all six pictures, but do <u>not</u> assume that the reader of the story can see the pictures.

Start the story with the words "*Letzte Woche . . .*"

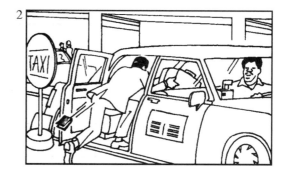

NOTES

Begin your response here.

_____

_____

_____

_____

_____

_____

_____

_____

_____

_____

_____

_____

_____

_____

_____

_____

_____

_____

_____

_____

_____

_____

_____

_____

_____

_____

Question 8
(Suggested time—15 minutes)

Directions: In this question, you are asked to write a formal letter in German based on the following situation.

Pretend that you rented a car while you were on vacation in Germany; you paid for it at the rental agency office in Munich. After you returned from your trip, you received in the mail another bill for the same rental. Write a letter in German to the car-rental agency; explain the situation and try to convince the agency to resolve the problem promptly. Include the following information:

- when and where you rented the car
- a description of the car you rented
- how long you rented the car and at what rate
- how you paid for the car rental
- what the problem is
- what you want the agency to do

Be sure to observe the appropriate degree of formality for such a letter.

NOTES

Begin your response here.

Question 9
(Suggested time—10 minutes)

Directions: In this question, you are asked to write four questions in German based on the following situation.

Pretend that Frau Waldner has just arrived from Austria to start teaching at your school. You are preparing to interview her, on a topic of your choice, for the newsletter of the school's *Deutschklub*. To help focus her thoughts, you plan to give her four of the questions in German that you will be asking her at the interview.

In the lined space provided on the next page, write in complete German sentences the four questions that you wish to ask.

Use a variety of question types. Ask

- one question that requires only a <u>short</u> answer, and

- three questions that require <u>longer</u> answers, such as an opinion, a description, a comparison, or a narration.

Be sure to observe the appropriate degree of formality for the purpose of your questions.

NOTES

Begin your response here.

First Question:

_____

_____

_____

_____

_____

Second Question:

_____

_____

_____

_____

_____

Third Question:

_____

_____

_____

_____

_____

Fourth Question:

_____

_____

_____

_____

_____

STOP.

THIS IS THE END OF THE TEST.

If you finish before time is called, you may go back and review your responses to questions 7–9 only.

Chapter 18

Sample Responses and How They Were Scored—
German: Productive Language Skills

▶ ▶ ▶ ▶ ▶ ▶ ▶ ▶ ▶ ▶ ▶ ▶

This chapter presents transcriptions of actual sample responses to the practice questions in chapter 17 and explanations for the scores the responses received. The sample responses are transcribed with errors. After you have finished answering the practice questions in chapter 17, review your answers in light of the scored sample answers. If you find it difficult to evaluate your answers and assign them scores, ask a colleague, a professor, or a practicing teacher for help.

As discussed in chapter 16, each constructed-response question on the *German: Productive Language Skills* test is scored on a scale from 0 to 4. The scoring guides used to score these questions are reprinted here for your convenience.

General Scoring Guides for the *German: Productive Language Skills* Test

Presentational Speaking Section

This scoring guide is used to evaluate responses in the Presentational Speaking section. The score range is 0 to 4.

4
- Is completely and easily comprehensible, even to an unsympathetic listener[1]
- Gives a complete and entirely accurate, relevant response, with appropriate elaboration, to all (or almost all) parts of the question
- May make sporadic errors, but they rarely or never interfere with communication
  - has strong grammatical control (no errors in basic, high-frequency structures; few errors in complex, low-frequency structures; no marked error patterns)
  - employs a broad, precise vocabulary adequate for almost all topics, with word choice that is generally idiomatic and varied and rarely awkward
  - has overall fluency: speech is occasionally or rarely hesitant, with frequent use of complex sentences and "connectors" when appropriate or required
  - may have a slightly nonnative pronunciation, with few or no phonological errors and no error patterns, but is always comprehensible

3
- Is generally comprehensible, even to an unsympathetic listener, but occasionally requires the listener's effort and interpretation of the intended meaning
- Gives a mostly accurate, relevant response to most parts of the question
- Is likely to make errors and/or error patterns, but they only occasionally interfere with communication
  - has moderate grammatical control (few errors in basic, high-frequency structures; some errors and/or error patterns in complex, low-frequency structures)
  - employs vocabulary adequate for most general topics, with word choice that is often idiomatic but occasionally awkward
  - has considerable fluency: speech is sometimes hesitant, with some use of complex sentences and "connectors" when appropriate or required
  - may have a markedly nonnative pronunciation with some phonological errors and/or error patterns, but is nearly or always comprehensible

---

[1] "Unsympathetic listener" refers to a native speaker of the language who is NOT accustomed to dealing with nonnative learners of the language. An unsympathetic listener does not make any special effort to understand the examinee.

2

- Is somewhat comprehensible to a sympathetic listener,[2] but often requires the listener's effort and interpretation of the intended meaning

- Gives a somewhat accurate, relevant response to some parts of the question

- Produces errors and/or error patterns that may often interfere with communication

  — has limited grammatical control (many errors and/or error patterns in basic, high-frequency structures; no control of complex, low-frequency structures)

  — employs a limited vocabulary, with word choice that is often unidiomatic and awkward

  — has limited fluency, with halting speech and mostly short, simple sentences; suggests inability to use complex sentences and "connectors" when appropriate or required

  — has a markedly nonnative pronunciation, with many phonological errors and/or error patterns, and is sometimes incomprehensible

1

- Is generally incomprehensible, even to a sympathetic listener, despite the listener's constant effort to interpret the intended meaning

- Gives an incomplete and/or mostly inaccurate and/or irrelevant response

- Produces errors and/or error patterns that very often interfere with communication

  — has very little grammatical control (many serious errors and/or error patterns in virtually all structures)

  — employs very little vocabulary, with some "formulaic speech" (memorized phrases, fixed expressions) used inappropriately

  — has virtually no fluency: speech is fragmentary and halting, interrupted often by long pauses and repetitions, and consists only of isolated words, memorized phrases, and fixed expressions

  — has a markedly nonnative pronunciation, with many serious phonological errors and/or error patterns, and is very often incomprehensible

0

- Is completely incomprehensible, even to a sympathetic listener, despite the listener's constant effort to interpret the intended meaning

- Gives an entirely inaccurate, irrelevant response or fails to respond at all

- Produces errors and/or error patterns that always interfere with communication

  — has no grammatical control (many serious errors and/or error patterns in all structures)

  — employs no vocabulary, not even "formulaic speech" (memorized phrases and fixed expressions)

  — has no fluency

  — has a markedly nonnative pronunciation and is always incomprehensible

[2] "Sympathetic listener" refers to a native speaker of the language who is accustomed to dealing with nonnative learners of the language. A sympathetic listener tends to make a conscious effort to understand the examinee, interpreting his or her speech for its intended meaning.

Presentational Writing Section

This scoring guide is used to evaluate responses in the Presentational Writing Section. The score range is 0–4.

4
- Is completely and easily comprehensible, even to an unsympathetic reader[3]

- Gives a complete and entirely accurate, relevant response, with appropriate elaboration, to all (or almost all) parts of the question

- May make sporadic errors, but they rarely or never interfere with communication

  — has strong grammatical control (no errors in basic, high-frequency structures; few errors in complex, low-frequency structures; no marked error patterns)

  — employs a broad, precise vocabulary adequate for almost all topics, with word choice that is generally idiomatic and varied and rarely awkward

  — has very few or no errors in mechanics, which rarely or never interfere with meaning

  — is completely coherent and well organized, with frequent use of complex sentences and "connectors" when appropriate or required

  — uses language that is appropriate for the intended task and/or audience

3
- Is generally comprehensible, even to an unsympathetic reader, but occasionally requires the reader's effort and interpretation of the intended meaning

- Gives a mostly accurate, relevant response to most parts of the question

- Is likely to produce errors and/or error patterns, but they only occasionally interfere with communication

  — has moderate grammatical control (few errors in basic, high-frequency structures; some errors and/or error patterns in complex, low-frequency structures)

  — employs a vocabulary adequate for most general topics, with word choice that is often idiomatic but occasionally awkward

  — makes some errors in mechanics (spelling, punctuation, etc.), but they only occasionally interfere with meaning

  — is generally coherent and organized, with some complex sentences and "connectors" when appropriate or required

  — is likely to use language that is appropriate for the intended task and/or audience

2
- Is somewhat comprehensible to a sympathetic reader,[4] but often requires the reader's effort and interpretation of the intended meaning

- Gives a somewhat accurate, relevant response to some parts of the question

- Produces errors and/or error patterns that may often interfere with communication

---

[3] "Unsympathetic reader" refers to a native speaker of the language who is NOT accustomed to dealing with nonnative learners of the language. An unsympathetic reader does not make any special effort to understand the examinee.

[4] "Sympathetic reader" refers to a native speaker of the language who is accustomed to dealing with nonnative learners of the language. A sympathetic reader tends to make a conscious effort to understand the examinee, interpreting his or her writing for its intended meaning.

— has limited grammatical control (many errors and/or error patterns in basic, high-frequency structures; no control of complex, low-frequency structures)

— employs a limited vocabulary, with word choice that is often unidiomatic and awkward

— makes several errors in mechanics (spelling, punctuation, etc.), which may often interfere with meaning

— is partly or often incoherent, with little evidence of organization; suggests inability to use complex sentences and "connectors" when appropriate or required

— is likely to use language that is inappropriate for the intended task and/or audience

1 ■ Is generally incomprehensible, even to a sympathetic reader, despite the reader's constant effort to interpret the intended meaning

■ Gives an incomplete, mostly inaccurate and/or irrelevant response

■ Produces errors and/or error patterns that very often interfere with communication

— has very little grammatical control (many serious errors and/or error patterns in virtually all structures)

— employs very little vocabulary, with some "formulaic language" (memorized phrases, fixed expressions) used inappropriately

— makes many serious errors in mechanics (spelling, punctuation, etc.) in virtually all structures, which very often interfere with meaning

— is mostly incoherent, with very little or no evidence of organization

— uses language that is inappropriate for the intended task and/or audience

0 ■ Is completely incomprehensible, even to a sympathetic reader, despite the reader's constant effort to interpret the intended meaning

■ Gives an entirely inaccurate, irrelevant response or fails to respond at all

■ Produces errors and/or error patterns that always interfere with communication

— has no grammatical control (many serious errors and/or error patterns in all structures)

— employs no vocabulary, not even "formulaic language" (memorized phrases and fixed expressions)

— makes many serious errors in mechanics (spelling, punctuation, etc.) in all structures, which always interfere with meaning

— is completely incoherent

Presentational Speaking Section
Constructed-Response Question 1—Sample Responses

We will now look at three scored responses to the first constructed-response practice question ("Sick on the Day of the Exam") and see comments from the scoring leader about why each response received the score it did.

Sample Response 1: Score of 4

> Hallo, ich bin Stefanie Lessing und ich bin eine Student in Ihren Vorlesung. Und ich wollte heute anrufen, weil ich sehr krank geworden bin. Und ich habe heute eine Klausur, aber ich fürchte, wenn ick nick konzentrieren kann, werde ich durchfallen. Ick bin den ganzen Tag heute zu Hause und ich hoffe, dass jemand zurückrufen konnen, damit ich noch ein Termin machen konn, kann, wenn ich das die Klausur schreiben kann. Ich hoffe, dass, ich hoffe, dass Sie meinen Situation verstehen und wenn ich mich erholen, kann ich die Klausur nochmal schreiben. Vielen Dank.

Commentary on Sample Response That Earned a Score of 4

The candidate is asked to leave a message in German on a telephone answering machine explaining why the exam has to be rescheduled. The tasks are to include as many details as possible and be persuasive in getting a new date for taking the exam. This speech sample is clearly comprehensible in spite of several ending errors (e.g., *Student* instead of *Studentin* or *ein Termin* instead of *einen Termin* and a few nonnative pronunciation errors: "Ick" or "nick"). The candidate is very persuasive when asking for an understanding of her situation and also offers a solution. The candidate shows strong grammatical control in basic sentence structures (e.g., *Und ich wollte heute anrufen, weil ich sehr krank geworden bin.*). However, in more complex structures, errors do occur (e.g., *Ich hoffe, dass, ich hoffe, dass Sie meinen Situation verstehen und wenn ich mich erholen [erholt habe], kann ich die Klausur nochmal schreiben [Werde ich die Klausur schreiben].*) Overall, the candidate clearly demonstrates proficiency.

Sample Response 2: Score of 3

> Guten Morgen, hier ist Erika Freitag. Ich bin ins Herr Schmidts Inglishklasse. Heute fühl ich sehr kranke. Mein Bauch tut mir weh. Es ist sehr schlecht. Ich denke, dass vielleicht ich nach dem Krankhaus gehen müssen. Aber heute haben wir eine Prufung und ich kann absolut nicht es machen. Bitte geben mir eine andere Prufung später. Das, die Prufung ist sehr sehr wichtig und ich mus es machen, aber ich kann nicht heut. Bitte rufen mir zuruch und dann werde ich ein andere Tage es machen. Danke.

Commentary on Sample Response That Earned a Score of 3

This is a generally comprehensible response, with moderate grammatical control. The sentence *Ich denke, dass vielleicht ich nach dem Krankhaus gehen müssen* can be understood, but has two errors: subject-verb agreement and structure of the subordinate clause. The correct sentence should have been *Ich denke, dass ich vielleicht ins Krankhaus gehen muss*. The candidate includes all assigned tasks and speaks with considerable fluency but without trying to use more complex sentences. The choice of vocabulary is adequate. Overall, this response suggests proficiency.

Sample Response 3: Score of 2

> Hallo, ich heiße Ute Nemig und ich bin seine deutsche Unterlüg und es tut mir Leid, aber ich bin krank. Ich bin sehr krank, mein Tag ist schlecht auf meiner Kopfschmerzen auch. Ich kann nicht die Prüfung machen, ich bin so krank, es tut mir Leid, und ich will, wellen ich werde Sie an ruft an und da wir eine andere Seit für die Prüfung zu machen. Danke.

Commentary on Sample Response That Earned a Score of 2

The short spoken sample is somewhat comprehensible but requires the listener's effort and interpretation of the intended meaning, especially in the sentence *Ich bin sehr krank, mein Tag ist schlecht auf meiner Kopfschmerzen auch*. Grammatical control is limited (e.g., . . . *und ich will, wellen ich werde Sie an ruft an und da wir eine andere Seit für die Prüfung zu machen*). Even though the vocabulary is adequate for the task, the choice of words is limited. Overall, the speaker is somewhat comprehensible. Errors often interfere with communication. The response suggests a lack of proficiency.

Constructed-Response Question 2—Sample Responses

We will now look at four scored responses to the second constructed-response practice question ("Stuck in the Elevator Door") and see comments from the scoring leader about why each response received the score it did.

Sample Response 1: Score of 4

> Es sieht so aus, als ob diese Situation in einem Gebäude stattfindet und dass darin diese Frau vielleicht arbeitet. Es konnte vielleicht ein Officegebäude sein und es sieht so aus, dass die Frau viel zu spät ist und es sehr eilig hat. Sie passt nicht auf, die Door des Aufzugs schließt und ihr Kleid steckt fest. Sie trägt sehr viele Sachen, sehr viele Bücher und noch eine Tasche. Sie ist sehr traurig, weil sie entweder ihr Kleid verreißt oder jemanden rufen muss, der ihr helfen kann. Oder sie muss warten, bis die Door wieder aufgeht, weil sie den Knopf sieht aber nicht drücken kann. Jetzt kommt sie noch später zum Meeting. Sie sagt sich selber: Wie dumm, dass ich hier stecke, dumme Door, ging viel zu schnell zu. Ich hätte nicht bis zur letzten Minute warten sollen und der Mann hätte mir auch helfen können.

Commentary on Sample Response That Earned a Score of 4

The response is complete and comprehensible. All five parts of the prompt have been addressed. If the candidate had not repeated her first thought twice, some more elaboration would have been possible; nevertheless, one could easily recreate this picture from the description given. The response shows strong grammatical control in *Es sieht so aus, als ob diese Situation in einem Gebäude stattfindet* or *Sie ist sehr traurig, weil sie entweder ihr Kleid verreißt oder jemanden rufen muss, der ihr helfen kann,* and especially in the last sentence, *Ich hätte nicht bis zur letzten Minute warten sollen und der Mann hätte mir auch helfen können.* Vocabulary is quite broad, but sometimes a bit awkward as in *dass darin.* It should be *dass diese Frau dort vielleicht.* The word *traurig* is not quite idiomatic; a better choice would have been *entsetzt.* Instead of saying *ihr Kleid verreißt,* one would say *ihr Kleid zerreißen muss.* The only repeated error is that "door" is used instead of *Tür,* but even an unsympathetic listener can understand what is meant. The candidate speaks fluently and very clearly, and the errors are sporadic and never interfere with communication. The candidate cleary demonstrates proficiency in describing this picture.

Sample Response 2: Score of 3

> Da sieht man ein Mädchen oder eine Dame mit ein langes Jacke und ihre langes Jacke ist zwischen den Turen eines Lifts in einem Haus. Sie hat lockige Haare und sie tragt, sie tragt viele Bucher, Papiere in den Handen und sie kann nicht gehen, weil ihre Jacke ist zwischen die Türen und die Turen haben jetzt noch nicht geoffnet. Ein Mann ging vorbei und ich denke, dass die Dame muss bis die Tur des Lifts offnet warten. Dann kann sie gehen. Sie sieht nicht glücklich, nicht froh aus. Sie weiss nicht was tun. Sie sieht die Knopfe. Wie kann ich sie drucken, dass die Turen offnen?

Commentary on Sample Response That Earned a Score of 3

The candidate tries to describe the situation depicted. There are five points that should have been addressed. Most of the assigned tasks are included, but the candidate does not talk about how this situation could have been avoided. Grammatical control is moderate. The candidate speaks with considerabe fluency. Sometimes, however, the candidate is hesitant and quite often avoids using the umlaut, as in *tragt, Turen, Bucher, Handen,* and *offnet* (which should be *trägt, Türen, Bücher, Händen,* and *öffnet*). This, however, only occasionally requires interpretation of the intended meaning. While basic structures are mostly correct, complex structures seem to cause a problem, as demonstrated in *Ein Mann ging vorbei und ich denke, dass die Dame muss bis die Tur des Lifts offnet warten.* The correct sentence should have been *Ein Mann ging vorbei und ich denke, dass die Dame jetzt doch warten muss, bis sich die Tür wieder öffnet.* The candidate tries to pack too much into the second sentence, thus making it an awkward run-on sentence. Adjectival endings in sentence one should have been corrected to *mit einer langen Jacke und ihre lange Jacke.* Overall, the response suggests proficiency but does not clearly demonstrate it.

Sample Response 3: Score of 2

> Die Frau ist bei ihrer Arbeit und sie ist in dem Ometer und sie hat auf, sie kam aus dem Elevator und ihre Jacke hat, ist, hat gestoppt und sie tragen, sie trägt viel und vielleicht sie sagen, was muss ich tun? Ich, meine Jacke ist, meine Jacke stuckt und vielleicht ich muss meine Jacke abnehmen und dann ich kann die Tur öffen und dann ich kann meine Jacke holen. ——— (long pause) Vielleicht als ich nicht so viele getragen, meine Jacke nicht stucken.

Commentary on Sample Response That Earned a Score of 2

Without seeing the picture that the candidate tries to describe, even a sympathetic listener would have trouble understanding what the speaker is trying to say. Errors like *ihre Jacke hat gestoppt* and *Vielleicht als ich nicht so viele getragen, meine Jacke nicht stucken* definitely interfere with communication. There is limited grammatical control, as in *sie trägt viel und vielleicht sie sagen, was muss ich tun*. The elements are all there, but the structure is unacceptable. The vocabulary is often unidiomatic (e.g., *stucken, Ometer*). The speech is halting and markedly nonnative. This response definitely suggests a lack of proficiency.

Sample Response 4: Score of 1

> Bei meiner Arbeit, mein Kleid, mein Kleider in die Aufzug stehen bleiben und ich hoffe, dass jemand will mir helfen. Wenn ich komme schneller aus die Aufzug, mein Kleider wollen, woll, will nicht stehen bleiben. Ahh, ich denke da, ich wünsche da, mein Kleider woll nicht in die Aufzug stehen bleiben.

Commentary on Sample Response That Earned a Score of 1

The candidate cannot describe the picture. The candidate basically uses only four words (*Kleid, Kleider, Aufzug,* and *stehenbleiben*) and tries to rearrange them but is unsuccessful. The entire short sample is incomprehensible, and errors interfere with communication at all times. This response clearly demonstrates lack of proficiency.

Constructed-Response Question 3—Sample Responses

We will now look at three scored responses to the third constructed-response practice question ("Placing a Plant in the Ground") and see comments from the scoring leader about why each response received the score it did.

Sample Response 1: Score of 3

> Mach zuerst die Schublade auf, nimm die Handschuhe aus der Schublade und zieh sie an. Jetzt bist du fertig zum pflanzen. Dann wegtrage Blumentopf aus Fenster und nimm die Pflanze aus dem Topf. Geh in Garten, grab ein tief Loch und tu Pflanze rein. Fülle Topf mit Wasser in Küche. Geh in Garten und gieße Wasser um Pflanze im Loch.

Commentary on Sample Response That Earned a Score of 3

Even though the response is quite short, all pictures are described; however, there is no appropriate elaboration. The candidate gives instructions to a friend and uses the correct form (i.e., the informal command form). There are hardly any errors in the sentence structure except in *Dann wegtrage Blumentopf aus Fenster* and *Fülle Topf mit Wasser in Küche*. The correct sentences should have been *Dann nimm den Blumentopf vom Fenster (brett) und trage ihn weg* and *Geh in die Küche und fülle eine Gießkanne (einen Topf) mit Wasser*. Articles are often missing, as in *in Garten* and *in Küche*, thus making it difficult for the listener to follow without making an effort to interpret what was said. The vocabulary is adequate. Overall, this response suggests proficiency, but does not clearly demonstrate it.

Sample Response 2: Score of 2

> Mach zuerst *die Schublade auf, nimm die Handschuh, mach und daaaa mach sie an die Hände, nehm die Pflanze in Fenster und nehm die Pflanze selbst aus Topf.* Mach Sie ein Loch am Hof, mach Sie die Pflanze im Graben. Mach Wasser ins Eimer und gieß des Wasser über dem Pflanzen.

Commentary on Sample Response That Earned a Score of 2

Without being able to see the six picture frames, even a sympathetic listener cannot imagine what is taking place based on the response. The candidate has been asked to give instructions to a friend about how to place a plant into the ground. Short sentences using the informal imperative would have been correct. In the second sentence, the candidate switches to the formal address of *Sie* but does not use the correct verb form with it. Grammatical control is limited and so is the choice of vocabulary. The candidate could have varied the choice of verbs more. Instead of *daaaa mach sie an die Hände*, the candidate could have said *zieh sie an*. Instead of *Mach Wasser ins Eimer*, *füll den Eimer mit Wasser* would have been a better choice. In fact, the candidate uses only three different verbs: *mach*, *nehm-nimm*, and *gieß*. The candidate also demonstrates very little command of prepositions: either the preposition is incorrect or the article following the preposition is missing or also incorrect (e.g., *in Fenster* should have been either *aus dem Fenster* or *im Fenster*; *aus Topf* needed the article *dem*; *über dem Pflanzen* should have been *über die Pflanzen*). Overall, the response suggests a lack of proficiency in describing this series of pictures.

Sample Response 3: Score of 1

> Mach zuerst *die Schuhba, Schublade auf und danach nehmen die Schublade und und stellt die Schublade in die in die in die Door.* Mach zuerst die Schublade auf, danacht nehmen die Pflanzen und stellt die Pflanzen in der Nähe von auf dem Fenster den Fenster. Offen der die Fenster und nehmen die Pflanzen auf der Pflanzenhalter und geht draußen und ein Hol gemacht und stellt die Pflanzen in die Hol und finden Wasser und nehmen das Wasser und auf die Pflanzen spillen.

Commentary on Sample Response That Earned a Score of 1

This response clearly demonstrates a lack of proficiency. The candidate is not able to describe what is going on in the picture series. The candidate starts out with the informal imperative, *Mach zuerst die Schuhba, Schublade auf*, but does not continue with it. Despite the listener's effort to interpret the intended meaning, the speech sample is incomprehensible. There is very little grammatical control. The speaker also does not have the vocabulary to give instructions about how to place a plant in the ground. The speech is fragmentary and halting and the test taker uses English words ("hole" and "spillen" from "spill") to describe what is depicted in two of the frames.

Constructed-Response Question 4—Sample Responses

We will now look at three scored responses to the fourth constructed-response practice question ("Daycare for Employees") and see comments from the scoring leader about why the responses received the scores they did.

Sample Response 1: Score of 4

> Ja ich glaube schon, dass Firmen mmmm, einen Kindergarten für die Kinder der Angestellten haben sollten. Ich sage das, da die Kinder ja irgendwo hingehen müssen, wenn die Eltern gehen arbeiten. Wenn man erwartet, dass die zu Hause bleiben, dann müssen die Eltern auch da bleiben und dann werden sie arbeitslos oder sie müssen Geld für babysittern geben. Ich glaube es ist auch wichtig für die mmm Erziehung der Kinder mit anderen zusammen sein. Die Kinder wollen lernen, und es hilft, wenn die auch mit andern Kinder sind. Die müssen dann mmm auch lernen wie sie andere Kinder behandeln müssen. Später können sie dann bessere Entscheidungen treffen,wenn sie älter sind und das hilft sicher den Eltern. Wenn die Kinder krank sind, können die Eltern sich auf die Arbeit konzentrieren und das tun, was die Firma von ihnen verlangt, weil sie wissen, dass die Kinder sorgen. Ich glaube auch, dass es gut ist, wann Vater oder Mutter in Pause das kranke Kind im Kindergarten sehen kann und sehen kann, dass das Kind gut gesorgt ist. mmm Vielleicht sollen die Angestellten etwas Geld geben müssen für den Kindergarten...

Commentary on Sample Response That Earned a Score of 4

The candidate is asked to state and defend an opinion on the question of whether companies should provide day-care facilities. Examples are supposed to support the ideas put forth. The candidate includes all of the assigned tasks with enough elaboration to make the point. The response is very comprehensible and requires interpretation of the intended meaning only in the following: *weil sie wissen, dass die Kinder sorgen.* The candidate may have wanted to say *weil sie wissen, dass die Kinder versorgt sind.* The vocabulary is well chosen; however, in some cases (e.g., *dann müssen die Eltern auch da bleiben und dann werden sie arbeitslos oder sie müssen Geld für babysittern geben*), the candidate should have explained his point a little more in detail and not tried to put everything into one sentence. A clearer sentence would have been *Wenn man erwartet, dass die Kinder zu Hause bleiben, dann muss mindestens einer von den Eltern mit den Kindern bleiben, das hieße, dass einer arbeitslos ist oder die Eltern müssen Geld für einen privaten Kindergarten bezahlen.* The grammatical control is extremely strong, as in the sentence *Wenn die Kinder krank sind, können die Eltern sich auf die Arbeit konzentrieren und das tun, was die Firma von ihnen verlangt, weil sie wissen, dass* . . . There are no errors in basic structures and only a few errors in complex sentence structures. There is no pattern of errors, but there are some minor mistakes, as in *mit anderen zusammen sein* (it should have been *mit anderen zusammenzusein*), *wenn die Eltern gehen arbeiten* (the verb-position should have been reversed to *arbeiten gehen*), or *wann* instead of *wenn*. However, these do not detract from the overall clear communication. The candidate speaks quite fluently with a very slight nonnative pronunciation pattern. Overall, this response clearly demonstrates proficiency in giving an opinion and supporting it with specific examples.

Sample Response 2: Score of 3

> Wenn in einer Familie beide Eltern arbeiten, ist es oft schwer zu entscheiden, was tun mit Kinder. Kinder können allein nicht sein im Tag, aber ein Babysitter ist teuer. Unternehmungen sollen einrichten Kindergarten für arbeitende Kinder, so dass die Eltern sorgelos auf Arbeit konzentrieren, da sie wissen, dass ihre Kinder versorgt gut sind. Ein glücklich Kind gibt der Firma glücklich Arbeiter. Die Arbeiter arbeiten besser, wenn sie wissen, wo ihre Kinder sind und sie müssen nicht früh weggehen, Kinder zu holen.
>
> Ich glaube, ein Kindergarten in der Arbeitsstelle ist gutes Management.

Commentary on Sample Response That Earned a Score of 3

Even though this response is not very long, the candidate states and defends her opinion well and includes at least two examples to support her ideas. Generally this response is comprehensible and requires only an occasional effort by the listener to interpret the intended meaning (e.g., *arbeitende Kinder*; the candidate most likely meant to say *für Kinder ihrer Arbeiter* or *Ein glücklich Kind gibt der Firma glücklich Arbeiter*). The candidate tried to put too much into one sentence. Sometimes the chosen vocabulary is a bit awkward, as in *sorgelos* (a better choice would have been *so dass die Eltern sich, ohne sich sorgen zu müssen, auf ihre Arbeit konzentrieren*). Sentence structure is generally good, with some errors in more complex sentences, as in *dass ihre Kinder versorgt gut sind*. The correct structure should have been *dass ihre Kinder gut versorgt sind*. Minor errors, as in *Ein glücklich Kind . . . glücklich Arbeiter (ein glückliches Kind, glückliche Arbeiter)* or *sie müssen nicht früh weggehen, Kinder zu holen (sie müssen nicht früh weggehen, um ihre Kinder abzuholen)*, do not detract from the general comprehensibility of the response. Overall, this response suggests proficiency in discussing the stated question.

Sample Response 3: Score of 2

> Ich denke dass Firme soll dass Firme Kinder solle für die die Leute das sie zahlen für arbeiten geben. Es ist wichtig, weil viele haben Kinder aber sie mochten auch arbeiten. mmm Und es ist auch teuer, wenn die wenn die eine Sitzer mmm haben. Also es ist es ist wichtig dass Leute mm haben diese Fasilitäten für ihre Arbeiter. mm Als ich ein Kind war meine Mutter hat nicht gearbeiten, aber, aber ich ich hoffe, wann ich haben Kinder mm wird meine , meine , mm Chef mein Chef ein Fasilitäten für ihn haben wenn ick arbeiten gehe und es ist besser für die Firma, ich komme zu Arbeit. Ja wann sie Day-care haben, dann komme ich jeden Tag und vielleicht wenn ich eine Sitzer hätte, mm vielleicht das Sitzer ist krank einmal und ich kann nicht kommen zu Arbeit oder ich kann nicht bezahlen ein Sitzer. Ein Sitzer ist zu teuer. Also ich kann nicht garnicht arbeiten ich muss bleiben Hause und mein Kinder versorgt. Firmen es ist besser vor mich und vor die Firmen Kindergarten haben.

Commentary on Sample Response That Earned a Score of 2

After a rough beginning (*Ich denke dass Firme soll dass Firme Kinder solle für die die Leute das sie zahlen für arbeiten geben*), the candidate settles down, and one hopes that the beginning of the next sentence is the beginning of an explanation. The response is somewhat comprehensible but often requires the listener's interpretation of the intended meaning. There is not one sentence that does not have more than one error. The word *Sitzer*, one would assume, is meant to mean "babysitter," but the word *Sitzer* does not exist in the German language. The candidate has some knowledge of the structure of the language but cannot put all the puzzle pieces together correctly. For example, in the sentence *Es ist wichtig, weil viele haben Kinder aber sie mochten auch arbeiten*, the subject-verb agreement is correct, but the placement of the verbs is incorrect. The correct sentence would have been *Es ist wichtig, weil viele Kinder haben, aber auch arbeiten möchten*. Overall, because of the many errors throughout the response and the often awkward word choice, a lot of interpretation is required, and therefore the response suggests a lack of proficiency.

Constructed-Response Question 5—Sample Responses

We will now look at two scored responses to the fifth constructed-response practice question ("Eating Contest") and see comments from the scoring leader about why each response received the score it did.

Sample Response 1: Score of 4

> Herr Meier hat ein neues Restaurant geöffnet und wollte es bekannt machen. Er hat sich überlegt, wie er das machen konnten. Er hat endlig entschieden, dass er eine Wettbewerb in Würstessen haben werden. Also derjenige, die der meisten Würsten in einer Stunde essen konnten, werden dann einen Preis finden und der Preis war ein kostenlos Essen für zwei in seinem Restaurant. Er hat so diese Wettbewerb in der Zeitung und im Radio bewerbt. Er hat funfundzwanzig Personen sind gekommen und einer war eine sehr dicker Mann und die andere die anderen war eine dreizehnjähriger Jungen und auch ein Deutschprofessor, der in der Nähe wohnte. Also es gab auch viele Zuschauer und Zeitungsreporter. Sie waren also auch ganz wichtig für Herr Meier. Also am Ende hat der Junge schließlich gewonnen. Und danach wollte er wissen, wo was zur Nachtisch gab.

Commentary on Sample Response That Earned a Score of 4

This response is completely comprehensible and does not require any interpretation. The speaker includes all major points. The spoken paragraph is a very good example of how to paraphrase a longer paragraph. The vocabulary used is very precise and describes the situation perfectly. The only unidiomatic word choice can be found in the following sentence: *Er hat so diese Wettbewerb in der Zeitung und im Radio bewerbt*. Instead of *bewerbt*, a better verb to use would have been *angekündigt*. The candidate's speech is occasionally hesitant and is marred by some incorrect endings and very few phonological errors (e.g., *Würstessen* instead of *Würsteessen* or *Wurstessen*). Nevertheless, this spoken paragraph clearly demonstrates the candidate's proficiency in German.

Sample Response 2: Score of 1

> Viele Personen haben in ein neues Restaurant geessen, gegessen. Die Name war Herr Meier's Restaurant. Viele Mensch waren da. Deutsche Professor, viele Zeitungsreporter, und vielen Junge. Zu essen, ja es gibt Wurst und es gibt Wurst und ein rädio war gestellt. Fertig.

Commentary on Sample Response That Earned a Score of 1

The speaker starts out in a very promising way with only one grammatical error in the first sentence. The candidate even partially corrects the statement *Viele Personen haben in ein neues Restaurant geessen, gegessen.* However, the response falls apart immediately afterward. The few short phrases are all inaccurate. The candidate covers only the very beginning of the story. Because of the brevity of the spoken piece, no level can be determined. Therefore, this response clearly demonstrates a lack of proficiency.

Constructed-Response Question 6—Sample Responses

We will now look at three scored responses to the sixth constructed-response practice question ("Visit to Sister City") and see comments from the scoring leader about why each response received the score it did.

Sample Response 1: Score of 4

> Ich möchte die Leute unserer Schwesterstadt ganz herzlich für die Höflichkeit und Gutmutigkeit bedanken. aaaa Alle die Leute, all die Einwohner meiner Stadt aaa interessieren sich sehr für Ihre Stadt und sie warten auf meine Wiederkehr, um zu lernen um ganz mit mir zu erleben, was ich hier erfahren habe. Und wir glauben in meiner Stadt, dass wir wirklich, aaa Glück haben, dass diese Verbindung zwischen unseren zwei Städten gemacht worden ist, weil wir wir lernen viel voneinander und besonders besser unsere Kinder einander besuchen können. Zum Beispiel mein Sohn war letztes Jahr hier und hat mit einer Familie, die Familie Spitt, gewohnt und wenn er wiedergekehrt ist, hat er seinen Freundin überzeugt, dass sie auch ein/ eine solche Reise machen soll.

Commentary on Sample Response That Earned a Score of 4

The candidate has been asked to represent a city, thank people for their hospitality, and explain how this trip will foster good relations between the two cities. This speaker includes almost all given tasks. The candidate's grammatical control is quite strong, but errors do occur, especially when the candidate chooses vocabulary that is correct in terms of content but not idiomatically used, as in *Ich möchte die Leute unserer Schwesterstadt ganz herzlich für die Höflichkeit und Gutmutigkeit bedanken.* The candidate should have said either *Ich möchte mich bei den Leuten . . . bedanken* or *Ich möchte den Leuten . . . danken.* The following sentence, *Alle die Leute, all die Einwohner meiner Stadt aaa interessieren sich sehr für Ihre Stadt und sie warten auf meine Wiederkehr, um zu lernen um ganz mit mir zu erleben, was ich hier erfahren habe,* is a great example of how well the candidate handles complex structures. The speaker's choice of vocabulary fits the tasks well most of the time. Overall, the candidate speaks very well and the listener does not have to make an effort to interpret what is being said. This response clearly demonstrates proficiency.

Sample Response 2: Score of 2

> Ich danke Sie unsere Schwesterstadt für wie nett Sie sind. Wir danken Sie viel. Es ist sehr nett, was du hast gemacht. Es ist auch sehr gut, dass ich follow hier. Diese Reise wäre es besser zwischen unsere Stadten machen. Wir kahn in, wir kahn, (long pause) wir kahn die anderen Stadte besser verstehen und besser kennen. Das is natürlich sehr gut.

Commentary on Sample Response That Earned a Score of 2

The candidate is trying to respond to the tasks given but is only somewhat comprehensible, even to a sympathetic listener. The candidate speaks in very simple sentences. Apart from the last sentence, all sentences are filled with errors. A great deal of interpretation is required to determine whether the speaker even includes some of the assigned tasks. The speaker's pronunciation is markedly nonnative, with many phonological errors. Overall, this response very strongly suggests a lack of proficiency.

Sample Response 3: Score of 1

> Danke fur den Einladen. mmm. Danke fur...den Wohnung und Essen, mmm ich bin fröhlich , ich will hoffen Sie, und ich will...will...Sie nach Amerika einladen.

Commentary on Sample Response That Earned a Score of 1

The candidate produces only isolated words and ends with a memorized phrase: *Ich will Sie nach Amerika einladen*. There is little, if any, grammatical control. The response is generally incomprehensible and therefore clearly demonstrates a lack of proficiency.

Presentational Writing Section
Constructed-Response Question 7—Sample Responses

We will now look at three scored responses to the seventh constructed-response practice question ("Returned Wallet") and see comments from the scoring leader about why each response received the score it did.

Sample Response 1: Score of 4

> Letze Woche ist ein Mann aus dem U-bahn gestiegen und direkt zum Taxi gegangen. Aber beim Taxi einsteigen ist seine Brieftasche aus seiner Jacke gefallen. Schade, daß er das nicht bemerkt hat. Glücklicherweise ist eine Frau vorbeigekommen. Sie sah die Brieftasche und nahm sie mit zur Bahninformationsstelle. Da gab sie die ab. Später rief der Mann, der die Brieftasche verloren hat, die Informationsstelle an und hat sich gefreut als er hörte, daß die Brieftasche da war. Er ist sofort hingefahren um die abzuholen.

Commentary on Sample Response That Earned a Score of 4

This short paragraph describes a story for the reader. The reader definitely can imagine what is happening, even without seeing the six picture frames. Occasional small errors (*Letze* or *beim Taxi einsteigen*) or wrong tenses (as in *verloren hat* instead of *hatte*) do not interfere with communication. The word choice is generally idiomatic (*Brieftasche, glücklicherweise*). The candidate clearly demonstrates proficiency in writing in German, especially when one reads the second-to-last sentence *(Später rief der Mann, der die Brieftasche verloren hat, die Informationsstelle an und hat sich gefreut als er hörte, daß die Brieftasche da war)*. Overall, the response clearly demonstrates proficiency.

Sample Response 2: Score of 3

> Ein Mensch stieg aus der U-bahn und nimm einen Taxi. Als er die Taxitür öffnete und herein einstieg, fell dein Geldbeutel am Boden. Der Herr bemerkte das nicht. Eine Frau, die an der selben Straße ging spazieren, fand den Geldbeutel und geht nach dem Informationbüro. Sie gab es der Frau, die in diesem Büro arbeitet. Später, ruft der Herr den Büro an, um seinen Geldbeutel zu suchen. Er war froh, das der Geldbeutel dort war und es geht (vielleicht fuhr) zu diesem Informationsbüro um seinen Geldbeutel zu benommen.

Commentary on Sample Response That Earned a Score of 3

The story is generally comprehensible but requires some interpretation on the part of the reader, especially when the writer uses the wrong possessive pronoun—*dein* instead of *sein*—or the wrong personal pronoun—*es* instead of *er*. The candidate shows moderate grammatical control and few errors in basic structures (*Der Herr bemerkte das nicht. Sie gab es der Frau, die in diesem Büro arbeitet* is fine, but then there is *fell dein Geldbeutel am Boden*). More errors appear in complex structures (e.g., *Als er die Taxitür öffnete und herein einstieg, fel* or *Er war froh, das der Geldbeutel dort war und es geht [vielleicht fuhr] zu diesem Informationsbüro um seinen Geldbeutel zu benommen*). Some of the words chosen are awkward, as in *benommen* instead of *bekommen* or *herein einstieg*. Overall, this response suggests proficiency.

Sample Response 3: Score of 0

> Letzte Woche von mir began es tage in a hurry. Er tat his wallet wenn er in einem Taxi fahren. Ein Freund er wallet gefundt dan gebringt to information in der Bahnhof. Der man von die Information und fand es wallet.

Commentary on Sample Response That Earned a Score of 0

These four sentences completely fail to communicate. If one cannot look at the six picture frames, one does not know what is going on. There is no grammatical control, and the vocabulary is minimal and interspersed with English words. The first sentence, *Letzte Woche von mir began es tage in a hurry*, cannot be interpreted even by a very sympathetic reader. Overall, this response clearly demonstrates a lack of proficiency.

Constructed-Response Question 8—Sample Responses

We will now look at three scored responses to the eighth constructed-response practice question ("Double Charged for Car Rental") and see comments from the scoring leader about why each response received the score it did.

Sample Response 1: Score of 4

> Mertz Rental-
>
> Ich schreibe Ihnen weil ich ein kleines Problem habe. Am 4. Juni bis zum 10 Juni habe ich von Ihnen ein Auto geliehen. Es war ein 1996 VW Golf—dunkel-blau. Ich hatte es nur für die sechs Tage in München und bezahlte 500 Dm da für. Sie haben es von meiner Bisa kredit karte genommen. Als ich wieder zu Hause war, fand ich im Briefkasten ein Brief, der sagte, das ich noch die 500 Dm bezahlen mußte. Ich bekamm aber auch von Bisa ein Brief, der sagte, daß ich es schon bezahlt habe. Ich hoffte daß Ihrer Brief ein misverständnes war, und bezahle kein Geld mehr. Wenn es noch Probleme gibt, rufen sie mich bitte an ((555) 846-9170)
>
> > Vielen Dank,
> > Kristina Dienstag

Commentary on Sample Response That Earned a Score of 4

The assignment was to write a <u>formal</u> letter in German, based on a given situation. Six points had to be included in the letter: a date, a description, a time frame, means of payment, the problem, and a solution to the problem. The candidate includes all assigned tasks with enough elaboration for the reader to understand what has happened. The writer also observes the correct level of formality, using the formal address *Sie* instead of the informal *Du*. There are no errors in basic high-frequency structures *(Es war ein 1996 VW Golf—dunkel-blau. Wenn es noch Probleme gibt, rufen sie mich bitte an)*. Word choice is idiomatic *(misverständnes* should be spelled *Missverständnis)*, and in spite of spelling errors, comprehensible. Errors like *bekamm* instead of *bekam*, *sie* instead of *Sie*, or *Am 4. Juni* instead of *Vom 4. Juni* do not interfere with communication. This response clearly demonstrates proficiency in spite of the errors.

Sample Response 2: Score of 3

> Sehr geherrte Automieter,
>
> Letzte Monat, während meine Reise nach Europa, habe ein gelben fünfundzwanzigjahrigen Citröen in Münich gemietet. Da habe ich fünf Mark für die Automiete bezählt. Wann ich zurück zu Hause kame, fande ich noch eine Rechnung für die Miete.
>
> Ich bin sicher, daß der Vermieter mich erinnern wird, weil wir beide zum Mittagessen gegangen sind.

Sample Response 2: Score of 3 (continued)

> Der Citröen, wie ich habe gesagt, war gelb und hatte 158 000 Milen am Ödometer. Ich habe es nur für einen Tag gemietet und bezahltete ich mit meiner Kreditkarte.
>
> Bitte, schicken mir keine mehr Rechnung.
> Deine Katerina Wangouh

Commentary on Sample Response That Earned a Score of 3

This letter suggests proficiency in spite of its many mistakes. All assigned tasks are included and are mostly relevant, except when the candidate claims to have paid only 5 DM for a one-day car rental. The correct level of formality is displayed as well. The sentence *Ich bin sicher, daß der Vermieter mich erinnern wird, weil wir beide zum Mittagessen gegangen sind* is correct in its structure, but it uses the reflexive incorrectly. It should have been *daß der Vermieter sich an mich erinnern wird*, and instead of *wir beide zum Mittagessen gegangen sind*, the idiomatic phrase should have been *weil wir zusammen zu Mittag gegessen haben* or *weil wir zusammen essen gegangen sind*. Another sentence, *Bitte, schicken mir keine mehr Rechnung*, is grammatically incorrect but generally coherent. The correct sentence should have been *Bitte, schicken Sie mir keine Rechnung mehr*. Overall, this response suggests proficiency in writing a letter in German.

Sample Response 3: Score of 2

> Liebe Reiseautoleute,
> Ich habe besuchen Deutschland zwei Monate für. Ich habe ein Auto gemietet wenn ich wäre im Munchen. Ich habe mein Mietengeld gegeben im Büro. Weil ich nur ein billige rote Volkswagen mieten, ich habe zwei hundert Mark pro tag bezahlen. Und ich habe das Auto für eine Woche mietet. Ich habe dass bezahlt mit mein Kreditkarte. Aber jetzt habe ich ein Problem. Wenn meine Reise sind fertig ich komme nach Hause und ich habe eine Brief gefunden. Es sagt dass ich muss 100m bezahlen für das Auto das Ich habe gemietet. Ich habe meine Kreditkarte schön bezahlt und ich weiss dass du bekommen die Geld. Bitte schicken mir kein mehr Bills weil habe ich dass schön bezahlt.
> Danke
> Andrea Thomas
> P.S.   Wenn du willst ich kann die Rezipt schiken von die Bill von mein
>   Kreditkarte

Commentary on Sample Response That Earned a Score of 2

This response addresses all the assigned tasks. However, only one sentence is structurally correct in this paragraph: *Aber jetzt habe ich ein Problem*. There are several errors that interfere with communication (e.g., *Ich habe besuchen Deutschland zwei Monate für* or *ich wäre im Munchen. Ich habe mein Mietengeld gegeben im Büro*). The reader has to make quite an effort to understand what the writer intended to say. The grammatical control is limited, subject-verb agreement is inconsistent (e.g., *meine Reise sind* instead of *meine Reise ist*), and verb endings are incorrect (e.g., *Ich habe besuchen* instead of *Ich habe besucht*). The candidate invents new vocabulary, as in *Reiseautoleute*, a word that does not exist in German. The sample overall suggests the writer's inability to construct complex sentences and to use connectors when required. This response suggests a lack of proficiency.

Constructed-Response Question 9—Sample Responses

We will now look at two scored responses to the ninth constructed-response practice question ("Questions for Frau Waldner") and see comments from the scoring leader about why each response received the score it did.

Sample Response 1: Score of 4

First Question:
Welches Fach/welche Fächer haben Sie auf dem Humbolt-Gymnasium in Graz unterrichtet?

Second Question:
Wenn Sie die Gelegenheit haben, eine Reise durch Amerika zu machen, welche drei Städte oder Orten sind Ihnen am wichtigsten zu besuchen, und warum?

Third Question:
Würden Sie bitte beschreiben, die Ähnlichkeiten und Unterschiede zwischen unserer High School u. Ihrem Gymnasium die Sie schon bemerkt haben?

Fourth Question:
Könnten Sie uns bitte erklären, wie man in Österreich zur Gymnasiumlehrerin wird. Wie lange muß man an der Uni studieren? Was/ wie lernt man über Pädagogik/Ausbildung?

Commentary on Sample Response That Earned a Score of 4

Question 9 asked the candidates to write four questions based on a given situation: <u>one</u> question that will require only a <u>short</u> answer and <u>three</u> questions that require <u>longer</u> responses. All four questions here are completely and easily comprehensible. The response displays strong grammatical control. Some minor errors, such as in question 3, where the verb *beschreiben* should have gone to the end of the sentence (*Würden Sie bitte die Ähnlichkeiten und Unterschiede zwischen unserer High School u. Ihrem Gymnasium, die Sie schon bemerkt haben, beschreiben*), or in the fourth question, where *zur* should not have been there at all, do not interfere with communication. The writer successfully uses the conditional in questions 3 and 4 but should have used it in question 2 as well. Overall, the candidate knows how to write simple questions but also handles complex sentence structures very well. This response clearly demonstrates proficiency in writing questions in German.

Sample Response 2: Score of 3

> *First Question:*
> Was ist die größete Unterscheid zwischen die Gymnasium in Österreich und einem High School in den USA?
>
> *Second Question:*
> Was vermissen Sie am meisten von Österreich?
>
> *Third Question:*
> Warum möchten Sie in den USA wohnen und was gefällt Ihnen hier am besten?
>
> *Fourth Question:*
> Wie würden Sie das amerikanische Schulsystem verändert?

Commentary on Sample Response That Earned a Score of 3

In spite of some errors, the candidate addresses all of the assigned tasks, and the reader can easily determine which question asks for a short reply and which questions ask for longer responses. Questions 1 and 2 are written quite awkwardly, but they are generally comprehensible. A more idiomatic version of question 1 could have been *Wenn Sie Gymnasien in Österreich mit High Schools in den USA vergleichen, welche Unterschiede sind besonders bemerkenswert?* Question 2 is a direct translation from English ("What do you miss most from Austria?"). Question 3 has no error, and question 4 is well written, except that the verb ending is incorrect. It should have been *verändern*. Since errors only occasionally interfere with communication and the writer knows how to pose/write questions, the response suggests proficiency in writing questions in German.

Chapter 19
Are You Ready?—Last-Minute Tips

► ► ► ► ► ► ► ► ► ► ► ►

Checklist

Complete this checklist to determine whether you're ready to take the test.

❏ Do you know the testing requirements for your teaching field in the state(s) where you plan to teach?

❏ Have you followed all of the test registration procedures?

❏ Do you know the topics that will be covered in each test you plan to take?

❏ Have you reviewed any textbooks, class notes, and course readings that relate to the topics covered?

❏ Do you know how long the test will take and the number of questions it contains? Have you considered how you will pace your work?

❏ Are you familiar with the test directions and the types of questions for the test?

❏ Are you familiar with the recommended test-taking strategies and tips?

❏ Have you practiced by working through the practice test questions at a pace similar to that of an actual test?

❏ If you are repeating a Praxis Series assessment, have you analyzed your previous score report to determine areas where additional study and test preparation could be useful?

The day of the test

You should have ended your review a day or two before the actual test date. On the day of the test, you should

- Be well rested

- Take photo identification with you

- Take a supply of well-sharpened #2 pencils (at least three) if you are taking a multiple-choice test

- Take blue or black ink pens if you are taking a constructed-response test

- Eat before you take the test to keep your energy level up

- Be prepared to stand in line to check in or to wait while other test takers are being checked in

You can't control the testing situation, but you can control yourself. Stay calm. The supervisors are well trained and make every effort to provide uniform testing conditions. Don't let it bother you if the test doesn't start exactly on time; you will have the necessary amount of time once it does start.

You can think of preparing for this test as training for an athletic event. Once you've trained, prepared, and rested, give it everything you've got. Good luck.

Appendix A
Study Plan Sheet

▶ ▶ ▶ ▶ ▶ ▶ ▶ ▶ ▶ ▶ ▶ ▶

Study Plan Sheet

See Chapter 1 for suggestions about using this Study Plan Sheet.

STUDY PLAN						
Content covered on test	How well do I know the content?	What material do I have for studying this content?	What material do I need for studying this content?	Where could I find the materials I need?	Dates planned for study of content	Dates completed

Appendix B

For More Information

►   ►   ►   ►   ►   ►   ►   ►   ►   ►   ►   ►

Educational Testing Service offers additional information to assist you in preparing for The Praxis Series Assessments. *Test at a Glance* materials and the *Registration Bulletin* are both available on our Web site: **http://www.ets.org/praxis/index.html.**

General Inquiries

Phone: 800-772-9476 or 609-771-7395 (Monday-Friday, 8:00 A.M. to 7:45 P.M., Eastern time)

Fax: 609-771-7906

Extended Time

If you have a learning disability or if English is not your primary language, you can apply to be given more time to take your test. The *Registration Bulletin* tells you how you can qualify for extended time.

Disability Services

Phone: 800-387-8602 or 609-771-7780

Fax: 609-771-7906

TTY (for deaf or hard of hearing callers): 609-771-7714

Mailing Address

ETS—The Praxis Series
P.O. Box 6051
Princeton, NJ 08541-6051

Overnight Delivery Address

ETS—The Praxis Series
Distribution Center
225 Phillips Blvd.
P.O. Box 77435
Ewing, NJ 08628-7435